PRAISE FOR *REBECCA'S COUNTRY*

'This is a fascinating and original interpretation of important (often trivialised) events. It places west Wales firmly within the general discussion of changes in the early nineteenth century and the transition to industrial society. Well told, with evocative detail and flashes of brilliance, it also has lessons for today and the ways we understand the paths of deindustrialisation.'
Huw Beynon, Emeritus Professor of Sociology, Cardiff University

'Written with the pace and drama of a thriller, this superb account of one of the oddest and most inspiring of insurgent movements is a timely reminder of a past that is too often sanitised and patronised.'
Owen Hatherley, writer, author of *Landscapes of Communism*

'Deeply researched and brilliantly written, Rhian E. Jones takes the cartoonish basics of the Rebecca we remember from school and recasts the story as a fast-paced thriller, full of colourful characters, windswept West Walian landscapes and bristling contemporary relevance.'
Dylan Moore, *Cwlwm* editor and author of *Driving Home Both Ways*

'*Rebecca's Country* is a meticulously researched history of protest in early Victorian Wales. Rhian E. Jones tells the gripping narrative of the people's fights for rights in a period of massive social and political change. She uncovers unheard voices and stories. This is a crucial history and brilliant contribution to our knowledge of modern Wales.'

Katrina Navickas, Professor of History, University of Hertfordshire and author of *Protest and the politics of space and place, 1789–1848*

'Vital to the understanding of the roots of Welsh radicalism. Jones' writing is a rare combination; affable and authoritative.'

Rachel Trezise, author of *Easy Meat* and *Fresh Apples*

'Fascinating, moving, and extremely well told by Rhian E. Jones, this is a story that not enough people know. A compelling treatment of an important subject.'

Lucy Worsley, Chief Curator at Historic Royal Palaces and author of *Queen Victoria: Daughter, Wife, Mother, Widow*

REBECCA'S COUNTRY

REBECCA'S COUNTRY

A WELSH STORY OF
RIOT AND RESISTANCE

RHIAN E. JONES

2024

www.uwp.co.uk

British Library Cataloguing-in-Publication Data
A catalogue record for this book is available from the British Library.

ISBN: 978-1-915279-74-3

Cover artwork by Andy Ward
Typeset by Agnes Graves
Printed and bound in Great Britain by Bell & Bain Ltd, Glasgow

The publisher acknowledges the financial support of the Books Council of Wales.

CONTENTS

PRONUNCIATION GUIDE TO WELSH NAMES AND PLACES

BY ANWEN HAYWARD

Welsh may look daunting at first, but in fact it is much easier to pronounce than it may appear at a glance. Welsh is a phonetic language, meaning that each letter is pronounced consistently, with no silent letters. Subsequently, almost every word can be read aloud on sight once the alphabet is learnt. As a general rule, emphasis falls on the penultimate syllable in each word.

WELSH CONSONANTS

The following consonants are pronounced the same way in Welsh as in English: *b, d, h, l, m, n, p, t*. Some letters are written as digraphs, meaning that two characters are used to represent one sound, e.g. *ff, ng, dd* – these are all considered single letters, and are pronounced differently to *f, n, g* and *d*.

c   always hard, as in *cat*, and never soft, as in *mice*

ch   an aspirated *c* sound, like the Scottish *loch*

dd   a voiced *th*, as in the English *the*

f   like an English *v*, as in *dove*

ff   like an English *f*, as in *four*

g   always hard, as in *glove*, never soft, as in *gem*

ng   always hard, as in *singing*, never soft, as in *angel* (and without pronouncing the *g*, asin finger)

ll   this digraph does not have an English equivalent sound, but is pronounced by pressing the tongue to the top of the mouth (the same position as for *l*) and blowing air through your teeth.

An English-based approximation would be to run together *th* and *l* sounds similar to the *thl* sound in *athletic*

r   always trilled, as in Spanish or Italian, or as pronounced in a Scottish accent

s   always sibilant, as in *snow*, never voiced, as in *rose*

rh an aspirated *r*, producing a sound like *hr*

th an unvoiced *th*, as in the English *think*, never as in *the*

VOWELS

a   as in *cat*

e   as in *met*

i   as in *pig*

o   as in *fog*

u   as in *peek*

w   as in *loot*

y   as in *dull*, or at the end of a word as *ee* (as in *fee*)

DIPHTHONGS

Diphthongs are pairs of vowels which are pronounced as a single syllable.

ae / ai / au	as in *eye*
aw	*as in cow*
ei / eu / ey	as in *pay*
ew	*eh+ooh*, said quickly so that each sound glides into the other
iw / yw	as in *stew*
oe / oi	as in *oil*
ow	as in *go*
wy	*ooh+ee*, said quickly so that each sound glides into the other

Pronunciation Guide to Welsh Names and Places

NAMES

Alcwyn Caryni Evans	ALC-win car-UN-ee EV-ans
Dai'r Cantwr	DYE-ur CANT-oor
Dic Penderyn	DICK pen-DER-in
Dynevor	din-EV-or
Jac Ty Isha	JACK tee EE-sha
John Dillwyn Llewelyn	JOHN DILL-win lloo-WEL-in [Welsh *ll*]
Lewsyn yr Heliwr	LEW-sin uh-r hel-EE-oor
Petrys Bach	PET-riss BARCH [Welsh *ch*]
Shoni Sguborfawr	SHON-ee sgee-BOR-vowr
Twm Carnabwth	TOOM car-NA-booth

PLACES

Aberystwyth	ah-buh-RUST-with
Bolgoed	BOL-goid
Cilgwyn	KILL-gwinn
Cwm Cile	KOOM KEEL-eh
Cwmgwili	KOOM GWILL-ee
Cyfarthfa	kuh-VARTH-vah
Dowlais	DOW-lice
Efailwen	eh-VILE-wen
Glyn Saith Maen	GLIN SIGH-th MINE
Llanelli	llan-ELL-ee [Welsh *ll*]
Llangolman	llan-GOL-man [Welsh *ll*]
Llanidloes	llan-ID-loyce [Welsh *ll*]
Llannon	LLAN-on [Welsh *ll*]
Merthyr Tydfil	MER-thirr TID-vil
Mynydd Sylen	MUN-idd SUL-en [Welsh *dd*]
Parc Eynon	PARK AY-non
Pontarddulais	pont-ar-DDIL-ice [Welsh *dd*]
Pontyberem	pont-uh-BEAR-em
Preseli	preh-SEL-ee

xi

Pwll-Trap	POOLL-TRAP [Welsh *ll*]
Rhayader	rhay-ADD-uhr [Welsh *rh*]
Rhydypandy	rheed-uh-PAN-dee [Welsh *rh*]
St Clears	sin-CLAIRS
Talog	TAL-og
Teifi	TAY-vee
Towy	TOW-ee
Trevaughan	treh-VORN
Ystomenlle	us-tom-EN-lle [Welsh *ll*]

PHRASES

canu'r pwnc	KAN-eer POONC
ceffyl pren	KEFF-il PREN
eisteddfod	eye-STEDD-vod [Welsh *dd*]
Mabinogion	mab-in-OG-ee-on
Mari Lwyd	MAR-ee LUID
tŷ unnos / tai unnos	TEE INN-os / TIE INN-os

FOREWORD

The world of the Rebecca riots can feel surprisingly near to our own. As Rebecca's rebellion was drawing to a close at the end of 1843, Henry Cole was producing the world's first commercial Christmas card, Ada Lovelace was developing the world's first computer program and Britain's first amusement park had opened on the Isle of Wight. Newspapers and journals including the *Economist* and the *News of the World* carried reports on the lives of the rich and powerful while, in streets, pubs, rented rooms and marketplaces across Britain, people grumbled and sighed – and occasionally took to the streets in protest – over unemployment, foreign policy and the rising cost of living. Other aspects of 1843 feel more extraordinary: the previous year had seen half a million people take part in a general strike; crowds of thousands had attended the hanging at Bedford prison of the 'Potton Poisoner' Sarah Dazley; and the newspapers were also breathlessly reporting on an unwelcome insurrection in the Welsh hillside.

I first learned about the Rebecca riots, like many Welsh children, in history lessons at school. By that point, in repeated retellings over a century and a half, the story's spiky contours had been smoothed into something resembling a fairy-tale: *Once upon a time, men in women's clothing struck down the villainous tollgates, and after the government waved its magic wand they all lived happily ever after.* It's a great story to tell, particularly if one's history is otherwise full of unsuccessful struggle, but what struck me in my later research into Rebeccaism was the extent to which, in the pursuit of a happy ending, significant aspects of the movement have been forgotten or underplayed. Opposition to tollgates is only one part of a fuller and more interesting story. At school I had been captivated by the history of radical popular movements, and although I subsequently managed to avoid an academic career, my enduring interest in both historical and contemporary popular protest eventually led me to publish a book on the subject, *Petticoat Heroes* (Jones, 2015). While that was an academic monograph, supplemented by independent writing and research, this book is a new attempt to tell the story of Rebeccaism with as much attention to story as to history.

Rebeccaism, in this retelling, is a wide-ranging movement concerned with defending the established rights of local communities and with popular opposition to social, economic and political injustice. It formed part of the conflict and resistance generated in eighteenth- and nineteenth-century Britain by the shift from a society regulated by paternalist obligations, popular customs and what the historian E. P. Thompson called a pre-existing 'moral economy', towards an economy, politics and society informed by industrial capitalism.[1] Faced with absent, negligent or actively oppressive local authorities, those who took part in the Rebecca movement were attempting to remedy their collective discontent by taking matters into their own hands. Rather than a single-minded campaign against tollgates, this looked more like an 1840s version of the 'Occupy' campaigns that arose after the 2008 financial crisis or, a decade later, the *gilets jaunes* of France. Like them, it was a broad, if not always coherent popular movement trying to call attention to economic and social inequality, and to the lack of attention by remote, incompetent or corrupt local elites to the problems of those they governed. In early Victorian Wales, protestors obscured their identity and proclaimed their allegiance using bonnets and petticoats rather than yellow vests or Guy Fawkes masks, and, rather than 'the 99 per cent', they called themselves 'the children of Rebecca'.

Many people have given accounts of the Rebecca riots, from Henry Tobit Evans's 1910 *Rebecca and her Daughters* to David Williams's magisterial *The Rebecca Riots: A Study in Agrarian Discontent* (1955), and from Pat Molloy's energetic *And They Blessed Rebecca* (1983) to David J. V. Jones's *Rebecca's Children* (1989) which first established the Rebecca movement as having been 'larger than we thought and less respectable'. In addition to a multitude of work by local historians and other enthusiasts on aspects of the events, available both in print and online, Rebeccaism has appeared in fact and fiction, on screen and stage, in poetry and even symphony.[2] I'm thankful to those who have previously told the story in their own way, and grateful to have been able to draw upon this material in addition to original historical sources in telling my own version. In all retellings, it's hard not to replicate the narrative beats, pacing and iconic events that history has already supplied for the story, but each retelling can still bring something new for both writers and readers.

Although Rebeccaism is a fascinating example of collective action, individual stories are important, too. Many moments of individual or community drama, humour or tragedy took place against the backdrop of Rebeccaism. The people we will meet in this story led lives that feel as modern as they do archaic: they spent their time working or looking for work, struggled to bring up children or support ageing parents, and thought and talked about old and new ideas, plans and beliefs. They celebrated special occasions, fell in and out of love, spread gossip and rumours, started businesses, kept up with events in the country and the world beyond their own, and discussed all of this with each other at work, chapel and market, in the pub or at political meetings. Together, they discovered ways to understand their world, including how it was changing around them and what they could do to shape it themselves.

Some of the major personalities of Rebecca's story are at least recognisable by name – in particular Shoni Sguborfawr and Dai'r Cantwr who have gone down in history as both heroes and villains. Some of the best impressions of the story come from relative outsiders, like *The Times* reporter Thomas Campbell Foster or the estate manager and reluctant observer Thomas Cooke. Other individuals who appear in the archives are not often focused on, but their involvement in particular events, or general journey within or alongside the events of Rebeccaism, paint a vivid picture of the movement and the motivations, conflicts, hopes and fears that participants brought to it. I have tried to bring some of these people to the forefront, even if only for a brief glimpse: Alcwyn C. Evans, the schoolboy who went on to tell his own story of the movement; Frances Evans, the young single mother who inspired the storming of a workhouse; the battle-ready women of the Morgan clan; Daniel Lewis who brightened up a grim lifestyle with pranks and poetry; Joseph Downes whose romantic ideas about Wales were shattered when he attempted to investigate it; even the 'pretty landlady' of a Radnorshire pub who shocked her local landowner with her support for Rebeccaism. Place, too, can be as useful a focus as personality: for the story as a whole, the often overlooked Glamorganshire, with its copper, coal and 'violent Chartist politicians', was as important a setting as the bleak Preseli Hills where the first man to play Rebecca staked out a living; the grand three storeys of Llanelly House where William Chambers Junior found his class sympathies torn; the Stag and Pheasant Inn at Five Roads which became a gang headquarters; or Carmarthen, the 'London of Wales', where high society and low life were thrown together.

I have also tried to emphasise the links between rural and urban, and industial and agricultural Wales, showing how the 'riots' were, in fact, a well-organised umbrella movement that connected farmers, labourers and industrial workers, as well as middle-class reformers and working-class radicals. Although 'Rebecca's country' of Pembrokeshire, Carmarthenshire and Cardiganshire can seem insular or isolated, the movement and responses to it were inextricably linked with the world outside it – not just industrial Wales and Chartist Britain, but revolutionary France and pro-independence Ireland – and with larger contexts, systems and structures including imperialism and colonialism. Beyond the success story of the defeat of the tollgates, looking at the movement's lesser-known aspects – its demands for financial support for unmarried mothers and children, for workers' rights or for national political reform – ties the events into wider struggles and historical narratives on welfare reform, gender relations and the development of working-class politics.

The Rebecca movement contained many quirks and idio-syncrasies, at times seeming strange or surreal to modern observers

– and to some observers at the time – but in fact solidly rooted in Welsh society and culture. Outside Wales, not only were the events a subject of contemporary political debate, but the imagery and aesthetics of 'Rebecca' became deeply embedded in popular media and the public imagination, inspiring comedy, satire and even playful imitation among groups and individuals completely unconnected with the events. These social and cultural aspects of the Rebecca riots mean that their story can be much more than a dry and solemn account of popular struggle, and one that is as lively, moving and intriguing as the events themselves.

Stories of the past can also tell us something about the present, and Rebeccaism strongly resonates with much of today's political turmoil, economic crisis and reactions to both. Many problems familiar to our Victorian ancestors – poverty, high rents, unemployment, the privatisation of common space, the policing of protest – either have never gone away or are making a stark return. In a world that can seem increasingly fraught and volatile, the study of historical responses to comparable developments is one of our few remaining ways to make sense of things.

SOME MAIN CHARACTERS

REBECCAITES AND ALLIES

BOWEN, MICHAEL: farmer's son, Trelech, Carmarthenshire

DAVIES, DAVID: *alias* Dai'r Cantwr, poet, lay preacher and labourer, Glamorganshire

DAVIES, ELIZABETH: farmer's daughter, Hendy, Glamorganshire

EVANS, ALCWYN CARYNI: schoolboy and later historian, Carmarthenshire

EVANS, FRANCES: farm servant, Carmarthenshire

HARRIES, JOHN: miller, Talog, Carmarthenshire

HUGHES, JOHN: *alias* Jac Ty Isha, farmer's son, Llannon, Carmarthenshire

JONES, JOHN: *alias* Shoni Sguborfawr, prize-fighter and labourer, Glamorganshire

LEWIS, DANIEL: poet and weaver, Pontarddulais, Glamorganshire

MORGAN FAMILY: tenant-farmers, Glamorganshire

REES, THOMAS: *alias* Twm Carnabwth, prize-fighter and farm labourer, Pembrokeshire

WILLIAMS, HUGH: barrister and Chartist, Kidwelly, Carmarthenshire

GENTRY AND ALLIES

ADAMS, EDWARD, JUNIOR: landowner, Middleton Hall estate, Carmarthenshire

CHAMBERS, WILLIAM, JUNIOR: magistrate and businessman, Llanelli

COOKE, THOMAS: estate manager, Middleton Hall estate, Carmarthenshire

GRAHAM, SIR JAMES: Home Secretary, London

GUEST, LADY CHARLOTTE: author and industrialist, Merthyr Tydfil, Glamorganshire

Some main characters

HALL, EDWARD CROMPTON LLOYD: acting High Sheriff,
  Cilgwyn estate, Cardiganshire
LOVE, COLONEL JAMES: soldier, Carmarthenshire
NAPIER, CAPTAIN CHARLES: Chief Constable, Glamorganshire
RICE TREVOR, COLONEL GEORGE: Deputy Lord-Lieutenant
  and MP for Carmarthenshire
WALSH, SIR JOHN: MP and Lord-Lieutenant, Radnorshire

OTHERS

BULLIN, THOMAS: toll-farmer, Swansea
DOWNES, JOSEPH: nature writer, Breconshire
FOSTER, THOMAS CAMPBELL: reporter for *The Times*
  newspaper, London/Carmarthen
O'CONNOR, FEARGUS: Chartist leader and proprietor of the
  Northern Star newspaper
THOMAS, MARGARET: labourer's wife, Hendy, Carmarthenshire
WILLIAMS, SARAH: tollkeeper, Hendy, Carmarthenshire

REBECCA, that brave Amazon!
Comes rolling o'er your brows;
And, like a mighty avalanche,
Destruction loud she vows
To your bastiles, and your police;
As fiercer on she rolls,
She wars against the system, now
She's conquer'd all the tolls ...
'Old Commodore' (E. P. Mead),
The *Northern Star*, August 1843

Oh! Then I see Queen Bec hath been with you,
She is the law's corrective, and she comes
In shape, alike the amazon heroines of old,
Athwart her prancing milkwhite steed
Led by her brawny children to the spot
Which needs the help of her corrective hand,
Her whip of horse's hide – the lash of wire
Her heels well spurred – her brows adorned
With graceless curls, and ringlets brown,
And in this state she gallops night by night
O'er Wallia's mountains and through Wallia's vales ...
But need I tell you more? Is not her fame
Throughout Europe sounded far? Hath not
Victoria's majesty from England's throne
Deigned recognition of our heroine's pranks
While troops at arms are sent to put her down?
But still she reigns – alike triumphant
And alike admired – she is that very Bec
That Welshmen long have sought
And now have found.
'TL', The *Welshman*, September 1843

PROLOGUE:
REBECCA'S ROOTS

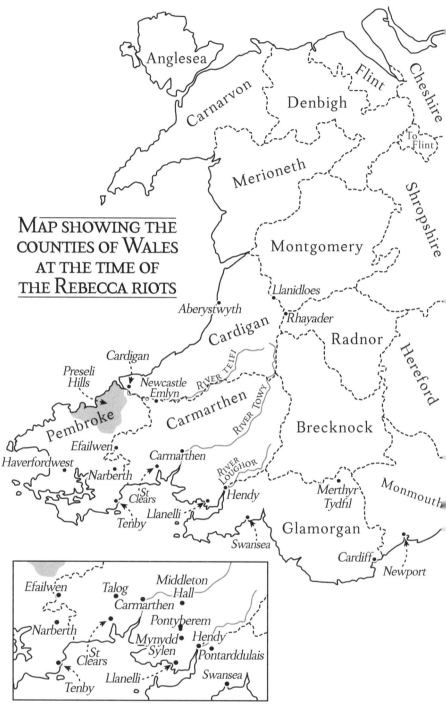

MAP SHOWING THE COUNTIES OF WALES AT THE TIME OF THE REBECCA RIOTS

Anglesea

Carnarvon

Flint

Cheshire

Denbigh

To Flint

Merioneth

Shropshire

Montgomery

Llanidloes

Aberystwyth

Rhayader

Radnor

Cardigan

Hereford

Cardigan

RIVER TEIFI

Preseli Hills

Newcastle Emlyn

Carmarthen

RIVER TOWY

Brecknock

Pembroke

Efailwen

Haverfordwest

Carmarthen

RIVER LOUGHOR

Narberth

Hendy

Merthyr Tydfil

Monmouth

St Clears

Llanelli

Tenby

Swansea

Glamorgan

Cardiff

Newport

Efailwen

Talog

Middleton Hall

Carmarthen

Narberth

Pontyberem

Mynydd Sylen

Hendy

St Clears

Pontarddulais

Llanelli

Tenby

Swansea

The three south-western counties of Pembrokeshire, Cardiganshire and
Carmarthenshire would become Rebecca's heartland, with significant action also
taking place in Glamorganshire to the south-east and Radnorshire to the north-east.

THE PRINCIPLES OF REVOLUTION

JULY, 1843

The flannel nightshirt John Morgan put on that night had once been white, but it had by now seen so much service that it was the same grubby grey as the sheep that grazed the slopes of Goppa mountain. It fell to his knees over his trousers and work-boots, both caked in the mud of the fields and country lanes. The red-striped shawl he wore was borrowed, as was the white cap on his head. Drawing a deep breath in the summer night's air, he raised his hands to his face and smeared it in a mixture of soot, flour and berry juice, until only his eyes were uncovered.

All the men gathered on the hillside that night – over a hundred, and some of them neighbours, some strangers and some friends – had come dressed for the occasion. Summoned from miles around by horns, rockets and flares that lit the night sky, they wore high-crowned black hats, white lace caps or old straw bonnets newly trimmed with feathers, ferns and ribbons. Their faces were painted in red, black, white or all three, veiled with handkerchiefs or scarves, or half-hidden behind glued-on beards of horsehair. Their work-clothes were now shrouded in white shirts, petticoats, shawls or bed-gowns, their coats turned inside-out, or cloaked with animal hides.

Their leader, mounted on a powerful white horse, was as usual looking more spectacular – dressed in the most immaculate white gown, the most magnificent bonnet. This figure, for as long as the night's adventure lasted, would take the name Rebecca, though the knot of men around them, consulting on whether it was time to set off, addressed them, too, as 'mam' or 'mother'. With a nervous grin, John reflected that Rebecca didn't much resemble his own mam, her face lined from years of work and worry, who had seen him off that evening with the familiar words of caution and a kiss for good luck.

As the group moved off at a signal from Rebecca, trooping on foot behind her horse, there was excited chat and even laughter, though with a grim and fearful edge to it. John took a firm grip on both his axe and his gun. Others carried scythes, reaping-hooks, pitchforks, saws and crowbars – well-worn implements picked up from the farmhouse, field or farmyard but now given a new and greater purpose. After a mile or so's tramp down the mountain to the road, announcing their approach by firing off guns and blowing ox-horns, in the hours just past midnight their target was in sight.

The tollgate that barred the village's main road was known to John, being the place he'd had to give up almost half his week's wages just to take his cart to market. Everyone had a similar story, if not about this gate then a different one of the multitude springing up everywhere, like weeds, taking their hard-earned money and giving back nothing but trouble. Yes, they had all complained, to each other, to the magistrates, to anyone who would stand still long enough to listen. But everyone knew complaining did no good. Nothing did, apart from this.

Everyone's eyes were on Rebecca as she halted her followers' march with an imperiously raised hand. Glancing up and down the road, John could see that these eyes included those of men and women peering cautiously and curiously from the darkened windows and doorways to each side. They also included the tollkeeper, who was already scurrying with an armload of his possessions from the tollhouse to the side of the road. Until he was out of harm's way, no one stirred, but then, at Rebecca's shout of 'Forward!', the crowd surged like a breaking wave towards the gate, accompanied by cheering and another round of gunfire. They did what they had come to do – like others had done first at Efail-wen, then in Carmarthen and then, it seemed, everywhere at once. The first stroke of the axe as it bit into the gate's top bar felt like a sigh of relief.

The next ten or twenty minutes – these things always seemed at once to take mere moments and to last forever – were a blur. As, at Rebecca's command, the crowd stepped back from their work of destruction, John found himself exhausted and exhilarated, looking with satisfaction at the rubble of the tollhouse walls, the sawn-off and fire-blackened stumps of the tollgate. There was no urgent need to retreat before the soldiers or police arrived – Rebecca always had enough scouts and look-outs to hear them coming from a mile away. Instead, the crowd dispersed slowly and gradually, melting away into the dawn, some to knock up the nearest pub for a well-earned glass of ale, others to snatch an hour's sleep before rising for the next day's toil, returning to their everyday identities as easily as they shed their night-time costumes.

John slept well, looking forward to the next day's headlines, no doubt reporting with even more disapproval on yet another triumphant night's work by the children of Rebecca. He could still recall reading the words of the *Carmarthen Journal*'s editors, sounding as much alarmed by events as they were outraged:

> We are everywhere asked, Who is Rebecca? We answer, Rebecca is an impersonality – a mere political abstraction, or if she has any corporeal form or essence, we say that she is AN EMBODIMENT OF THE PRINCIPLES OF REVOLUTION.[1]

Only a matter of weeks ago, he had felt alone and powerless, at a loss for how his family – or anyone – could afford to live in these increasingly hard and desperate times. But now he was part of Rebecca's ever-growing family, and – despite the anger of the magistrates and gentry, the denouncements from the press and the pulpit, the skirmishes with soldiers and police, and the threats of arrest, imprisonment and worse – it was at last getting easier to breathe in what was rapidly becoming Rebecca's country.

A WORLD TRANSFORMED

'In sublimity and grandeur, there are few spots superior to this. I had the good fortune to see it in its happiest moment,' sighed the Jersey clergyman Corbet Hue in 1810, recording his visit to Devil's Bridge Falls in the heart of the Cambrian mountains.[2]

This view was a typical one of Wales in the early nineteenth century. These were years in which Wales had become a desirable tourist destination, ideal for wealthy British holidaymakers looking for a getaway at a time when the French Revolution, followed by the Napoleonic wars, had rendered their usual habit of travel to the Continent less inviting. The country's presentation as a place of unspoilt natural beauty also made it attractive to those who disliked the changes being wrought in other parts of Britain: the spread of industrial towns and cities, the noise, grime and pollution produced by the furnaces and smokestacks of the new factories, mines and mills, and the growth of a new class of increasingly restless workers whose labour – along with the products and profits from centuries of slavery overseas – made it all function. By contrast, in narratives from the Revd William Gilpin's *Observations on the River Wye* in 1782 to Edward Pugh's 1816 *Cambria Depicta*, the country shimmered as a sleepy and unchanging land. Victorian Romantics like Samuel Taylor Coleridge thought fondly of Wales, as they did of parts of Scotland and Ireland, as a place uncorrupted by modernity and its industrial turn, which they saw as transforming and degrading not just the natural environment but the very soul of man. On a trip to Wales, visitors could marvel at its thoroughly un-modern dramatic mountain scenery, intriguing ruined forts and crumbling castles. These latter relics – markers of the country's occupation by the Romans and, nearly a thousand years later, the Normans – lay pleasantly scattered between 'soft ridges of hills' and 'lovely little rural towns'.

The Welsh people, and their lifestyle and language, were often featured as just another part of the scenery. As tourism developed into a boom industry of its own throughout the early nineteenth century, mass-produced prints and postcards offered depictions of the mountainous landscape, the market-day or *eisteddfod* festival, and the female figure in 'traditional' Welsh dress, posed behind the spinning-wheel or harp or in the doorway of a quaint hillside cottage. A traveller in 1836 recorded his first impressions of 'a truly Welsh scene':

It was market day and the display of wares in the open street, the peculiar costume of the people and their singular dialect, completed a picture novel in the extreme ... my road onward was enlivened by a few picturesque groups of brilliant Welsh beauties mounted on their strong rough horses.[3]

But the natural landscape that presented its beauty and charm to visitors was also a harsh one, offering little to those who lived on it and strove to make a living from it. The poverty and grind of everyday life in Wales was longstanding, but usually absent from tourist or romantic narratives, and when aspects of it did break the surface, it could be an unsettling experience. The Scottish novelist Catherine Sinclair, touring Wales in 1833, tutted as her carriage was mobbed by local children who 'here seem universally addicted to begging, as in Ireland ... They are not, however, quite ragged enough to be picturesque.'[4] Armand-Louis-Bon Maudet de Penhouët, a French aristocrat who paid a visit to the ruins of Neath Abbey while in exile in 1796, described his encounter with a group of women and children who had been using the building for shelter:

> As soon as I entered into one of the vaulted outer parts, several women came out of holes that communicated with it; they surrounded me, and the further I advanced, the more the troop augmented: they carried almost all of them infants on their backs, and the tone of voice in which they begged of us could be compared only to that of those women who headed the rebels at Paris.[5]

This comparison of the poor in Wales to those who had taken part in the French Revolution – an event still unfolding at the time its aristocratic author wrote down his impressions – was the most vivid and shocking comparison he would have had to hand, but it illustrated the extent of poverty and desperation in the Welsh countryside beneath its picturesque façade, and the people's ability to disrupt proverbial ideas of their country's placidity.

In 1844, an essay in the English literary and political journal the *Quarterly Review* looked back on the last few years in Wales. It began by characterising the Welsh people, as usual, as quiet and obedient:

> No quarter of the British Islands has, for a long course of years, occasioned less disquietude to its rulers, or attracted less public attention to its internal concerns, than the principality of Wales. The inhabitants of the mountainous and agricultural districts, of which so large a part of that country consists, have been chiefly known to the English neighbours as a patient, industrious and hard-faring race, tenacious of the traditions and customs of their forefathers, disliking change, and not easily aroused to enterprise [...] While England, Scotland and Ireland have successively raised spectres... no cry of 'Justice to Wales' has been echoed from Snowdon or Plinlimmon.[6]

Snowdon (now known by its indigenous name, Eryri) and Plinlimmon – again, the country's mountainous features stood in as markers for its men and women. But, as the magazine went on to report, over the course of a single year all this had utterly changed. By the end of 1843, Wales had become the setting for:

> a formidable insurrection, overawing the law, invading the most sacred rights of property and person, issuing its behests with despotic effrontery, and enforcing them by the detestable agents of terror, incendiarism, and bloodshed.[7]

What on earth had happened? In some ways, the events that became known as the Rebecca riots were little different to events that had already happened outside Wales. The changes of the previous fifty years had brought tension and unrest to almost every part of Britain, as industrialisation's transformation of how people lived and worked made the country's divides in wealth and quality of life more glaring. Across Nottinghamshire, Lancashire and Yorkshire, textile workers smashed machinery and set factories ablaze in a bid to prevent their impoverishment by new industrial technology. In Kent and East Anglia, agricultural workers rioted over harsh working conditions and the advance of mechanisation. And the new pro-democracy movement of Chartism sprang up across the whole of Britain, demanding that ordinary people be listened to in a political system that only gave influence and power to a privileged few.

To observers seeking a break from their country's industrial turmoil, Wales could seem invitingly remote from all this, but, as became clear in the early 1840s, it was nothing of the sort. For over a year, newspapers in Britain, and even beyond, were full of one particular protest movement. Wealthy landowners fled their country estates, urgent questions were asked in Parliament and by the Queen, and hundreds of police and soldiers were sent in with orders to suppress a potential revolution. These restless territories were not the northern industrial districts of Luddism, or the burning hayfields of south-east England's Captain Swing, but the hill-farms of south-west Wales, where tens of thousands were now rioting, demonstrating and marching under the banner of 'Rebecca'.

WORK

For a century before the Rebecca riots, Wales's population, like that of the rest of Britain, had been growing, but in 1843, 80 per cent of the country's inhabitants still lived in 'village-towns' of fewer than 1,500 people, and sometimes as little as a few hundred. Where people gathered to live and work in larger numbers, they did so around hubs of business, industry and transport: in the growing industrial towns of Swansea and Llanelli or established market towns like Carmarthen. All of these, however, existed in the shade of the intensive development of the iron and coal districts in Wales's south-eastern quarter.

In 1767, as Britain's Industrial Revolution was beginning to gather steam, John Guest had moved from Shropshire to manage a single furnace for smelting iron at Dowlais, in the hills above Merthyr Tydfil at the north-eastern edge of Glamorganshire. By the time of Rebecca, less than eighty years later, Guest's grandson was in charge of a huge – and hugely profitable – ironworks that was on its way to becoming the largest in the world. With the valley floors now shorn of their dense ancient woodlands and cleared of their scattered homesteads, shafts were sunk deep into the land's seemingly inexhaustible seams of coal and ragged settlements thrown up around the mines, and the expanding iron foundries and steelworks they supplied, to house their tens of thousands of workers. Merthyr Tydfil's population, which had numbered less than 8,000 in 1801, exploded to almost 50,000 in the next fifty years, making it the largest town in Wales.

By the 1840s, Guest's works at Dowlais formed part of an industrial powerhouse that supplied the world with iron, coal and steel. From Merthyr at the northern tip, the advance of industrialisation swept down through the valleys of Glamorganshire, spreading east into Monmouthshire and west to Swansea, Neath and Port Talbot at Carmarthenshire's south-eastern border. Along ribbons of railway and canal, and shipped overseas from docks at Newport and Cardiff, the Welsh valleys poured forth their contributions to Britain's economic and imperial development: track for the country's expanding railway system, fuel for the factories, cannon and shot for the British navy.

The power of the new industrialists, in Wales as in England, was overtaking the fading glory of the rural gentry, both in the kind of money they made and the semi-feudal influence an 'ironmaster' could exert. The iron and coal companies owned not only the sprawling industrial works but the houses their workers lived in and the company shops where they were obliged to spend their wages, and there was little to obscure the stark contrast between those who owned the means of production and those who lived by selling their labour. The coalfield's availability of wages and work itself were subject to the coal trade's slumps and fluctuations in price, to say nothing of the work's exhausting and dangerous nature. The close-packed rows of workers' terraces, on rough and unpaved roads, were built with little consideration for quality, privacy, overcrowding or sanitation. Tough and disorderly townships like Merthyr were places where, according to horrified observers, 'no one would live for choice, except to make money'.[8] By the time of Rebecca, the town was described in one government report as 'the most depraved and uncivilised locality in Wales'.[9] Its aesthetics alone upset conventional notions of the idyllic Welsh landscape: '[Merthyr Tydfil] is built on the face of bleak and abrupt hills, and the enormous mining operations and iron works here carried on have heaped up around it gray and smoking mounds of ashes and dross ...'[10]

But making money, then as now, could make you overlook or endure a lot. The coalfield and iron belt drew in workers from all over the world, particularly Ireland and Spain, but many of its workers were also Welsh, moving in from more rural areas in the west and often returning to their home parishes as opportunities for work in either part of the country ebbed and flowed. These back-and-forth patterns of migration meant that customs and behaviour from agricultural and industrial Wales permeated both areas along with their people, often giving rise to more changes in culture and ideas.

The industrial population's demand for food, drink and other consumables provided a valuable market for the producers of rural Wales, and the higher wages available in good years meant that industrial workers could bring themselves and their families up in the world, even if only by inches. The money that wasn't needed for necessities, or sent back home to support relatives, flowed into the coalfield's abundance of pubs, entertainment and consumption. Observers like the Monmouthshire-born Alfred Russel Wallace, who had grown used to seeing industrial workers grimy and half-naked in the mines and furnaces, looking 'more demon than man', were startled to see them on their days off, having dropped some disposable income on flashy waistcoats, silk handkerchiefs and suits 'that would not disgrace an English gentleman'.[11]

Pembrokeshire, Carmarthenshire and Cardiganshire, the south-western agricultural counties that would become Rebecca's territory, had a longer established and less intense pace of life than that of the industrial districts. Men here dressed more soberly than some of their coalmining cousins, in suits of homemade cloth, lace-up boots and low-crowned hats, smartening up for market, fairs or chapel with brightly coloured waistcoats, buttons or scarves. Tourists were particularly taken with the way that rural women dressed, in colourful flannel shawls, striped or plaid dresses, black-and-white chequered aprons and the famous tall black hat. Visiting Carmarthenshire, Alfred Russel Wallace was further struck by their ability – with their hats off – to carry their daily domestic burdens:

> The women and girls carry great loads upon their heads, fifty or sixty pounds weight, and often much more. Large pitchers (like Grecian urns) of water or milk are often carried for long distances on uneven roads, with both hands full at the same time. They may be often seen turning round their heads to speak to an acquaintance and tripping along with the greatest unconcern, but never upsetting the pitcher.[12]

The position of women in Rebecca's country wasn't only domestic. Younger women usually found work as servants at larger farms or manor houses, where their duties could range from managing the dairy to driving the horse-drawn plough. Some ended up as the heads of their own household or farm, often taking over the running of the place after death, illness or injury claimed a husband or father, but just as many lived independently, renting or owning small plots of land, giving school lessons in barns or lofts, taking in laundry and mending, or managing guesthouses and pubs. Single and widowed women dominated the area's stocking trade, buying wool from farms and turning it into garments to sell at markets or fairs, and many brewed their own beer, selling it on the doorstep to neighbours.

Rebecca's country was still sparsely populated in many areas, but had growing centres in market towns like Narberth,

Haverfordwest and Aberystwyth, and smaller towns like Fishguard, Milford Haven and Cardigan rounding the south-west's coastal corner. Larger towns like Cardiff and Swansea, and the fast-rising regional hub of Carmarthen, had a thriving middle class of shopkeepers, bankers, teachers, lawyers and clergymen. Meanwhile an equally fast-growing 'underclass', who lacked work, shelter and support, lived in desperate straits on the hillside or the streets, sleeping under rags and often surviving, like the women and children in the ruins of Neath Abbey, by begging or turning to crime.

The hills and moorland between and beyond these population centres were sprinkled with farmsteads and cottages of various size, quality and longevity. The poorer of such houses, built of mud or stone with thatched roofs, had minimal furnishings, often a single room with one or no windows, packed-earth floors and bedding of straw mattresses and homemade blankets. Open peat fires were used for boiling water or baking bread, and filled the place with acrid smoke. The house, both for space and warmth, was often shared with pigs and chickens, and washing and other necessities were done outdoors, with clothes washed at the side of streams or rivers then beaten against the rocks to dry them.

In the better-off farmhouses, the roof could be tiled and the floor paved with clay or stone, and the kitchen, described by one visitor as 'the theatre of the Welsh farmer's domestic life',[13] could give pride of place to a tall clock or a sideboard or dresser stacked with spotless crockery. Bibles and hymnbooks shared space with newspapers, and clothes were hung from ceiling-beams between flitches of bacon or joints of beef, along with a piece of rennet for cheesemaking. The kitchen could be partitioned by a bed, wardrobe or dresser from a 'best' room where visitors were entertained and the 'good bread' – white and wheaten rather than the regular barley bread – was served.

Farms tended to be run by one or two generations of a family with a few live-in or casually employed farmhands, servants or unpaid helpers, and were based around mixed meat and dairy production,

13

growing and harvesting crops and vegetables, and sheep and cattle grazing. The latter were now mostly breeds from over the border in Herefordshire, the native cattle being described as 'very small ... ill-shaped, and unprofitable for the dairy', while the Welsh mountain sheep remained a 'small, hardy, and intractable race'.[14] Welsh cobs and ponies, similarly tough and compact, were given several jobs from ploughing to carrying the family to market or chapel. Farmers had to work with, and sometimes against the land, bringing in lime to fertilise the leached soil and using carts rather than wagons to negotiate ploughing the steep hillside.

Ploughing, tilling, sowing, planting and harvesting were still mostly done by hand with the same carts, scythes and reaping-hooks that had been in use for generations. This was in spite of the growing encouragement by the gentry and their estate managers for tenant-farmers to modernise and mechanise – which usually involved laying out money for expensive agricultural equipment. This was a risky investment when tenancies were insecure, and farmers were reluctant to give their landlords any excuse for recouping the increased value of the farm in the form of a rent rise, or eviction to re-let the more profitable farmland at a higher rate. For farmers, as many landowners complained, short-term self-sufficiency took precedence over any spirit of speculation or enterprise.

The rhythms of the working day, too, were ancient, revolving around the seasons, the weather and the sun's duration rather than the externally disciplined patterns of clocking-in at factories or shift work in the mines. Farming families, labourers and servants all began their day before dawn, with a breakfast that could consist of boiled oatmeal, barley bread and sometimes the leftover cheese or potatoes from the previous day's dinner, and sustained themselves throughout the day on cups of milkless tea. Butter from the dairy and meat from the livestock were eaten less often than they were taken to weekly markets by famers' wives or dispatched to dealers and drovers at the farm gate for transport by foot through Hereford and Gloucester for sale in England or for export at Bristol. Men and women – and children – all worked on the farm, although for wives and daughters the working day was interleaved with equally vital household tasks and childcare.

The rural Welsh economy of the early nineteenth century was both casual and complex. Individuals could rent their own patch of land on neighbouring farms in exchange for helping out with the harvest; small farmers near the coast had shares in small boats so they could fish for part of the year; and farmhands or servants on larger farms often spent the slack farming season going on the road to look for work in the coalfield, in larger towns in and outside Wales, or even to London. The growth of tourism offered new opportunities for seasonal work in service or leisure industries, as holiday hotspots like Tenby and Aberystwyth hosted regattas, dances and sporting contests, along with brass bands and theatrical troupes to entertain their wealthy visitors. By the 1840s there were also a handful of coalmines and ironworks in the south of Carmarthenshire, these smaller concerns owned by local landowners rather than the coalfield's industrialist-kings. For those who preferred to stay closer to home rather than brave the industrial frontiers of the valleys, these offered better-paying employment than work on the land, although in harsher and more dangerous conditions. Lead mines in Cardiganshire pulled in a notable population of migrant miners from Cornwall, while in Glamorganshire copper ore to be processed at the huge Swansea copperworks arrived both from Cornwall itself and later – to the protests of Cornish miners and Swansea workers – from Chile and the slave-worked mines of Cuba.

The Rebecca riots would draw people from all walks of life, all ages and all levels of the economy. Men like John Hughes and Michael Bowen, the eldest sons of families who owned larger farms employing farm servants and farmhands, could expect to make a steadier living than Thomas Rees, a part-time farm labourer who occupied a tumbledown cottage on the Preseli hillside, or Frances Evans, a live-in farm servant. Others like Daniel Lewis, a young weaver from Pontarddulais, did not live off the land but off their craft skills, whether carpentry, tailoring, cobbling, spinning or smithing.

15

... AND PLAY

People in 1840s south-west Wales played as hard as they worked. Pubs, marketplaces, and town and village squares were crowded with professional and amateur entertainers trading on their various talents, from ballad-singing to boxing. The area's farmers, labourers and craftsmen were often musicians or lay preachers on the side, as well as taking part in the Welsh tradition of folk poetry, composing verses on their daily life and to mark community events from successful harvests to weddings and funerals. Neighbours met regularly at chapels and markets or paid calls to each other's houses, individually or en masse, for births, weddings, funerals, seasonal celebrations or simply gathering round the hearth on a cold and damp evening. Particularly where there was no local manor house or chapel, larger farmhouses became focal points for community activity. This made it no surprise when established farmers began to act as community leaders or were looked to for local decision-making, as was to happen under Rebecca.

In communities where most people had little, social life was built on an unspoken reciprocity, expressed in more and less formal ways. For neighbours and relatives, news of a birth or death in a family meant visiting to catch up over a cup of tea or slice of bread and cheese, but also bringing the household something of your own that you could spare, whether a few shillings or a pound of sugar. The custom of the 'bidding wedding' allowed a couple without a dowry to hire a local 'bidder' to announce the marriage and invite friends and neighbours, each of whom would contribute a small sum to cover the cost of the celebration and to set up the new couple with enough money to build a house or buy their own farm. Like an informal system of mutual aid, there was an understanding that this money would end up recirculating when other biddings happened in the same community.

The social calendar, like the working day, reflected the requirements of the season. At the huge county fairs that took place throughout the year, busiest in May and September, business could be mixed with pleasure, with crowds buying and selling farm produce, livestock, and other goods and services – including their own labour. Like the smaller weekly markets that took place in larger towns, county fairs were the cogs that kept the machine of the rural economy running. Visitors came from Wales and far beyond to attend, and small fortunes could be spent on drinking, dancing, exhibits and entertainment. The latter included boxing matches of the kind where local men, such as Thomas Rees, who would later help to kick off the Rebecca riots, competed for prizes and a small degree of fame. In the background, stallholders hawked everything from children's toys to handmade gingerbread to allegedly healing elixirs, while wandering preachers argued with political agitators over how to set the world's problems to rights, and travelling players set up their portable theatres to put on a production of the latest farce or tragedy. Matches were made between young people with or without the knowledge or permission of their parents, while other hopeful youngsters stood in rows to be assessed as suitable for hiring as farmhands or domestic servants, on contracts that would give them board and lodging for a year. Deals were struck, horses raced, poetry composed, pockets picked, new dresses, suits and bonnets shown off, and all the latest news and gossip caught up on over a drink – often several. Saturday markets in towns like Carmarthen reflected in miniature the raucous communal enjoyment of fairs, as one observer wrote of the day's aftermath: 'all the surrounding roads and lanes were then positively dangerous owing to the vagaries of homeward-bound drunkards and the loose horses lost by their tipsy owners, or by the wildly-driven gigs of inebriated farmers.'[15]

Festivals marked both the religious and agricultural calendar, seeing communities celebrate the coming of spring and winter, midsummer and the harvest as well as holidays like Christmas and Whit Monday. Like county fairs, these celebrations could get wild, with boxing matches, cockfights, bull-running and horse-racing taking place against a backdrop of bonfires, fireworks and flaming torches lighting the hillsides. Participants drank, danced and paraded in costumes, masks and painted faces, with popular 'queens' and 'mayors' from the community crowned for the occasion, while unpopular figures – from annoying village busybodies and quarrelsome married couples to members of the local gentry – were mocked or even burnt or hanged in effigy.

These Bacchanalian aspects – all thoroughly disapproved of by the gentry, clergy and local authorities, who favoured 'manly English sports' over 'Welsh debauchery' – would take on a new form during Rebeccaism. The area's particular blend of religious and secular observance was reflected in customs like the Mari Lwyd, a wassailing tradition still continued today in some parts of Wales, in which a horse's skull mounted on a pole, dressed with colourful ribbons, was carried from house to house by equally dressed-up processions of neighbours with songs, contests of improvised poetry and a call-and-response routine. It was reflected, too, in the persistence of older folklore and superstition surrounding the desolate moorlands and bleak mountainsides, where claims of ghosts abounded and corpse-candles were glimpsed as a portent of death.

LIVING ON AND OFF THE LAND

Most people in south-west Wales in the 1840s made a living from the land, but a handful of the area's families did so in a different sense – they owned it. The great landed families of Carmarthenshire, Cardiganshire and Pembrokeshire had vast manors which stretched across the country, encompassing whole towns and villages along with rivers, woodland, parks, mountains and mines. They built mansions on the coastal plain or in lowland valleys, and purchased second homes in larger towns like Carmarthen and Aberystwyth. Below these dynasties were the lesser gentry, with smaller estates of between 3,000 and 10,000 acres, sometimes struggling to afford their upkeep but still deriving from them a social status and influence over life in their communities, not to mention an income of thousands of pounds each year, largely in rents. Next in line were freeholders, whose land was bought from the Crown or consolidated from commons or waste land. Even fifty acres could grant a family community status – sometimes considered more important than the land's economic value – as they provided jobs or housing on their property, or simply allowed the landless poor to plant a few rows of potatoes in exchange for help with the harvest.

As landowning families themselves were at pains to point out, not all estates were equal. Some large estates gave their owners valuable arable land or the right to mine for minerals, while others consisted only of barren open moorland and common or waste land where poorer farmers, cottage-dwellers and squatters staked out living space and scrapped over pasture for their sheep and cattle. Land that was suitable for this use was scarce, and getting scarcer as landowners took advantage of new Acts of Parliament which allowed them to enclose common land for private use. In Carmarthenshire, more common land was enclosed in the 1830s and 1840s than anywhere else in south Wales. Even with the privatisation of new land for farming or mining, most landowners were still reliant on rental income to sustain their estates and their lifestyle, which made them reluctant to lower their rents even at a time of economic crisis like the one that led to Rebecca's rise. But, by living off rents and tithes, or leasing parts of their estates for mining, forestry or metal extraction, these landed families didn't have to worry about keeping a roof over their head or putting food on the table.

The Welsh landed gentry were famously obsessed with their lineage, and their real or fabricated descent from the country's medieval nobility or from even earlier ancestors. The Dynevor family of Carmarthenshire claimed descent from Rhys ab Thomas, who had been knighted by Henry VII for his support in the Wars of the Roses. Such dynasties were a product of power struggles in wider British history, and of consequent punishment or reward meted out by the victors, who could seize and redistribute land, titles and offices of state to their allies – or indeed seize them back when the same allies fell out of favour. Ancient houses like the

Dynevors were powerful and influential, but had been built on ambition, patronage, networking and luck, and had to use the same means to maintain themselves.

For the gentry, property changed hands and wealth was gained through marriage and inheritance, but both could prove unexpectedly tricky. In marriage, considerations of money and status came before love, and matches were often directed by parents who opposed or punished 'undutiful' marriages that brought no social or financial advantage to the family. Inheriting titles and land wasn't always straightforward – a family's title could lapse if there was no male heir to pass it on to; a maverick or vindictive parent could bequeath their estate arbitrarily to a male relative or friend instead of their children, as would happen in the events that brought the Chambers family to Llanelli. Family wealth could be squandered by extravagance, lost through bad business decisions or wiped out by debt, leaving a younger generation to inherit a title with little else to the name, or stranding them in a crumbling mansion or dilapidated estate with no money left for its upkeep. Even without the folly, fickleness or failures of older generations, running an estate and supporting a household could take its toll, and few of the gentry were financially minded enough to keep on top of things without professional help from bookkeepers or estate managers. Late in life, Edward Lloyd of Rhagad estate in Merioneth passed on some mournful advice to his son: 'Know exactly the state of your affairs and keep regular and intelligible accounts (Would that I had done so).'[16]

Beyond the country's ancient dynasties, some landowners in Wales represented the vast new wealth generated not only through the Industrial Revolution, but its entanglement with empire-building and slavery. Nathaniel Phillips from London, a former rum merchant in Jamaica, bought Slebech estate in Pembrokeshire in 1793. Other estates were themselves developed with the help of money made through colonial expansion and exploitation: William Paxton, formerly the East India Company's Master of the Mint in Bengal, purchased Carmarthenshire's Middleton Hall estate in 1789 and built a neo-classical 'hilltop palace' surrounded by landscaped parkland. By the time of Rebecca fifty years later, the estate had been sold to Edward Hamlin Adams, whose family had been planters in Barbados since the seventeenth century and who had also made his own fortune through the supply of slaves for government projects in Jamaica.

Wherever the gentry's money came from, they spent it on the maintenance of their houses and estates, entertaining each other's families, travelling to the Continent or further afield, employing tutors and governesses for their children and sending them to English public schools or local grammars and later university, or embellishing the grounds of their mansions with lakes, hothouses, ornamental gardens and game reserves. Money was also spent on race-meetings, fox-hunting, gambling, drinking and mistresses – a lifestyle that owed as much to the hedonistic and indulgent Regency era as it did to the Victorian drive for respectability and moralism which showed itself in charitable donations of money, fuel or food to the local poor and philanthropic or cultural endeavours, including the stewardship of agricultural societies and promotion of *eisteddfodau*. Occasions like family birthdays or weddings, or the succession of an heir to an estate, could be made into public celebrations, with musicians hired for open-air concerts and meat and ale distributed to the community so that they could join in the jubilation. These paternalist aspects of the gentry's role would be increasingly eroded as the country's ruling class became integrated into the world of the English aristocracy, leaving Wales for seasons in London or Bath where the trip's expense might pay off in social and political connections, marriage agreements, or just the chance to expand one's art collection or fashionable wardrobe.

'FRESH BUTTER AS WELL AS THE GENTRY'

Rich as well as poor were affected by the changing world of the early nineteenth century. Across Britain, tension was growing between the older gentry and the newly enriched industrialists who were able to buy up property, land and even whole estates from cash-strapped landed families. In Wales, the still-powerful Dynevor dynasty had an estate in the woods above the Towy marked out by the ruins of its twelfth-century castle, but in the coalfield some industrialists were now building brand-new castles of their own, like the Crawshay family's cod-medieval construction, built in 1824, that overlooked their ironworks at Cyfarthfa. The gentry began to place greater emphasis on their titles and ancestry as a means of distinguishing themselves from these industrial upstarts – even if they were happy to offer a daughter (or, less usually, a son) in marriage, bestowing a title and land in exchange for a share of industrial wealth. Within the ranks of the gentry themselves, petty divisions over family status and the recognition of it became increasingly vital, going as far as who could sit in the most prominent pew at church – with some families even paying to ensure the privilege – as well as the order in which each family's coach should arrive on the drive at a ball, and whose daughter could dance with whose son inside the lamplit and wood-panelled ballroom.

The gentry's position in general in the early nineteenth century could also feel fragile – at least to them. For the British landed elite as a whole, the impact of the French Revolution was shifting their attitude towards the poor of their communities from benevolent paternalism to paranoid suspicion. The unprecedented social and political upheaval in France had seen the rapid spread in Britain of radical movements in support of popular democracy, whose members were observed in alarmist reports to be displaying the revolutionary Tricolour flag, addressing each other as 'citizen', and donning red 'caps of liberty' as they demanded political reform. Defenders of the status quo, like the *New Times* newspaper in 1819, issued dire warnings that British radicals who adopted these conventions 'shall not stop there in their imitation of French example'.[17] In Britain, 1819 was the year of the Peterloo Massacre in Manchester, which vividly illustrated these tensions and fears and the brutal response they could inspire in a panicky governing class which responded to movements for change with military repression and prosecutions for sedition. By the 1830s, revolutionary democratic protests had, once again, rocked France, and their waves rippled out to Britain's shores, re-energising British radicals to campaign for political reform and better working and living conditions in their own country.

Wales wasn't unaffected by all this. The rebellion in France had famously been welcomed by the Glamorganshire-born Revd Richard Price, whose 1789 sermon *A Discourse on the Love of Our Country* compared it favourably to England's own Glorious Revolution. Published and picked up widely, the speech triggered a retort from Edmund Burke in his foundational text of modern conservatism *Reflections on the Revolution in France*, while members of Price's London congregation, including Thomas Paine and Mary Wollstonecraft, wrote their own responses in support of Price. In 1795 Haverfordwest in Pembrokeshire had seen a mass riot over rising food prices, in which the local labouring population declared 'they would have fresh butter as well as the gentry, and would live as well as the gentry'. One of the women who took part proclaimed, using rhetoric that could have come straight from the streets of revolutionary Paris, that 'in less time than a twelvemonth, she should see the downfall of all the clergy and of every rich person'.[18] In 1816 Aberystwyth on Wales's west coast was convulsed by anti-enclosure riots while the south-eastern coalfield was paralysed by a strike over wage cuts. The following few years saw another major coalfield strike, as well as widespread disturbances across Wales aimed at preventing the export of food and grain from deprived localities; in Carmarthen, the yeomanry were called in to deal with a hungry 'mob' attempting to stop the export of the area's cheese.

In the south-east's mines and ironworks, the 1820s and 1830s saw the Scotch Cattle's drives for industrial organisation – an early attempt at trade unionism – while, in 1831, the ever-troublesome town of Merthyr Tydfil was occupied for over a week by workers protesting over unemployment, low pay and debt. The Merthyr Rising involved, reputedly for the first time in European protest, the raising of a red flag, and the demands of those who took part included both *Caws a bara* ('Cheese and bread') and *I lawr â'r*

Brenin ('Down with the King'). The Merthyr rioters occupied their town for around a week, fending off the military, destroying a debtor's court and redistributing pawned property. The rebellion was eventually put down by force, with its leader Lewsyn yr Heliwr transported and, on the Prime Minister's orders, the twenty-three-year-old participant Dic Penderyn hanged at Cardiff jail. The drama of these decades meant that by the end of 1831, there were military garrisons established across the whole of Britain, beginning with tumultuous industrial towns like Manchester but soon spreading to the Welsh coalfield as well as Cardiff and Brecon. This wasn't enough, however, to prevent a deadly second 'rising' taking place eight years later in Newport.

In 1844 the *Quarterly Review*, still intent on painting the Welsh as a naturally placid people, explained the previous years of unrest in the country's iron and coal districts by claiming that they resulted from a 'newly formed population' modifying the 'native characteristics' of the Welsh.[19] But the newly formed population that was worrying these commentators had been called into being by the economic changes imposed on Wales itself, leading people down paths shaped by new economic demands, pressures and opportunities. The power of industry was changing not only the landscape of Wales but also the people themselves.

While there was little reason – so far – to fear a similar level of threat in rural Wales to that of insurrectionary Merthyr, the gentry of the three counties of Pembrokeshire, Carmarthenshire and Cardiganshire weren't immune to the alarmist effect of rumours and paranoia. This meant that by the 1840s a number of landowners had withdrawn from their local estates, choosing to spend their time in London, taking little direct interest in the management of their land except in terms of the income it provided, and leaving their properties in the hands of agents and estate managers. This physical distancing further encouraged the breakdown of deference, as did the gentry's increasing drift towards Anglicanism and the English language, which distanced them culturally from the overwhelmingly Nonconformist and Welsh-speaking farmers and labourers.

While the gentry in 1840s Wales had problems and anxieties, these paled into insignificance when compared to the problems of those without money, status and connections – and crucially, without land. Those who rented or worked on the land, whether tenant-farmers, labourers or cottage-dwellers, found a common cause of complaint with each other, and with the landless poor, against those who owned it. These complaints were not precisely over land ownership but more about changes to its management or use. Larger landowners facing financial difficulties, or just wanting to increase their capital, could ignore traditional customs and rights as they tried to increase their income. In Rebecca's time, estate owners had begun not only to enclose an increasing amount of formerly common land but also to crack down on unauthorised use of their land for grazing, gleaning or house-building, and enforced a stricter collection of rents and dues, often bringing in land agents and gamekeepers as an additional layer of policing.

The country's population growth meant a higher demand for land in general, which pushed newer settlements onto less cultivated wasteland on the hillsides, where many poorer people lived in conditions of near-destitution. This demand also meant rent increases for farms by opportunistic landowners. In the early 1800s, leases for many farms had changed from being lifelong to being renewed each year, which further sharpened the insecurity that tenant-farmers felt with the threat of eviction now ever present. With decreasing land to spare, an increasing amount of struggle happened on waste or marginal land to which no one had a legal right but which was fought over by rival farmers, cottage-dwellers and squatters needing space for housing, pasture or cultivation. This created work for lawyers, surveyors, bailiffs and rent collectors – and it created protest. Landowners encroaching on the residue of the commons, farmers looking to expand their fields, shepherds seeking a larger area to graze their flock, the landless poor building an unauthorised roof over their heads, were all coming into conflict as poverty and insecurity escalated.

UNHEARD VOICES

In the years both during and after Rebecca, the question was often asked that if life in Wales was so harsh, and economic and social problems multiplying so quickly, why hadn't the people affected tried to change things by raising their complaints through the proper channels, before taking matters into their own hands in such an extreme way? Under the political system of the early nineteenth century, this was much easier said than done.

The Welsh gentry held power not just as landowners but as those in charge of justice, welfare, policing and the courts. High up in this system were the Lords-Lieutenant of each county in Wales, a prestigious position held for life and usually given to members of a leading county family – like the Dynevors in Carmarthenshire. A local Lord-Lieutenant, somewhat like an MP, was meant to provide a bridge between local and national government. They could influence the appointment of magistrates to administer the law in a specific county – and when they did, they ensured the judiciary reflected the interests of the landed class. Magistrates, who were often gentry themselves, harshly punished offences against private estates like poaching, and frequently conducted trials in English even when they involved defendants who spoke only Welsh.

As overseers of the collection of county rates and taxes, magistrates often spent these opaquely or corruptly, ordering bridges built or road improvements on their own land or for their own convenience when travelling. Many neglected their duties entirely, failing to turn up to judicial meetings and court cases or, when they did, proving incompetent, drunk, or both. Shortly before Rebeccaism, the petty sessions at Llandilo, for instance, had been inquorate on over thirty occasions in three years. Complaints raised during the Rebecca movement – and dating back much earlier – focused on the 'great abuses [in] the appropriation of the county stock' by magistrates and the 'unbearable' treatment of defendants at petty sessions:

[W]e are treated like dogs, we are told to hold our tongues or go out of the room, that the law that is dealt out to us is the law of the magistrates' clerk, and not the law of the Queen, and the magistrates' clerks charge us what they please.[20]

In response to these conditions, the early nineteenth century had seen mass campaigns for political reform, which included working-class organisation and wider movements for democracy. This culminated in the passing of the 1832 Reform Act, which opened up political influence and careers to the middle classes. The new wealthy industrialists now shared power with the landed gentry, with a section of the middle classes given a greater degree of influence – but for those lower down the social scale, there was very little change. Only three years after the Reform Act, the hated New Poor Law was introduced, and working-class reformers felt they had been sold out by their middle-class allies, who had accepted a share of political power for themselves rather than pushing for a new and fairer system of distributing influence that would include the whole population.

The few magistrates who attempted to fulfil their duties conscientiously in the 1840s, like William Chambers Junior at Llanelli, faced difficulties with a vastly expanded population, increasing unrest and few resources to keep order. With no national police network established until 1856, chief constables were, again, chosen from the gentry or yeomanry of a county. They were assisted by petty or regular constables drawn from the local population, who were low paid, unpopular and largely ineffective given their frequent reluctance to execute warrants against their friends and neighbours, either from sympathy or fear of reprisals. At times of unrest or when trouble was expected – times which included county fairs and elections as well as strikes and lockouts – magistrates could enlist special constables, who were recruited from the local community under the 1831 Special Constables Act. If nervous about any kind of mass gathering among the people, magistrates could also read the Riot Act, which had been passed in

1715 to increase the powers of local authorities. Reading the Riot Act would call in the military – either the local mounted yeomanry or, if they were garrisoned nearby, professional soldiers – to clear an assembled crowd by any means necessary.

When local magistrates were also, in their other capacities, landowners who charged high rents, employers who cut wages and Poor Law Guardians who implemented the workhouse system, there was little sense of an impartial authority to appeal to. Rebeccaite protestors were often asked to take up their complaints on the tollgate system or the level of rents with the relevant authorities, but there seemed little point in doing so when the relevant authority could frequently be the subject of your original complaint wearing, often literally, a different hat. Nonetheless, there was no shortage of complaints from farmers and labourers throughout the 1830s and 1840s, voiced in individual grievance petitions and court cases, as well as in pamphlets and broadsides. The writer of a letter to *The Times* in 1844 attributed Rebeccaism to 'the supercilious insolence of the squirearchy' and offered a vivid picture of 'the state of society in our rural districts':

> Could a Kentish yeoman, or a Yorkshire farmer, take his stand in a Welch town during an assize week, and see a Welch squire issue from his inn, followed by a tenant or two, he would blush with indignation. The 'master', as he is still slavishly designated, striding along, snuffing and snorting, ready to burst with self-importance, and the poor serfs, hats in hand, bowing and crouching at every step![21]

Even observers whose sympathies lay entirely with the gentry, like Herbert Vaughan of Golden Grove estate, writing in the 1920s, still recognised the power they held in the early nineteenth century:

> [Until some forty years ago] the gentry or the squirearchy – call them what you will – were the real rulers of the countryside. They interpreted the law at Petty Sessions;

they were responsible for all local administration at Quarter Sessions; they constituted in fact a ruling caste, and on the social side the wives and daughters and mothers of these magistrates shared their rule.[22]

After the 1832 Reform Act hadn't gone far enough for many reformers, efforts for deeper changes had poured into movements like Chartism, but even a decade later at the time of Rebecca, the growing forces of democracy still had few legitimate ways to express themselves. The mid-nineteenth century saw a rise in complaints about not only landlords and magistrates, but also the MPs representing south-west Wales, who throughout the 1840s were notorious for their lack of attendance at or interest in parliamentary debate, their interests roused only when particular acts of Parliament threatened their rights as landowners. That MPs in the area were absent or negligent was a problem of the wider political system, which was geared, yet again, towards the representation and protection of the landed interest.

At the time of Rebecca the three counties of Pembrokeshire, Cardiganshire and Carmarthenshire were represented by four MPs, with another four borough MPs, elected by 15,000 voters. With those able to vote comprising only 5 per cent of the local population, this was one of the weakest mandates in Britain. Local politicians in Wales, as in Britain as a whole, were sometimes from opposing party factions but tended to represent the same class and principles. Whig or Tory party labels were less important than personality, connections and family influence. Dynastic families like the Dynevors passed on seats in Parliament from father to son, and the gentry monopolised local politics for personal or family prestige and a place within the wider networks of favours, patronage and social connections that also made up national politics.

Carmarthenshire's local politics revolved around the feuding of gentry-led factions, the 'Reds' and the 'Blues' – not with the political associations these colours might bring to mind today, but representing two sides of the same semi-feudal coin. The 'Reds' were associated with the Dynevor family, three generations of whom sat as Tory MPs between 1754 and 1852, and the 'Blues' with the Whig houses of Cwmgwili and Golden Grove. Each faction fielded their own candidates in elections, pouring family money and resources into their campaigns and ensuring that independents had no chance of breaking through. Elections could last days, with candidates splurging on posters, pamphlets and propaganda, ribbons and cockades in their party colours, and lodgings, drink and entertainment for their supporters as they trooped into town to the polls, encouraging them to cheer their own candidates and heckle, slander or even physically attack the other side. Candidates could win political support through gifting their local area a new civic building or park, granting loans to individuals, or offering civic offices if elected – and could, of course, then maintain that support by threatening to withdraw their patronage or call in their loans. Tenants on their land and men in their employ were assumed to vote as directed, and could be threatened with eviction or the sack if they failed to do so. Once elected, there was little or no accountability; in Carmarthen, meetings of the council were conducted in private with members having to take an oath of secrecy.

As those who took part in the Rebecca riots would discover, direct action could offer greater and more immediate influence than exchanging their vote – if they even had one – for a barrel of beer at election time or under threat from their landlord or boss.

THE DOWNWARD SPIRAL

In the years before Rebecca emerged in 1839, a series of unproductive harvests due to bad weather, combined with a fall in the price of cattle and butter, had whittled away the already small capital that tenant-farmers had. When employment was good, more money was circulating and farmers could expect to charge higher prices for their produce, which meant they could cover their own higher rents. But when prices and wages collapsed in the early 1840s, rents stayed high – and so did tithes, poor rates and county rates, all of which either remained constant or increased over the period. To offset this fall in income, larger farmers sublet or re-mortgaged their land, or sold or pawned what livestock, clothes and possessions they could, to buy themselves time until the slump in agricultural prices was over. Farmers also looked to reduce the money they spent on their labourers by cutting wages and offering fewer jobs – regardless of the fact that labourers had their own rent, taxes and tithes to pay and food to afford.

In times of individual need, neighbours could offer loans, share food or lend goods to each other – but when a whole community was faced with the same sharp drop in income at the same time, disaster set in. Mutual loan customs like the bidding wedding broke down when no one had any money to spare, and families were unable to save or to set up their children with their own farm, let alone lend to their neighbours. Those unable to work on a family farm or set up their own, and those who lost their land as rents rose to an unaffordable level, switched to becoming labourers on other farms – accepting greater precarity and a fall in their wages – or packed up and headed east to the industrial districts for work. But in 1839–41 the crisis in agriculture was joined by an industrial depression which saw wages in the mines and ironworks collapse, cutting off the temporary escape route to the coalfield and driving up both rural and industrial unemployment.

'Everything is not much, but all these things come together,' explained a farmer at the government's eventual Commission of Inquiry into the causes of Rebeccaism.[23] His words provided a rejoinder to the testimony of George Rice Trevor, MP for Carmarthenshire and heir to the Dynevor estate, who told the same commission that the reasons for the unrest 'appear to me to be so numerous, and yet in many cases so trifling, that it is difficult to say which of them predominates'.[24] While Trevor may have viewed the multitude of material demands crowding in upon the population of his constituency as 'trifling' when seen in isolation, their cumulative effect could feel catastrophic. A contemporary editorial in the *Welshman* newspaper captured the growing sense of crisis:

Distress and ruin are progressing with giant strides all over the country. The manufacturers are stopping work because they cannot sell their goods; and their workmen are thrown upon the parishes and cease to buy the food, clothing and provisions which the farmers have to sell. This produces distress among the farmers, besides a heavy increase in their poor rates; and then as the farmers find they cannot dispose of their cattle and their corn, they will by degrees cease to produce them; up will go the prices to those few of the public still able to buy, and then will come in a flood of corn and cattle from foreign countries which will [...] put the finishing stroke to [the farmer's] misery, unless his landlord will give up his rents – a thing not very likely to happen.[25]

As the economic squeeze got stronger, those who could scratch together the cost of travel made their way to the coast and the ships bound for America, Canada and Australia, hoping to start a new life far from Wales. Those left behind did what they could to tighten their own belts. They sold a greater proportion of their livestock and dairy produce to cover rent and bills than they used to feed themselves, and even better-off tenant-farmers began living, like the cottagers and squatters on waste land, hand to mouth, stretching out meat to flavour broth or gruel and mixing their oatmeal with more water than milk. There was little chance of luxuries like butter, bacon or even cheese, let alone the roast meats and fresh fruits, pastries, wine and beer that still loaded the tables in the big houses when the gentry entertained with dinners and dances. Such a poor diet inevitably affected people's strength and energy, which in turn affected their ability to work and earn money, setting in motion a vicious cycle of impoverishment. The still abundant flow of travellers and tourists to the area began to remark on the physical fragility of the south Welsh 'peasantry', not only in comparison with Welsh workers in the coalfield, but with agricultural workers in comparable circumstances in England.

Unsurprisingly, rates of death from ill-health rose as swiftly as rates of emigration. So, too, did the suicide rate, as resilience battled despair, while others who no longer felt able to cope turned to petty crime, heavy drinking or both. But the economic crisis and political shifts were even affecting the definition of crime: gleaning for fuel or food on newly enclosed land was now treated as theft, rather than custom. As enclosure had made ordinary people into trespassers, so the Game Act of 1831 made many into poachers, as legal changes meant that the new private rights of the few to land and its produce overrode the older traditional rights of the many. Conflict with landowners' agents like bailiffs or gamekeepers could turn violent as the lines between customary sustenance, self-defence and crime became blurred.

Meanwhile, many of the gentry were absent, and not simply because they were holidaying at Bath Spa. Across Cardiganshire in particular, mansions stood almost permanently empty, their occupants increasingly nervous of contact outside their bubble. The gentry's withdrawal, arguably, just exacerbated matters – had they remained engaged with their community, there would have been traditional duties to fulfil: not only civic and judicial roles as magistrates, but also less formal philanthropic and paternalist functions. The fact that they effectively abandoned these roles eroded the community respect they had formerly been able to rely on and contributed to the search for new forms of authority and ways of 'setting things right'.

In the absence of leadership from the gentry, some of the longer established farming families arose as community leaders. These figureheads began to take decisions on local matters and could call meetings to discuss solutions, including protest. Many of these families were chapel-going Dissenters, and Tory voices like the *Carmarthen Journal* worried that they were fomenting an independent layer of authority, ready to usurp the Church and the aristocracy. In reality, they were mostly trying to hold together a fraying social fabric in the absence of the traditional social contract between a dutiful landowner and a contentedly deferential population. What they had instead, in addition to their own economic worries, was a neglectful, if not wholly absent ruling class and a people torn between despondency and rage. The age of Rebecca was ready to begin.

PART ONE:
REBECCA RISES

1
THE FINAL STRAW

THE FIRST REBECCA

Thomas Rees who lived at Carnabwth, a stone cottage on the slopes of Pembrokeshire's Preseli Hills, was not the likeliest of rebel leaders. Thirty-three years old in 1839 and a father to three young children, he worked as a casual labourer on local farms but was better known as a prize-fighter, winning small amounts of money, food or drink by taking part in boxing contests and exhibitions at county fairs throughout Pembrokeshire, Cardiganshire and Carmarthenshire. Alongside this rough-and-ready lifestyle, he found time to be devoutly religious, and was well known by his neighbours as a passionate reciter of the *canu'r pwnc*, an ancient form of choral chanting that formed part of the Whitsun services at Pembrokeshire's Baptist chapels.

Rees's cottage, near Glyn Saith Maen farm in the parish of Llangolman, was a *tŷ unnos* – a house built in a single night. Structures like this had become common in rural Wales over the eighteenth and nineteenth centuries as population growth, poverty, and the enclosure of smaller farms, commons and waste land by private landowners drove people to scrape out a living on whatever scrap of land they could find. While some saw no better option than leaving the land entirely and joining the growing numbers of unemployed and homeless people on the streets of larger towns like Carmarthen, those who chose to cling on threw up rough dwellings on the hillsides, the outskirts of villages or the edges of their remaining commons. These cottages weren't much to look at – mostly built of stone cemented with clay or mud, a thatched roof with a hole for a chimney, and little furniture or bedding – but they were better than sleeping in a hayloft, stable or barn in between your casual shifts on a farm, and at least you could call them your own.

The tradition of *tŷ unnos*, although it had no basis in official British law, held that a person was entitled to the freehold of whatever shelter they could build over the course of a night, as long as smoke rose from its roof at dawn, and of the land within a stone's throw of it. They were often built by individuals with the help of fellow squatters, sometimes to provide a newly married couple with a household of their own. The custom annoyed both landlords and tenant-farmers, as these new dwellings could cut across the boundaries of their fields and interfere with the places where their livestock grazed. But the high number of court cases which took place over these homes had ruled that if squatters were allowed to remain on the land for more than one generation then they had established a legal right to it. Before this could happen, farmers and landlords often took matters into their own hands, getting rid of *tai unnos* and those who lived in them by pulling the houses down around them.

So Twm Carnabwth, as he became known, knew a few things about poverty, precarious work and existing in the margins of an increasingly poor and divided society where even the roof you had built over your head could come under threat at any moment. He might, therefore, have been intrigued to see, in the spring of 1839, the posting of handbills around his neighbourhood, calling for a public meeting 'to take into consideration the propriety of the toll gate' at the nearby village of Efail-wen.

ROCKY ROADS

South-west Wales, like many places across the country at this time, had roads that were rudimentary and barely maintained. For getting around your own farm or estate, or for visiting neighbours, chapel or the pub, you could manage well enough on foot, by using the narrow footpaths and cart-tracks over the hillside, or the paths used by drovers taking animals from farms to local markets and fairs or over the border for sale in England. But for travelling further afield, or for the business of buying and selling heavier loads at market, you needed horses, wheels or both.

The main roads were necessary for mail-coaches, farmers' carts and the gentry's carriages alike. While roads outside major cities had never been perfect, by the mid-nineteenth century they were being used by an increasing number of vehicles and needed a greater level of repair and maintenance. Road upkeep had previously been down to the local parish authorities, who tried to keep on top of things by requiring all able-bodied men to spend one day each year repairing the roads in their neighbourhood. This wasn't professional roadbuilding of the sort developing in London; instead of tarmac, rubble, broken slates and tiles were thrown into the mud to form a rough surface for the road.

In 1835, the Highways Act was passed, with the intention of improving things by permitting tolls on travel to be charged in order to pay for road maintenance. But rather than funding upkeep and improvements via a national tax, the new law placed responsibility in the hands of local turnpike trusts. Typically run by a board of trustees made up of local gentry and businessmen, who appointed their own surveyors, accountants and clerks, these trusts were allowed to raise money for roadbuilding and repair from government borrowing and private capital, then to recover the costs of their creditors by charging a toll from those who used the road, plus whatever further profit they felt like making. The trusts were meant to be a solution, but they were soon causing problems of their own.

People might have expected the new trusts to bring in professional road-surveyors and builders, assess the area's needs and channel their findings into practical improvements – but they seemed more preoccupied with making money. Their administration was chaotic, with accounts barely kept and rarely published, and there was no limit on the number of gates they could install. The rights to collect tolls were auctioned off to the highest bidder and used to maximise profits as well as recuperate costs. South-west Wales, moreover, was exceptional for having a number of different trusts with separate owners operating in the same locality. In the early 1840s, several of these trusts had been taken over by professional toll-collectors who raised the number of gates and became more exacting – some might say excessive – in the collection of tolls.

Some trusts, like the Whitland in Carmarthenshire, began to put up gates and bars on roads which they themselves did not repair, but the parishes did, effectively taking money for nothing. Information announcing a new gate was published in the local press, but if farmers and other local workers didn't read the newspapers on that particular day, the first they knew of the changes was when they found a barrier – as simple as a chain or bar, or as elaborate as a newly built tollhouse and gate – suddenly blocking their usual route to market or to work. With tollgate-keepers often paid on commission, encouraging them to collect more and higher tolls when they could, and trusts looking to turn a profit for their shareholders by any means possible, this was a system open to abuse.

A particular problem for Welsh farmers was the toll placed on the movement of lime, which was used as a whitewash for buildings and as fertiliser or to counteract acidity in soil, its alkaline leached by the heavy Welsh rain. Blocks of limestone were shipped in bulk to the south-west coast, where they were burnt in kilns to turn them into useable material. 'Lime roads' running from the coastal kilns into the hills allowed farmers to pick up and cart the lime back to their farms – but these roads had now quickly become studded with tollgates. When lime-burning season began in May, farmers would assemble at midnight at the nearest tollgate and set off for the coast, hoping to get to the kilns and back in a day to avoid paying a toll twice. A return journey to transport lime from the coast back to a farm could cost as much as five shillings – about half of a farm labourer's weekly wage. To add insult to injury, lime was meant to be charged at half-toll, or free if being taken back to a farm for agricultural use, but many tollkeepers simply ignored this clause and demanded the full toll before they would let farmers through their gate.

It wasn't just about lime, or just about farmers. Roads were used to get to local markets to buy or sell produce, to travel to work, or simply to visit other parts of the country. Many poorer people rented patches of land from local farmers to grow potatoes or other crops, and when the crops were ready to pick, needed to bring them back home by cart – which now meant passing through tollgates, and being charged for transporting produce that you had grown yourself. There were even cases of people being fined for evading tolls by driving their cart or livestock by a less convenient but toll-free route, and there was soon an increased number of 'side-bar' gates, placed strategically on by-roads to catch out any travellers who tried to bypass the main roads. Complaints made about all this to local magistrates – who, again, were often tollgate trustees themselves – were dismissed or ignored.

TOLLGATES AND WORKHOUSES

Efail-wen, on the border of Pembrokeshire and Carmarthenshire, was the site of a tollgate managed by Thomas Bullin. In his late thirties and originally from Surrey, he had settled in Swansea, from where he ran a network of tollgates throughout Wales and England. Rather than a tollkeeper who did the more mundane – and soon to become dangerous – work of staffing the gates and collecting tolls, Bullin was known as a 'toll-farmer': he leased the gates from the trusts and hired people – often his own relatives – to manage their daily operation. Frequently paying over the odds to convince the trusts to give him the lease of their gates, he then clawed back his investment by raising the level of tolls and putting up more gates, often without the knowledge of the trusts, let alone their permission. Having outsourced their duties to Bullin, the trusts then took little notice of the way he ran things.

In 1839, one of Bullin's new gates had just been placed on the only remaining untolled road out of Efail-wen, on a turnpike road that led north from Narberth to Cardiganshire. For the already hard-up local farmers, this spelled financial disaster: they now couldn't leave the area to bring lime back from the coast without paying a toll, nor, equally crucial to their income, could they freely take their produce or livestock to market. And if farmers wanted to hire farmhands from out of town, they would also need to find the money to pay for their journeys in and out. On top of this, they began to wonder where the money from this new tax was being spent: since the state of the roads was as bad as ever, the money clearly wasn't being used for repair and upkeep – so where was it going, apart from into the pockets of the toll-farmers?

By July, when Twm Carnabwth heard about it, there had already been not one, but two attacks on the Efail-wen gate. And, back in January, there had also been an attack on the newly built workhouse at Narberth, in protest at the New Poor Law. These things were more closely connected than they might seem – certainly more than they would later seem to the local authorities. Since the 1600s the welfare of the poor in Britain had been, like the upkeep of the roads, the responsibility of their local parish, with 'poor rates' collected by the local authorities from the community and then doled out to the local poor in each parish in the form of money, clothing or food. But from the late eighteenth century, industrialisation and population growth meant that there were more of the poor than there had been before, and the parish system was increasingly unable to cope.

The 1834 Poor Law Amendment Act, like the Highways Act, was intended to improve things but tended to make matters worse. Under the new system, parishes were instructed to set up Poor Law Unions, with each union administrating a local workhouse: forty-seven Poor Law Unions were created in Wales. The Unions were administered by Boards of Guardians who, usually consisting of local landowners and magistrates and their appointees, placed their own economic interests first and foremost, using their decisions to reduce the poor rates they had to pay for the workhouses by 'removing the idle and desperate from the parish' and making them the responsibility of another. They also prioritised setting inmates of the workhouse to work to pay for the running of the place, thereby reducing the amount needed for their upkeep from parish rates.

Beyond the feelings of the 'idle and desperate' themselves, the new system was unpopular for its complexity and endless paperwork, and there were frequent complaints that salaried middlemen often enriched themselves at the expense of both givers and receivers of relief. As unemployment and impoverishment intensified across Britain in the late 1830s, the growing numbers of poor people could no longer rely on parish relief but, under the New Poor Law, were faced with either the workhouse's impersonal bureaucracy and harsh regime or destitution.

It was one more problem for ordinary people to deal with in these years of crisis, and while the problems of the Poor Law weren't unique to south-west Wales, the problem of the tollgates was. It might have been impossible to demolish the workhouses, the landed estates or the vagaries of the rural economy itself, but – as more and more of the local population were beginning to argue – something could certainly be done about a bar across a road.

2
RESPECTABLE RADICALS, ROUGH MUSIC

FILLING A DESERTED SEAT

Nineteenth-century reformers could be respectable members of society as well as radical firebrands, and one example of this was provided by William Chambers Junior. Educated at Eton and Cambridge, he had arrived in Llanelli in 1827 to join his father, who was almost as new to the town. Their formerly grand, but now decaying residence, Llanelly House, faced the imposing parish church of St Elli's and backed onto what had once been a large and elaborate garden stretching as far as the river Lliedi with 'all sorts of fruit trees in perfection', as well as stables and a dairy. The three-storey townhouse formed part of the estate of the Stepney dynasty, which, despite its size and splendour, had lain neglected for over fifty years as the family abandoned the town in favour of aristocratic life in London.

The tourist narratives that lauded the beauty of the Welsh landscape further west were less kind about Llanelli, calling it 'an ugly populous town near the sea'[1] and a 'miserable village [...] famous for nothing but a deserted seat of the Stepneys'.[2] This judgement was a little harsh; by the time the Chambers family moved into the dilapidated Llanelly House and set about smartening it up, the town around them was also polishing its image, expanding from its existing industrial base of tinplate production into a significant seaport that also exported coal and copper. By 1830, a more impressed guidebook was able to record that:

> the improvement in [Llanelli's] appearance has kept pace
> with its prosperity; many old and unsightly habitations have

been removed, and new ones erected on their site, with ranges of handsome shops; a new and convenient market-house has also been built, which is well attended on the market days.[3]

The Chambers family had reached Llanelly House by a convoluted route, though it was one that many gentry of the era would have recognised. Its original owners in the Stepney family had come to Wales from London in the sixteenth century and formed a fruitful alliance with the Vaughans, a clan, who, like the Dynevors, claimed descent from ancient Welsh nobility. But Sir John Stepney, the eighth baronet of the line, had died unmarried in 1811. Just as Llanelly House, with its stucco fronting and tall panelled sash windows, was more Georgian than Victorian in style, so Sir John had been more of a Regency rake of the old school than a respectable patriarch. Having fallen out with his relatives over his dissolute lifestyle, he left a complicated will that aimed to deal them a financial blow by tying up the rights to his property in other legacies. These were left to no less than six different people, all unrelated to the Stepney family, and all of whom died in quick succession in the following few years and without producing heirs themselves.

Eventually, in 1824, the estate ended up passing to William Chambers Senior, one of Sir John's three illegitimate sons. The inheritance came as some surprise to Chambers, who was then fifty-one and living humbly enough in Kent. Rather than continuing the Stepney tradition of absentee landlordism, Chambers chose instead to move into the family mansion with his own teenage son. William Chambers Junior was, like his father, illegitimate, although Chambers Senior sought to cement his newfound respectability by belatedly marrying the boy's mother two years after they settled in Llanelli.

The family's dubious origins didn't endear them to the more established Welsh gentry like the Vaughans and Dynevors, to say nothing of the embittered remnants of the Stepney line. And, as strangers to Llanelli stepping into the prominent role of landowners and landlords, neither father nor son had a smooth transition into life in the town. In 1829, while down from his first term at Cambridge, Chambers Junior set off one night on a pub crawl in the company of the family's coachman and gamekeeper. Ending up in the Square and Compass tavern in Water Street in the early hours of the morning, with his spending money exhausted, Chambers staggered across the road to knock up a closed pawnbroker's shop, drunkenly demanding to be let in so that he could pawn his coat in order to buy a cup of coffee. Unfortunately for him, the building was both owned and occupied by the town's constable, who descended to the street, grabbed Chambers by the lapels and, when Chambers tried to fight back, punched him to the ground with what he later recalled as 'the hardest blow I ever felt'. In the resulting court case, the constable was unrepentant and noted that, in addition to Chambers being drunk and disorderly, his family 'have raised my rent and they buy nothing at my shop'.[4]

The Chambers were also embroiled in a long-running feud with Llanelli's vicar Ebenezer Morris, already the kind of man known to his neighbours and congregation as a 'colourful character', who objected to the alterations these newcomers were making to the town. In 1832 when the Chambers were invited to a private showing at Wombwell's Travelling Menagerie of Wild Beasts which had set up at Parc Eynon, the vicar arrived drunk at the same showing and commenced insulting Chambers and his family by likening them to the hyenas on display. The Chambers, wanting to avoid a confrontation, withdrew from the scene, only for the vicar to catch up with them at the doors of Llanelly House itself where he assaulted Chambers Senior. When the local police arrived they found a furious Chambers Junior threatening, in the timeless sign of readiness for a physical altercation, to take off his coat, before they calmed him down and wearily took the vicar into custody.

By 1839, when he founded the Llanelli Reform Society, William Chambers Junior was thirty years old and married to a naval captain's daughter, with his drunken sprees and street-fighting days a thing of the past. After his family's rocky entry into the town's society, and perhaps bearing in mind the town constable's complaint that his family raised rents while buying nothing from local suppliers, he had decided to give something back to the community. He spent £10,000 on establishing a pottery, built to the rear of what was now his family's estate, and accompanied with quality housing for the factory's workers, many of whom had migrated across the border from the long-established potteries in Staffordshire.

Chambers's motivations here weren't purely philanthropic, but tied to the endless wrangling over property and inheritances that had originally brought his father to Llanelli. The Stepney family had begun a complex legal battle to have the estate returned to them, in the course of which it had emerged that Chambers, being an illegitimate son, wouldn't be able to inherit the estate that Sir John Stepney had – in a roundabout way – bequeathed to his father. Building the pottery was, therefore, an insurance to maintain his commercial interests in Llanelli and to have something of his own to fall back on. Its contribution to the industrial development of the town, however, was at last making the family more popular in its civic life, and would make Chambers Junior a prominent figure – for good and ill – in the years to come.

MORAL AND PHYSICAL FORCE

Despite being a friend to local business, and a member of the minor gentry himself, in politics William Chambers Junior was pro-Reform, in favour of a more equal distribution of political power and influence, including extending the vote to ordinary people. There wasn't necessarily any contradiction here. The Reform movement of the early nineteenth century, and the Chartist movement that grew alongside it, had always been split between what was known as 'moral force' – the conviction that calm and rational political arguments would persuade those who held power and wealth to distribute it more evenly – and 'physical force' – the tendency which argued that constitutional pressure was not enough and that reform would only be won through action that openly threatened the position of the ruling classes.

In the same year that Chambers founded the Llanelli Reform Society with a genteel dinner and drinks at the town's Ship and Castle inn, another part of Wales was witnessing a pro-Reform action that ended in the worst bloodshed for a generation. In the summer of 1839, Parliament's rejection of a Chartist petition signed by over a million people had generated indignation in the movement, and doubts about the efficacy of moral-force persuasion began to spread. November of that year saw the Newport Rising, led by the former mayor of Newport, John Frost, but backed by physical-force Chartists from the coal and iron towns of the Glamorganshire and Monmouthshire valleys. It began as a demonstration in protest at the arrest of several Newport Chartists and ended in an armed stand-off outside the town's Westgate Hotel, where twenty-two demonstrators were shot dead by the military and dozens more injured. It was the deadliest clash between the state and the people since the Peterloo Massacre twenty years earlier.

The Newport Rising marked the peak of Chartist unrest in Wales, but earlier in the same year the rural town of Llanidloes in Montgomeryshire had been occupied by local Chartists protesting at the collapse of the town's textile industry. For five days in May 1839, the demonstrators seized control of the town and forced the release of three local activists who had been arrested and held in the Trewythen Hotel. A detachment of troops was sent in to restore order, which it managed with none of the carnage that would distinguish Newport a few months later. In court, the Llanidloes Chartists were defended by Hugh Williams, a high-profile radical lawyer from Kidwelly who in 1836 had founded the first Chartist branch in Wales – located, perhaps unexpectedly, not in the militant coalfield but the rural market town of Carmarthen.

William Chambers Junior, like Hugh Williams, felt that he had more in common with respectable moral-force Chartists than with the Valleys hotheads shot on the steps of the Westgate Hotel. But it would be surprising if the legacy of Newport, either as caution or as inspiration, failed to influence agitations like Rebeccaism, which took off around the same time. As the movement grew, Chartist leaders like Feargus O'Connor and Bronterre O'Brien would not have many compliments to pay to Rebecca. But the Chartists of Llanidloes showed that, in Wales, opposition to political injustice and economic crisis was not just a concern of the industrial coalfield. This was vividly demonstrated when, just a few days after the Llanidloes riots and a few months before the Newport Rising, the tollgates in Pembrokeshire and Carmarthenshire began to burn.

EFAIL-WEN

Tollhouses were usually simple structures – one-storey buildings, often circular, built of wood or stone with a thatched roof and windows that overlooked the road, allowing approaching traffic to be seen in both directions. At a time when housing and steady employment were becoming scarce, the job of tollkeeper could provide both, in exchange merely for raising and lowering the bar or chain across the road on payment of a toll or, even more simply, opening and closing the gate. But the job would soon look less attractive as it became more complicated and more perilous.

The destruction of the tollgate at Efail-wen took three separate attempts, although the first had seemed conclusive enough. After a meeting on 13 May of around 400 people, the attendees set off towards the tollhouse and gate on foot and on horseback, with a cry in favour of 'free laws, and free travelling to coal-pits and lime-kilns'.[5] They spent three hours on the work of demolition, leaving the tollhouse torn down to within a yard of the ground, the gate broken into pieces and the gate-posts sawn off. The trust in charge, baffled by an attack that seemed to have come out of nowhere, acted quickly to rebuild the house and gate, only for the gate to be destroyed again in a similar manner on the night of 6 June. After this, a group of constables was set to guard the tollhouse and its chain across the road, which had temporarily replaced the destroyed gate.

Despite the police presence, a third and final attack took place in broad daylight on a Wednesday afternoon in July, after another meeting openly advertised by public placards. The attackers had painted their faces in black and red, some had stuck on beards or wigs made of horsehair, and all were dressed in an odd-looking assortment of outfits – white petticoats or gowns pulled on over their work-clothes, flannel shawls flung around their shoulders, and women's bonnets or nightcaps on their heads. At the head of the crowd was a figure, dressed in the same striking style, who the *Carmarthen Journal*'s later report described as a 'distinguished' leader. This was Twm Carnabwth, who, according to local legend, had borrowed a dress for the occasion from the only woman in the neighbourhood sufficiently statuesque to have one that would fit his prize-fighter's frame. This woman was known by her neighbours as 'Great Rebecca of Llangolman', or 'Big Becca'.

When they caught sight of the advancing crowd, some of them on horseback, variously blowing horns, banging pots and pans and brandishing sledgehammers, the police around the gate did not stay to confront them, but rushed to fetch reinforcements from the Pembrokeshire yeomanry. On their return, as the crowd scattered just as fast across the fields around the shattered tollhouse, the only prisoner taken was Morris David, a blacksmith in his eighties, whose lame leg had prevented him escaping quickly enough. Taken in chains to Haverfordwest jail, he refused to identify any other rioters, and was eventually released due to lack of evidence. Despite an investigation by local magistrates, no admissions of responsibility were made or convictions achieved for any of the three attacks, and on 23 July a meeting of local trustees, gentry and magistrates advised the trust not to re-erect the gate.

Aside from a handful of craftsmen like Morris David, the Efail-wen rioters were a collection of local farmers and their hired labourers. Twm Carnabwth wasn't part of an established farming family like the Bowens of Trelech or the Hugheses of Llanon, whose sons would also play the role of Rebecca at future occasions, but families like this needed the labour and the strength in numbers of men like him, who had their own reasons for disliking the gates and were happy to help out in getting rid of them. Although Twm seemed to play no further recorded part in the riots, his presence at the start of them was instrumental in the path they took, and he – along with 'Big Becca' – may even have given them the name that would make them famous.

PROTEST OR PANTOMIME?

The name given to the rioters' leader, and the way they dressed and acted, instantly caught the imagination of those who saw them. The *Quarterly Review* wrote condescendingly about the seemingly incongruous nature of Rebecca's costume:

> All the movements of the assailants had been directed by a leader mounted and disguised, like his body-guard, in female attire, or with a shirt thrown over the clothes, and having, like them, his face blackened and shaded by a bonnet, or by flowing curls or other head-gear ... Is any germ or feature of [Rebeccaism] to be discerned in any prevailing usage, or legend, or ancient tradition of the district? Who suggested to the mind of the plodding and unpoetical Welsh farmer the idea of the mounted Rebecca heading the charge of her sylvan chivalry, rallied in an instant from their mountain ambush, and dispersing again with the rapidity of ghosts at dawn?[6]

The roots of Rebeccaism's costume and symbolism did, in fact, lie deep in Welsh 'ancient tradition' and folk culture, if not in the classical literary references with which the *Quarterly Review* was more comfortable. The form the riots took was drawn from the social life and cultural world around them, and specifically the ritual known as the *ceffyl pren* or 'wooden horse'. The *Quarterly Review*, while denying that this custom could have influenced Rebeccaism, nonetheless helpfully described it at length:

> The *Ceffyl Pren*, which has not unfrequently afforded much trouble to the local authorities, consists of a procession

headed by a man wearing the disguise of a horse's head, sometimes the skeleton of a real head covered with a sheet or cloth, sometimes a head made of wood, which is placed upon the man's shoulders. Thus accoutred and attended by his rabble train, having their faces blackened, and torches in their hands, the 'Ceffyl Pren' makes his visitations by night to the houses of those who, for any domestic misconduct, such as is occasionally visited with 'rough music' in England, or from any other causes have made themselves obnoxious to popular disfavour.[7]

In fact, those closer to the action – both those who took part in the riots and those who tried to suppress them – did tend to reference the *ceffyl pren* when trying to explain the form Rebeccaism took. The *Welshman* newspaper claimed that the attacks on tollgates had 'stepped into the place of the old-fashioned Ceffil-prens, and is thus favourably looked upon by the large mass of the community'.[8]

Drawing on familiar customs like the *ceffyl pren* lent political actions a frame of reference that their participants – and their audience – could easily understand. Indeed, many forms of protest across pre-industrial Britain could seem more like folk-rituals, carnivals or even pantomimes. For centuries, protestors had cross-dressed or worn animal masks and skins, carried effigies of unpopular figures or other objects to symbolise their reasons for protesting, and given themselves a soundtrack of 'rough music' produced from everyday items by blowing horns, ringing bells and drumming on pots and pans. This kind of protest was an evolution of a ritual that had various forms and names in various places across Britain and Europe, but was commonly known as *charivari* – local variants on the term included 'skimmington', 'shivaree', 'riding the stang' and the Welsh *ceffyl pren*.

Charivari was essentially a public shaming ritual used by communities to uphold local traditions and to express moral outrage at breaches in social norms and conventions. Originally these offences could include domestic violence or adultery, but charivari's elements also became incorporated into protests against enclosure of common land and other political and economic issues – like tollgates. As with original charivaris, these protests were intended to uphold customary rights, to draw public attention to a breach in the moral, social or political code that a community was used to and to resolve it. The word's broader meaning, of humorous or irreverent protest or critique, even made it into the name of the satirical magazine founded in 1841, a kind of nineteenth-century *Private Eye*, called *Punch, or the London Charivari*.

The rural communities where charivari evolved had, like south-west Wales, other festivals and carnivals where parading and dressing in colourful costumes and masks formed part of the event. These costumes symbolised the freedom of the occasion, and expressed that, during this period, those who took part were free from everyday rules and laws. Many costumes, including cross-dressing or wearing animal masks and hides, were meant to symbolise 'the world turned upside-down', suspending normality – including aspects of social and political relations – for a temporary period of anarchic enjoyment. In systems structured by rigid social and political hierarchies, occasions of organised chaos like this could act as a useful pressure-valve, allowing those who took part to get their daily frustrations off their chests. This exposure and mockery of power structures through inverting them, however, was understood to be only time-limited, with things returning to their 'proper' order after the carnival or festival's end.

Blame for Rebeccaism was variously put on Welsh 'peculiarities' – the people's language and religion – and on politically militant 'outsiders'. But the movement was homegrown, and, although a response to specific local circumstance, it both echoed and reflected similar unrest going on all over Britain, given its own particular south-west Welsh spin. The costume and ritual that became the movement's trademark – dressing up, masking or play-acting certain roles – were borrowed from older folklore and festival, but Rebecca's children were putting these familiar things to new use to make their social and political points. Using costumes that traditionally expressed freedom from law and order worked on several levels: it was a practical way of disguising their identity but, more subtly, it enabled them to defy the new laws put in place by landowners and tollgate trusts, and to demonstrate, through topsy-turvy aspects like cross-dressing, that the changes being imposed by the new laws meant, to them, a world turned upside-down. And, just as in carnival, wearing costumes and masks – particularly those which blurred and played with the boundaries of identity – was a way of creating a liminal space and a larger-than-life persona in which protestors could carry out extraordinary actions that were considered divorced from their 'normal' respectable selves.

3
MEN IN THE MIDDLE

SHOT BY BOTH SIDES

If life in 1840s Carmarthenshire was hard for the rural poor, and sometimes harder than might be expected for the local gentry, Thomas Cooke felt they both had it easy compared to him – the middleman.

The early nineteenth century had seen a movement among the British landed classes to invest in new methods of agricultural improvement, in order to get more out of their land and the tenants who lived on it. In Wales, many landowners began to employ agents from England or Scotland to run their estates more efficiently: cultivating better crops, tidying up the boundaries of fields and, of course, extracting greater profit wherever they could. For the land agents themselves, 'efficiency' could mean keeping up with the advances in agricultural science reported in the latest issue of the *Agricultural Gazette* or the *New Farmer's Journal*, teaching these new methods to tenant-farmers and strategically planning for the future use of the land. It could also mean collecting rent and other payments or debts due to the landlord from tenants, enclosing areas of formerly common land for private cultivation and cracking down on poaching, gleaning the fields for food, cutting turf for fuel and the building of *tai unnos*. All of this made land agents less than popular with ordinary people, and they often found themselves seen as nothing more than henchmen doing the landowner's dirty work.

This was the context in which Thomas Cooke arrived in Carmarthenshire in the summer of 1841. He was forty-three and, upon his father's death twenty years earlier, had inherited a family estate of his own in Northamptonshire. In another twist of inheritance fate, however, his father's will had left almost all the family fortune to Cooke's six sisters, leaving his son with few resources to maintain and run the estate and to support his ageing mother. With a failed attempt to find work in Canada's Nova Scotia already behind him, Cooke felt his only option was to try to make a living by running other people's estates for them.

As Cooke approached Middleton Hall through its surrounding parkland in the August sunlight, the white 'hilltop palace' of a mansion enclosed by lakes and stables and with a walled garden to its north, he tried to look on the bright side. He had been promised a decent wage of £200 a year – the equivalent of just under £30,000 today – and, even if he anticipated being disliked by the estate's tenants, he had a good impression of his employer, Edward Hamlin Adams, although the man was elderly and ill. But after settling in, Cooke took a closer look at the estate and was dismayed by its lack of cultivation. Its meagre produce had fetched only a small sum in the preceding year and the whole place, like the Llanelli seat of the Stepneys, seemed to have been left to almost terminal neglect.

In less than a year, Cooke's already gloomy outlook grew darker. Edward Hamlin Adams finally succumbed to illness and the estate passed to his eldest son, Edward Adams Junior. After meeting his new boss, Cooke wrote to his mother about him with a mixture of fury and despair:

> He knows but little or nothing of business – detests farming, – is meanly suspicious of every living creature – is an infidel, and frequently a scoffer at all religion, – is fickle, and capricious in the extreme, and exceedingly irritable – he is all smiles and sunshine, one day, and perhaps in a few hours after, will be just the reverse ... He has invariably treated me with respect – but if he ever treats me, as I have seen him treat others, I would leave him, even if I and all my family were driven to a workhouse the very next day.[1]

Edward Adams Junior, a young man around half Cooke's age, was noted locally for several things, from his deep interest in archaeology and heraldry to his vegetarianism and, as Cooke intimated, his 'infidel' scepticism towards religion. He also claimed to be liberal in his politics, and in 1835 had called himself 'a Loyal Reformer, and a Friend to the Dissenter and the Farmer', but now professed he 'took no active interest in public affairs'.[2] In his even younger days, he had published a radical pamphlet supporting the secret ballot and calling on tenants to stand up for their rights against the Tories and the landed classes. Cooke may have cynically wondered if his employer still held this position now that he was such a locally prominent member of the landed classes himself. Perhaps more alarming than his political leanings, or his vegetarian diet, Adams Junior was also known to be interested in firearms, an expert shot and prone to challenging men to duels.

Bearing in mind his employer's tempestuous and trigger-happy nature, Cooke confined his problems with him to the written word. In quieter moments between bargaining with tenants and wrestling with the estate's account-books, his letters to his mother were the only place he allowed himself to unburden himself on the subject of Adams's infuriating combination of neglect and micromanagement. One moment, he wrote, his employer was heading off to London, promising to be back within two weeks but in fact staying away for twice as long, and the next, he was keeping Cooke awake until three in the morning as the two of them worked their way through estate business. These all-nighters were no problem for Adams, who kept aristocratic hours: staying up for whole nights sustained by coffee and cigars, then sleeping the day away, taking breakfast in the early afternoon and dining around ten at night. He was known to occasionally sit up until dawn, to check on the time his employees arrived for work. Cooke, finding himself expected to stay up late but also to rise at a respectable hour to carry out his duties on the estate, couldn't keep up. He grumbled privately:

> Mr Adams himself is so very tedious, in transacting business; dwelling hours without end, on the most trivial matters, never seeming so well satisfied, or pleased, as when

he has got me in the Office (tied to the table leg as I am apt to think it) and hindering me from going about my most important matters of business. This being one of his many strange peculiarities.[3]

Cooke found the estate's tenants and the local community peculiar, too: the way they spoke in Welsh, even in church, and their stubborn refusal to adopt the new agricultural practices that were improving farming methods in England. As he stuck with grim determination to doing his job, things weren't going to get much easier.

ST CLEARS

As the winter of 1842 set in, with an economic crisis that hit agriculture, industry, commerce and finance all at once, Thomas Cooke had spent just over a year on his new estate. He noted bleakly that the weather itself had been harsh on the countryside in general, and the produce of Middleton Hall in particular. In addition to this, in south-east Wales, the closure of ironworks and laying-off of workers was leading to a fall in demand for farm produce from the surrounding country, reducing the estate's potential income even further. Even more worryingly, the industrial workers had responded to the lay-offs with a mass strike, and many were taking a renewed interest in the Chartist movement, whose radical politics promised an alternative to the conditions that left workers at the mercy of employers.

A Chartist convention held in London in April 1842 included a pro-Reform petition signed by 36,000 people from south Wales, and, particularly after the Newport Rising, the interest in Wales of the movement's national leaders had grown. In the summer of 1842 the Chartist newspaper the *Northern Star*, which had been established in 1837 by the Irish Chartist and former MP Feargus O'Connor and amassed a working-class readership in the tens of thousands, carried an interview with some Welsh farmers. It captured the impact that falling incomes and fixed outgoings were having on agricultural workers, as well as the industrial workers who formed Chartism's base. The financial burdens complained of included the continued demands for rents and tithes from landowners like Cooke's employer, but the farmers had also clearly identified a new problem – the tollgates and their tax on travelling:

> The average price of wheat was about 89 pence a bushel; now the price is 6 shillings.; butter, which used to sell at 8 and 9 pence per pound., is now selling at almost 2 pence ... Whilst THE TITHES [...]which were calculated on the former price of agricultural produce, NOW REMAIN A FIXED BURDEN UPON THE LAND [...] AND RENTS HAVE NOT FALLEN IN ANY DEGREE WHATEVER... [but most] prominent cause of grievance is the toll-bar tax. It is now impossible to get to Abergwilly, for instance, a distance of six miles from where we were then standing, without paying three turnpikes – a tax on the farmer who goes there with his cart and two horses with his market produce ... It is too hard; we can't bear it.[4]

In this atmosphere, anyone putting up a new tollgate should have expected trouble – and no one seemed happier to invite trouble of this kind than the notorious toll-farmer, Thomas Bullin. His target this time was St Clears, a market town nine miles from Carmarthen on the river Taf. The town was mostly notable as a bottleneck for traffic between Carmarthen and Haverfordwest, not least for seasonal traffic to and from the huge Whitland Fair. Bullin persuaded the directors of the Main Trust that a new gate just outside the town would be an obvious way to make a profit.

The new gate, known as the Mermaid Gate from its position near the Mermaid tavern, was opened at midday. It had only been standing for a matter of hours before its destruction. On the same night several other gates nearby were destroyed, with the attackers, as at Efail-wen, dressed in women's clothing and disguised with painted faces and large horsehair beards, and, again, led by a figure referred to as 'Rebecca'. Patrols of rioters on horseback stopped the traffic on the roads around the area while the work of demolition took place. On the following day, drovers heading to Narberth Fair from Carmarthen were halted on the road, and asked, on the grounds that they had no toll to pay thanks to the destruction of the tollgates, if they would make a donation to the rioters' cause instead.

CAT AND MOUSE

In England's north and Midlands at the end of 1842, strikes and riots were also breaking out as industrial workers faced similar conditions to the lay-offs and wage cuts in the Welsh coalfield. This meant that when the magistrates in Carmarthen wrote to the Home Office in London requesting troops to protect the tollgates, none could be spared from the industrial districts to help. The most they could manage was to send a detachment from the London Met, thoughtfully led by George Martin, a Welsh speaker. The policemen arrived in Carmarthen on 20 December and were lodged at the Blue Boar Inn on Water Street, where they met with local special constables and began to organise patrols, somewhat settling the minds of the magistrates.

But as the new year dawned, a kind of pantomime was staged at the Carmarthenshire village of Pwll-Trap. The tollgate here had been destroyed several times in the previous few months, and replaced each time by the trust that owned it. But, at midnight on 2 January, it went down for good. This time Rebecca was not the Romantic heroine described by the *Quarterly Review*, but more of a grandmotherly dame. As the crowd of rioters approached the tollgate, their leader tottered towards the barrier, leaning on a walking-staff. She turned to address her followers in a quavering tone of surprise, and began a routine of call-and-response:

'Children, there is something put up here; I can't go on.'
'What is it, mother? Nothing shall stop your way.'

'I do not know, children. I am old, and cannot see very well.'

'Shall we come on, mother, and remove it from your way?'

'Stay a minute. Let me examine it ... it seems like a great gate put across the road, to stay your old mother's progress.'

'We will break it, mother! So nothing will hinder you on your journey.'

'No, let me see. Perhaps it will open – no, children, it is bolted and locked, and I cannot go on. What is to be done?'

'It must be taken down, mother, because you and your children MUST pass.'

'Off with it, then, my dear children. It has no business here.'[5]

In less than ten minutes, the gate was levelled and the crowd had dispersed. A few hours' ride away from this comic production, the London policemen were still in their lodgings at the Blue Boar, with no idea that their services might be needed.

The Carmarthen magistrates, with some exasperation, wrote again to the government for military, rather than police, assistance but were again refused. They then sent a further message to Pembroke docks, where a detachment of the Royal Marines was billeted. This request had more success, and thirty marines arrived at St Clears a few days later. No sooner had they started patrolling the area than they received a note warning them that Rebecca was about to attack a gate at Trevaughan, six miles away. Rushing over to Trevaughan, they found the gate still standing and the countryside around it completely devoid of armed farmers in dresses. But on returning empty-handed and puzzled to St Clears, they discovered the remains of another tollgate, which had been razed to the ground in their absence.

This was the start of a confused cat-and-mouse game that would go on for months, in which attempts at military intelligence and information-gathering proved no match for the Rebeccaites' communication networks and in-depth knowledge of the area.

Confusion was worsened by the authorities' general state of jumpiness and the lack of coordination between different parts of the national government. When the marines were ordered back to Pembroke docks a few days later, for instance, they found they had been joined unnecessarily by reinforcements from Bristol – while similar missives had been ignored by the Home Office, the magistrates' panicked request for help had made the Board of Admiralty fear an armed uprising was imminent in Wales.

The magistrates, reaching their wits' end, brought in thirty of the Castlemartin Yeomanry, who arrived in St Clears on 21 January, and spent weeks patrolling and guarding gates there with no sign of Rebecca. It was only once they left the area that Rebecca showed her face again – this time to make a genuine appearance at Trevaughan.

4
'FAITHFUL TO DEATH'

A DAMPER OF ALE

In August 1843, the *New Zealand Gazette and Wellington Spectator* carried a small news item in its 'English Extracts' section:

> Two of the rioters in South Wales have at length been apprehended, and committed to the county goal at Haverfordwest for trial at the ensuing Pembrokeshire assizes. The names of the prisoners are Thomas Howells, a farmer, Llwyndrissy, Llangan, and David Howell, a miller.[1]

It had taken several months, but Rebecca and 'the state of south Wales' were now making headlines on the other side of the world. The story these few lines referred to had begun the previous January near the Trevaughan Bridge in Whitland, Carmarthenshire, where local tollkeeper William Rees was experiencing sleepless nights.

Rees had been working as keeper of the Trevaughan tollgates for less than two years, but during his short tenure the gates and tollhouse had been repeatedly visited by rioters, and after an attack in January the broken windows of the tollhouse had still not been repaired by its trustees. With the yeomanry patrolling, Rees should have felt safe, though he could be forgiven for not trusting the soldiers after how inefficient they had proved so far. But now the soldiers had departed entirely and, unable to calm his nerves about the prospect of the rioters returning, Rees had taken to sleeping at the houses of friends nearby rather than remaining at his place of work. On 13 February he was spending the night at the house of David Thomas. At around midnight, both men were settling to sleep when another neighbour, Rees Isaacs, burst in at the cottage's door. Gasping for breath, he told them that 'Rebecca was at the gates'.

A quarter of a mile away at the Golden Lion inn, Lewis Griffiths had also been trying to get an early night, worn out after spending a solid four days at Whitland pig fair. Sleeping off the evening's ale in a ground-floor room of the pub with two other drovers, he fuzzily awoke to sudden chaos: a buzz of urgent conversation, a shout of 'Becca is come!' and a crush of people streaming out through the pub's front door. Struggling to sit up and narrowly dodging a glassful of beer in the face, flung by a man who was urging everyone to wake up and get down to Trevaughan bridge, Griffiths pulled on his boots and cautiously followed the crowd. Reaching the bridge, he saw a group of men, dressed in petticoats and white headdresses, pulling the tollgate apart and carrying its fragments to the river.

Back at Trevaughan, William Rees had scrambled out of David Thomas's house and into a neighbouring garden with a better view of the tollhouse. From there, he could do nothing but watch as around twenty people fired off guns and ran across the fields towards the river, carrying bits of timber – the remains of his house and its tollgate – which they pitched into the water. Seeing stones being thrown at curious neighbours who were peering out of their windows, Rees kept his distance until the rioters dispersed, before he warily approached the tollhouse. Standing nearby to examine the destruction – the house's roof pulled off and its entire front wall torn down – he spotted three men returning from the river. As their eyes met, Rees recognised one of them as Thomas Howell, a local tenant-farmer he had known for three or four years.

There was a moment's awkward silence as Howell looked apologetically at his neighbour, whom he had just helped to render both jobless and homeless. He decided to offer what comfort he could by suggesting he buy Rees 'a damper of ale'. As the two men headed off to find the nearest pub that was still open after midnight, Howell tried to dodge any personal responsibility by blaming the abstract figure of Rebecca, telling Rees: 'It is hard on you to lose your house, Rebecca has done bad work to pull down the house.' Rees replied wearily, looking forward to his ale: 'Yes, and I am very cold.'[2]

MAKING HEADLINES

Trevaughan was significant because this wasn't an attack on a new tollgate, like the response to Thomas Bullin's opportunist erections at Efail-wen and St Clears. Trevaughan was a gate which had been around for years, and its demise suggested that the rioters were now not just preventing any new expansion of the toll system, but trying to push back against the existing system as a whole. The local trusts, becoming more seriously worried by this, began to issue public statements defending their operations and justifying the charging of tolls. The local magistrates swore in dozens of special constables to protect the remaining gates, as well as offering a substantial reward of fifty pounds for information on any of the attacks. Although tempting in a country where farmhands earned a few shillings a day, no one was yet urged to take up the offer.

Appearing alongside the trusts' defensive statements in the press were letters and statements by the rioters' supporters, including the Carmarthenshire lawyer Hugh Williams. His closeness to some of the rioters, combined with his Chartist politics, was already leading some to speculate that he was orchestrating the whole thing, including taking the role of 'Rebecca' himself. This was an attractive theory for those looking to pin the blame for what was happening on a single radical mastermind, but it ignored the amorphous and leaderless nature of the movement that was taking shape; 'Rebecca' would not turn out to be one individual who could be definitively unmasked. As a line of thinking, it also betrayed a certain patronising attitude towards the agency of ordinary people, like those expressed even fifty years later in the *Welsh Gazette* as contributors continued to argue over Hugh Williams's alleged part as Rebecca:

> I put it to the common sense of your readers as to whom was the most proper, most likely and most reliable person to act as leader Rebecca? Thomas Rees, of Pembrokeshire, a great muscular pugilist, a frequenter of fairs and festivities for rounds of fights? Surely such a character was an uneducated

man, whom no well respectable man would be guided by. Or a well-educated lawyer, whose job was to champion and defend all those misguided and fiery patriots who found themselves caught within the meshes of the law?[3]

Contemporary newspapers also carried their own editorials both summarising the debate on the unrest and offering their own opinion, which varied according to the politics of the paper in question. While conservative outlets like the *Carmarthen Journal* raged against the 'daring outrages' committed against the property of the trusts, the more liberal *Welshman* reminded its readers of the causes behind the actions:

> The condition of the farmers is becoming every day more unfortunate. The high prices of four years have given them high rents, high poor rates, and an income tax. To these sources of misfortune they have superadded a ruined population, and masses of customers wholly impoverished, whilst on every side they are surrounded by increasing pauperism amongst their own unemployed labourers.[4]

On the ground, attacks continued, with several gates destroyed at Narberth by around sixty people. The crowd, it was reported, was again 'headed by an athletic female on horseback, who gave the command with considerable coolness and promptitude'.[5] In these early descriptions, before the movement was investigated in detail, Rebecca's dress and presentation could be taken at face value by those reporting on the events – what was more important was the actions Rebecca was leading.

Completing their work in around twenty minutes, the Narberth rioters rode off with a triumphant firing off of their guns. The attack was witnessed by several people who left their nearby cottages to watch, but no one interfered and, as was becoming usual, no one came forward to offer information or identification to the authorities.

THE TREVAUGHAN TWO

One of the few who did give information, motivated by the reward money on offer, was Lewis Griffiths, the pig-drover who had witnessed the attack at Trevaughan. His evidence resulted in the arrest of the tollkeeper's friend Thomas Howell, as well as David Howell, a miller who lived on the small tenement of Bower Hill. These arrests provided an opportunity for magistrates to stress how serious the situation was – but the Rebeccaites were taking the arrests seriously, too. On 6 March, with Thomas and David held at Haverfordwest jail, two more gates were attacked at Robeston Wathen and Canaston Bridge – illustrating that Rebecca was now as much at home in Pembrokeshire as Carmarthenshire. As they demolished the gates, the rioters were reported as saying, should any harm come to the two prisoners, 'that they would show no mercy to anyone, but would harry the whole country'.

Four days later, the trial of the two Howells took place at the Lent assizes at Haverfordwest. Under the headline 'THE REBECCA AFFAIR', the *Welshman* reported that the courtroom was so crowded that their reporter could not get a seat 'without subjecting himself to serious inconvenience'.[6] In court, it emerged that there had been a mysterious disappearance of other witnesses from the Golden Lion who had been summoned by the prosecution, including the pub landlord's son and two of the barmaids. Undaunted by this, the trial began with a fierce denunciation of the riots from the presiding judge, aimed at cautioning any farmers who might have taken part, or who might be thinking about doing so in future:

> There has prevailed in this and the adjoining county, what I may term a war of extermination against the toll-gates ... Roads in this country are almost necessaries of life, and they cannot be kept in repair, unless funds are raised for the purpose. Lawless men may just as well invade your farms, because you cannot give away the produce of them,

as that people should destroy toll-gates because the keepers of them exact the tolls which are lawfully demanded for passing over the roads.[7]

After witnesses proved that Thomas Howell had been at the Golden Lion 'when the cry came that Becca had arrived', Lewis Griffiths was called as the principal witness against both men. He recalled seeing them both take part in the attack on the tollhouse and gate, excusing his own presence there by stressing that 'I am not a daughter of Becca. I went there to see what was going on'.[8]

The solicitor for the defence proceeded to rubbish Griffiths' evidence, claiming he had been drunk on the night in question and had now accused two men at random in order to get the reward money. Summing up, the judge again cautioned his listeners that 'if persons thought themselves aggrieved or oppressed, it was only making bad worse to take the law into their own hands. The course was to petition Parliament', but he concluded that the jury's decision should rest on whether they believed Griffiths' statement. It took the jury, composed of local men, around ten minutes to decide that they did not. The verdict of not guilty for both prisoners was followed by an immense cheer in the courtroom, 'which with great difficulty was silenced'.[9]

Leaving the courthouse having lost both his reward money and his local reputation, Griffiths was 'hissed and hooted' by a host of women and girls who, unable to find a seat in the packed courtroom, were awaiting the verdict on the street outside. The watching crowd, like a theatre audience, made it clear who they regarded as the villain of the piece. Community solidarity like this, mixed with the disorganisation and incompetence of the local authorities and those they brought in, was a recipe for disappointment for anyone hoping the anti-tollgate movement would be short lived. On the contrary, the scattered and seemingly random attacks on a handful of gates now seemed to be cohering into a more organised campaign.

'AND THEY BLESSED REBEKAH'

As the summer of 1843 approached, after six months of unrest, almost thirty gates destroyed, a handful of arrests and no convictions, 'Rebecca' was becoming a household name. 'She' was recognised at the head of the crowd at tollgates, in denunciations from the authorities and in the local newspaper reports that had begun to follow the movement's progress, widening its visibility with headlines like: 'OUTRAGEOUS PROCEEDING – REBECCA AND HER DAUGHTERS'; 'INCREASED STRENGTH OF REBECCA – MORE GATES DESTROYED'; and 'REBECCA AND HER LEGIONS'. Even the *Illustrated London News* had carried a brief mention of the events, along with an illustration of men, dressed in women's smocks, bonnets and headscarves, attacking a gate. While this early image was simply captioned 'The Welsh rioters', future depictions, showing Rebeccaites in tall black hats to mark them out as Welsh 'women' in particular, would be titled 'Rebecca Rioters, or 'Becas'. References to the leader of any riot as Rebecca, and to 'her' followers as 'daughters', became a recognised shorthand in public discussion and press discourse.

Rebecca's name was also appearing as a signatory to threatening communications. Only a few days before the trial and acquittal of Thomas and David Howell, the tollkeeper brother of the toll-farmer Thomas Bullin had received a disturbing letter. Its spelling was imperfect, but its meaning was clear enough, and it was signed: 'faithful to death, with the county – Rebecka and childrens':

> TAKE NOTICE. I wish to give you notice, espesial to those which has sworn to be constables in order to grasp Becks and her childrens [...] they impose so much on the county only pickin poor labrers and farmers pocets, and you depend that all the gates that are on these small roads shall be destroyed, I am willing for the gates on the Queens Roads to stand it is a shameful thing for us Welshmen to

have the sons of Hengist have a Dominion over us, do you not remember the long knives which Hengist hath invented to kill our forefathers and you may depend that you shall receive the same if you will not give up when I shall give you a vicit ...[10]

By referring to the legendary Saxon figures of Hengist and Horsa, the letter-writer was taking a swipe at the Bullin family's origins in England. But the letter also made a more practical point that the gates being objected to were not those on the main highway, the 'Queen's roads', but the hated 'side-bars' on smaller local roads. The letter finished with a flourish that made clear the lack of respect that awaited the numbers of police now swarming into Wales: 'As for the constables and the poleesmen Becka and her children heeds no more of them than the grasshoppers flying in the summer ...'[11]

Even more unsettlingly, Thomas Bullin himself had been sent two illustrations, on ruled paper torn out of a memorandum book. One showed a man without a head, with the inscription 'Receipt for the interest I took in the matter', while the second showed several people marching with clubs and pickaxes, with the heading 'Coming to visit St Clears' gate, when we think proper'.

The letter-writing campaign, whoever – or however many people – lay behind it, was targeting not only tollgates but also workhouses. In January and February, more notices had been sent to the beleaguered Narberth workhouse, warning of an attack by Rebecca unless better food was given to its residents.

Although Rebecca's name was gaining recognition, the explanation behind it was still a matter of dispute. At the trial of the Howells, the prosecuting solicitor stated that:

The rioters for the most part disguise themselves as women, and one of them, taller than the others, is called by them Rebekah, or shortly 'Becca, and is looked up to as their leader: and it is said that they blasphemously refer their authority to the 60th verse of the 24th chapter of Genesis, 'And they blessed Rebekah, and said unto her, Thou art our sister, be thou the mother of thousands of millions, and let thy seed possess the gates of those which hate them.'[12]

He did not draw on the 'Big Becca' origin of Twm Carnabwth's nickname at the destruction of Efail-wen tollgate, but claimed instead – as many others were doing – that its inspiration was the Bible. Alcwyn Caryni Evans, who was a schoolboy in Carmarthen at the time of Rebecca and later produced his own chronicle of the events, put forward an additional God-given reference from the Book of Isaiah: 'I will break in pieces the gates of brass, and cut in sunder the bars of iron.'[13]

As with other local stereotypes, the levels of religious commitment in early Victorian Wales could often be overstated, but this Biblical explanation soon caught the imagination. Not only did it provide those taking part in attacks with the highest level of justification – for the chapel-going Welsh, divine authority surely overruled any law passed by the state – but it also allowed the authorities to rail against the vulgar and blasphemous boldness of applying a divine warrant to a protest movement. Both theories about the name – one irreverently secular, the other reverently scriptural – were equally useful for explaining Rebeccaism. After all, Twm Carnabwth, the first Rebecca, was as familiar with the Bible as he was with the boxing-ring, and the movement he had helped to start would continue to be fuelled by elements of both.

PART TWO:
TAKING THE REINS

5
A THOROUGH REVOLUTION

THE LONDON OF WALES

As early as 1724, the market town of Carmarthen on the north-west bank of the river Towy had been called 'the London of Wales'. For decades it had been the country's largest town, though by 1843 it was falling behind Merthyr Tydfil and Swansea as their populations swelled with new industrial workers from Wales and outside it. Carmarthen's nickname reflected not only its size and economic importance but also its flourishing civic, commercial and social life, which drew people in from the surrounding hills and farmland for business, culture or adventure. Like London, Carmarthen's streets weren't paved with gold, but they were at least paved – along with gas lighting and a supply of running water, both of which were unusual and impressive at the time. A guidebook of 1844, *Pigot's South Wales Directory*, remarked that the town's main streets 'contain a large proportion of good houses, and though not perfectly regular, they possess an aspect of comfort and respectability'.[1]

Carmarthen's streets were also lined with over a hundred pubs, three circulating libraries, a dozen hair-dressing salons and shops whose bow-windows were bursting with everything from baked goods to silverware to fashionable hats and umbrellas, brought in by steam-packet to Carmarthen's dock from Bristol and further afield. More basic supplies could be purchased on Wednesdays and Saturdays at the market which covered two acres in the centre of town, its stalls 'abundantly supplied with every necessary of life' including meat, corn, butter, cheese, vegetables, flannel cloth, hats and shoes, locally produced by the hill-dwelling farmers and craftsmen who came to town both to buy and sell. The town's post-office on Spilman Street received and dispatched letters to and from collection points in Bristol, Milford Haven and Ireland.

A regular mail-coach between Carmarthen and London itself departed from Spilman Street at 6 a.m., passing through Brecon, Monmouth, Gloucester and Cirencester where it picked up and dropped off post and passengers along with the news of the day.

Like any capital, Carmarthen contained variety, and was a place where different social worlds could and did collide. One local writer described the 1840s as a time when the upper- and lower-class pursuits of 'balls, dancing, the theatre, hunting, drinking, dressing, and donkey-racing, flourished together'.[2] The banks of the Towy were home to a tight-knit fishing community whose members traversed the river in coracles, catching salmon and sewin in a way of life that stretched back centuries. Further into town, a growing middle class – bankers, lawyers, clergymen, shopkeepers and clerks – rubbed shoulders with the local gentry when they ventured out from their country seats to give parties, hold business meetings, take in a concert, lecture or play, or simply relax in their smart townhouses on Picton Place or Waterloo Terrace. Elsewhere, the town's taverns, alleyways and slums were home to the notorious 'Carmarthen mob', which consisted of the less respectable lower classes, the homeless and landless poor, petty and organised criminals, freelance ballad-singers, poets and musicians, sex workers, drifters and radical agitators – with some individuals combining several of these roles. The more infamous of the area's troublemakers showed up in police records under a variety of *noms de crime*: David 'Snag' Davies, Mary 'Trump' Hughes and Elizabeth Jones, a fencer of stolen goods who, 'having derived her *alias* from some fancied resemblance of her Majesty',[3] was known on the streets as Queen Victoria.

Carmarthen was the first town in Wales to have one of the newly established police forces which Robert Peel's government was trying to develop across the country. These were formed in the mould of the London Metropolitan Police, itself patterned after the Royal Irish Constabulary set up to suppress unrest against British rule in Ireland. Carmarthen's police force was small, but the town kept it busy – in addition to its crime rate, Carmarthen was a hotbed of political radicalism, and had already played a leading part in the Welsh Chartist movement and the campaign for political reform.

In the general election of 1831, pro-Reform rioting suffused Carmarthen, with the local MP physically attacked at the town hall for having voted against the First Reform Bill. In the autumn of the same year, after the Merthyr Rising in May and June had rocked the Welsh coalfield, Parliament's rejection of the Second Reform Bill set off violent protests across Britain, including again in Carmarthen. The next year saw even the town's better-off inhabitants holding a pro-Reform meeting and threatening to stop paying taxes in a bid to pressure the government into accepting the Bill. The eventual passing of the Reform Act a few months later was received with jubilation across Wales, with bands playing in the streets and church bells ringing. In Carmarthen, copies of the anti-Reform *Carmarthen Journal* were burnt in the street.

A decade after this, a still-restless Carmarthen had grown into a regional capital. It formed the political and administrative centre, main market, and transport and communications hub for the whole of the Towy valley. People and produce, news and newspapers, gossip and goods flowed through it on a daily basis. Other significant towns like Swansea, Haverfordwest and Cardigan were within an hour or so's reach by horseback, and coaches departed daily to Cardiff, Newport, Bristol and Gloucester. And the town's traffic brought in a tidy profit for the local tollgate trusts, six of whose boundaries met at Carmarthen. The main entrance into the town was the Water Street gate, leading down from the hills towards the marketplace, but the trusts had gradually thrown up gate after gate on smaller paths into town until in 1843 Carmarthen was ringed like a fortress, with entry only on payment of a toll.

PROGRESS AND PROMISES

In Llanelli, around an hour's ride from Carmarthen towards the south coast, William Chambers Junior was approaching both his mid-thirties and his goal of civic respectability with quiet satisfaction. In part due to his family's efforts, the town was rapidly coming to rival the regional capital for its size, economic significance and expanding middle class. Chambers's father, in addition to setting up a gas company and a mechanics institute for the town, had also poured time and money into restoring Llanelly House to its former glory. These were signs of the family attempting a legitimate entry into the local gentry, overcoming their social insecurity – which still caused tension with those above them – by symbolically stamping their presence on the community.

To a certain extent, this was working. Chambers Junior was now a magistrate, with only fading memories of his younger self's drunken misadventures and the local resentment of his family – although, in a memorandum of complaints made to him about the local clergy, he remembered enough of the early friction to note an additional reminder against the Revd Ebenezer Morris's name: 'Conduct to my father, wild beast show.'[4] In 1841, the establishment of his pottery had been marked with a public dinner at the Ship and Castle inn – the same place where, two years earlier, he had founded the town's Reform Society. At the dinner, around sixty of the town's prominent businessmen and politicians 'vied with each other to show their gratitude to Mr Chambers for conferring such a material benefit and improvement on the place'.[5] Two years on, the products of Llanelly Pottery had not only found a market locally but were being exported to Europe, America and Australia.

Beyond business, Chambers took his duties as a magistrate more seriously than many of his peers – although they gave him a low bar to clear. By devoting time to his casework on the complaints or questions local people brought to him, he was developing some insight into wider social issues and the economic problems facing his community. Along with competition for land and the falling prices of farm produce, he critically noted – as Thomas Cooke had done at Middleton Hall – the general resistance from farmers to helping themselves by adopting the new agricultural methods. But he was also conscious of the people's lack of 'confidence in [the] honesty and capabilities'[6] of his fellow magistrates, the clergy and the boards of tollgate trusts, and the growing popular distrust of the gentry – a social divide, with a sharpening political edge, that reflected the wider cultural divisions between church and chapel attendance and the use of English and Welsh.

In the spring of 1843 Chambers might have felt secure in his own social position, but he couldn't help but be aware that among ordinary people magistrates had become more unpopular than usual. One of Chambers's fellow magistrates, Timothy Powell of Pencoed, had made himself particularly disliked due to his out-spoken opposition to Rebeccaism, which had seen him intervene in the demolition of a gate at St Clears, where he tried to arrest a rioter himself. He found himself repaid for this one Sunday afternoon in May when the Powell family returned from church to find a corner of their estate ablaze, the high winds carrying the fire far enough to destroy four acres of valuable yew trees. This news was disturbing enough, but then Chambers received an anonymous letter in his own capacity as Chairman of Llanelli's Poor Law Union. He spread the paper out on his desk and deciphered the scrawl; the letter ordered him to release the poor from the local workhouse – or, it threatened, Rebecca's children 'will clean it out when they come'.[7]

It was difficult to know how seriously to take a letter like this. With no identifying details or any real specifics about the threatened attack, it was as likely to have been written by some powerless crank looking to spark anxiety for those above them as by an organised leader of incipient rebellion. And in any case, how could one man respond to it given the impenetrable bureaucracy attached to the workhouse system? Chambers may have concluded that the hitherto scattered disturbances would come to nothing, and that the rioters wouldn't take it into their heads to redirect their targets from tollgates to larger state property.

But, as it turned out, Rebecca was true to her word. In Carmarthen, she had issued another written notice, pasted up on walls and in the market square, stating that the Water Street gate barring the main entrance to the town should come down – and at the end of May, it did. At 1 o'clock in the morning, the keeper of the gate had returned from taking a toll when he heard the sudden approach, on the road leading down from the hills, of what sounded like a huge crowd of men and horses. Before he could reach the door, it was flung open against the wall and 'Rebecca' swept into the room, accompanied by another man in similar costume who identified himself as Rebecca's sister, Charlotte. Behind the pair, around 300 'daughters' could be seen crowding the torchlit road outside.

Armed with swords and firing off shotguns, they laid into the tollgate. The only person to approach them as they worked was a local drunk, who they gently turned away, saying 'Go about your own business, there's a good fellow, you are not wanted, we are enough here already'. The rest of Carmarthen's inhabitants thought it wise to stay indoors, and the police refused to risk their lives by taking on the crowd without military reinforcements – of which, as usual, none could be found in time. The town's magistrates, furious with the police, gave orders to rebuild the gate. Little attention was paid to the tollkeeper, his nerves still jangling from the previous night's encounter, who recalled hearing the ominous pronouncement from Rebecca that 'more things than tolls required adjusting'.[8]

TROUBLE AT TALOG MILL

In 1839 when the first tollgate fell at Efail-wen, twenty miles east in the village of Talog in the hills above Carmarthen, Thomas Thomas had been busily raising funds from friends and neighbours to erect a Baptist chapel. By 1843 Bethania Chapel, built to a simple and square design, had been opened to serve the small community and to act as a venue for meetings and speakers. It was established enough to be included on the list of stops made by Moses Roper, a former slave in North Carolina and now an activist for slavery's abolition in the US, on his speaking tour of Britain.

Like many of his neighbours, Thomas Thomas had been pleased to see Carmarthen's Water Street gate go down, whether or not he had taken part in its destruction. As the keeper of Talog's general store and post-office, he was at the centre of cross-currents of local

news and gossip, and he had heard from the previous keeper of the
Water Street gate that the new keeper was overcharging, asking for
2½ pence per horse rather than the previous charge of 1½ pence.
This rumour only added to the neighbourhood's excitement at
seeing notices posted locally, signed by Rebecca and warning
people not to pay a toll at Water Street, even with the gate rebuilt.
The next time he took his cart into town, Thomas was ready to
obey Rebecca's law rather than the state's.

Perhaps predictably, this didn't work out well for him, or for
Talog's miller John Harries and another local cart-driver, Samuel
Bowen, who all tried the same thing. John Harries found himself
fined for refusing to pay the toll and, when he also refused to pay
the fine, a warrant was issued by the town's magistrates to recover
the costs – adding that if Harries couldn't come up with the
money, his possessions to the same value would be seized instead.
After two attempts by Carmarthen's tiny police force failed to
execute the warrant, David Evans, the road surveyor for one of
the Carmarthenshire tollgate trusts, was sworn in as a special
constable. Under cover of darkness, he led a band of other specials,
police and bailiffs on a seven-mile trek from Carmarthen into the
hills towards Harries's home.

After walking for three hours, the town's forces arrived in Talog
just before dawn. They compelled Harries's daughter to open the
locked mill-house and began to lay hold of the family's furniture
and other possessions. Outside the house, the voices of neighbours
and Harries himself could be heard raising the alarm. As the police
loaded the seized goods onto a cart and prepared to leave, they
were startled by the sound of a bugle, and then further startled as
hundreds of figures began to materialise from the early-morning
mist – enough to completely surround them. The apparitions were
variously disguised, some in masks or with their faces painted,
others under women's caps and horsehair wigs, and they were
armed with scythes, guns and crowbars.

The few police issued with pistols moved to draw them, but the
crowd were quicker. One of the constables, with a hatchet and two

muskets held to his face, was instructed by a short and thick-set man – the 'Rebecca' for the occasion – to hand over one of his pistols and fire off the other. The whole company then marched four miles east to Trawsmawr, the home of local magistrate David Davies.

On arrival, 'Rebecca' ordered the police to produce the warrant for Harries's arrest, had it read in both English and Welsh, and asked if Davies had signed it. On being told he had, 'she' responded 'that is all we want to know'. The crowd then demolished an ornamental wall around Davies's estate. They gave the police and bailiffs the choice of joining them in the work, or of being stripped of their clothes and sent back to Carmarthen – they opted for the former.

A CALL TO ARMS

Fully clothed but deeply shaken, David Evans and his men returned from the fiasco at Talog to face the infuriated magistrates, who once more wrote off to the Home Office to request military assistance. But they weren't the only ones moved to action by anger. In the hills outside Carmarthen, indignation was growing at what was seen as an armed incursion by the town's authorities, on top of the fines and attempted arrests of their neighbours, and on top of the already unjust charging of tolls. On 14 June, 200 locals gathered to discuss what their response should be. They issued a demand for the local tollgate trust to produce its financial statements, to justify where all the money was going. The meeting also sent two delegates to ride north-west and pay a somewhat surprising call – to Edward Crompton Lloyd Hall, son of the High Sheriff of Cardiganshire.

Hall was heir to the small estate of Cilgwyn, near the market town of Newcastle Emlyn on the river Teifi where Carmarthenshire bordered Cardiganshire. The estate had passed to his family via another complicated will, this time left by a friend of Hall's father. Hall, now in his mid-thirties, had grown up in West London and been educated at University College London before becoming a barrister, but had been called back to the family estate to assist his ailing father with his duties as High Sheriff of the county.

In 1843 Hall was living in the estate's expansive grounds at Emlyn Cottage, a Gothic dower-house built fifty years earlier to a design by John Nash. Like Edward Adams of Middleton Hall, he had become known as something of a radical, advocating reform and the secret ballot – which made him popular among a section of the local population – but also advocating that the Welsh language be abandoned in favour of English, which did not. And like his friend and fellow magistrate William Chambers Junior, Hall was the scion of a family from outside Wales who had now settled among the lesser gentry of the three counties, but who still held an uneasy position on the periphery, the subject of occasional distrust from both his more solidly upper-class peers and the people.

It was both Hall's background in law and his radical politics that made the Talog farmers see him as a potentially useful ally; their meeting's delegates had come to ask for his legal advice on how to examine the accounts of the trusts, should their demand to see them be met. But, as Hall learned as he listened to his visitors, this advance on an administrative front was to be accompanied by a physical show of strength. At the same meeting, a call had been issued to all farmers, along with their families, labourers and farm servants, to assemble a few days later at the Plough and Harrow, an inn on the road from the hills north of Carmarthen into town. The summons extended to all, even those known to be critical of Rebecca's actions, who were warned in no uncertain terms, in letters delivered anonymously to their farms, that 'No excuse will be taken' for not attending on Monday 19 June:

> Non compliance will bring vengeance on your head and most likely you will be launched into eternity without the least warning and you shall see whether your threats, your loaded guns and pistols, your cursing and swearing at the people's good cause will avail you something in that day … If you will exert yourself in the people's cause all well and good, if not Monday will decide your fate.
>
> Yours &
> Becca[9]

From the Plough and Harrow, the Rebeccaites planned to march downhill into Carmarthen to retrieve the fines taken for non-payment of tolls at the Water Street gate, and to present their broader complaints to the magistrates.

News of the upcoming demonstration spread like wildfire by letter, word of mouth and notices pinned to house doors, public walls and shop-windows. At Talog's Bethania Chapel, John Harries himself announced it from the altar after service, and further afield town criers spread the call through marketplaces and village squares. On 17 June Harries, his fine and the attempted seizure of his goods having made him a neighbourhood *cause célèbre,* paid a call to a local magistrate. He took along a letter signed by himself and Thomas Thomas. Its legal language amateur but its position clear, the letter read: 'Sir– As we have been unlegally fined for refusing to pay Water-street gate, no refuse being made, we give you this offer if you are intending to pay the money to-day is the day.' Unless the money was returned, the letter concluded, they were coming in two days' time to request it in a far less polite manner.[10]

For Carmarthen's magistrates, news of the upcoming march concentrated the mind. The most recent mass demonstration in their memories was the Chartist march on Newport, just over three years earlier, which had ended in unprecedented bloodshed. Already on 16 June, in Blaen-y-Coed, a special constable had been shot at – who knew what havoc might be unleashed by a march on the regional capital? There was too little time to write, yet again, to the Home Office, but a request for help was sent to Cardiff, where a detachment of the 4th Light Dragoons was stationed.

Back at Cilgwyn estate Edward Crompton Lloyd Hall, fresh from giving legal advice to his visitors, was seized by an uneasy mixture of guilt, class loyalty and general dread. He sat down at his writing-desk to scribble the first of what would be his many alarmed letters to the Home Secretary warning of what might be to come: the farmers of Talog, he wrote, 'only want leaders to effect a thorough revolution'.[11]

6
LOVERS OF JUSTICE

A BAD TIME FOR THE GIRLS

Before she became a daughter of Rebecca, Frances Evans had become a mother. In 1843 she was working as a farm servant in the Carmarthenshire hills. Many young women from the area's poorer families worked in such roles at local farms or manor houses, with some even forced into service as young as nine to bring in income. At some point during Frances' service, she had spent a few days away from the farm, and been discharged from Carmarthen workhouse after giving birth there to her illegitimate child.

For many women and girls in Rebecca's country, becoming pregnant out of wedlock meant your options could be bleak – but this hadn't always been the case. The previous system of poor relief in Britain had allowed single women with young children to collect regular financial support either from their local parish or from the fathers of their children, but after 1834, under the 'bastardy clauses' of the New Poor Law, fathers – or men that women claimed were the fathers of their children – were no longer obliged to offer either marriage or maintenance payments, and the mother now needed to corroborate her paternity claim by evidence other than her own. In rural Wales, where premarital sex had once attracted little stigma, offers of marriage after pregnancy were now becoming thin on the ground. This change in the law didn't mean that there was any less sex outside marriage, but it did mean there were a lot more unmarried mothers.

The new law added to existing imbalances of power between not only men and women but the upper and lower classes, too. Sons of wealthier farmers – or the farmers themselves – seducing and abandoning their family's servant girls; men of the gentry feeling entitled to pursue any woman who crossed their path; or married men of any class having affairs, were socially embedded dynamics, and any of them could have accounted for the situation in which Frances Evans found herself. So, too, could the conditions of life on smaller farms, where younger male and female servants, often living away from their parents for the first time, shared overcrowded living and sometimes sleeping quarters. The duties of many female servants included isolated work outdoors – in far-off outbuildings or fields, grazing sheep or cattle on the lonely hillside, or transporting farm produce down quiet country lanes – where they were vulnerable to sexual harassment, assault and rape from strangers, employers and even their fellow servants.

Under the older system of poor relief, however, women who became pregnant outside marriage could at least expect some money for their child's upkeep. The new bastardy clauses denied them even this, and, as witnesses at the 1844 Commission of Inquiry later testified, they left women exposed to 'all the temptations of a life of vice', while 'the man evades or defies the law, with a confidence and effrontery'.[1] The new law led to cases like that of a farmer interviewed by the *Cardiff and Merthyr Guardian*, who said that the father of his daughter's child was 'a young man, who is very respectable, and able to maintain the child, but will not give a farthing ... I must send her to the workhouse'.[2] A female farmworker in Haverfordwest told her employer bluntly that 'It is a bad time for the girls, Sir, the boys have their own way'.[3]

With less chance of either marriage or financial support, both women and their children had a bad time. The New Poor Law decreed that, instead of local parish authorities providing assistance for single mothers, they were now instead directed to a workhouse if they wanted food and shelter. The workhouse's assistance was conditional not only on work from those who entered but also on the separation of families – including parting husbands from wives and parents from children. While some women went into the workhouse with their children, many mothers in south-west Wales, unwilling to be separated from them, were left destitute, ending up begging from door to door and even starving in the streets, while increasing numbers of children were abandoned at the gates of workhouses by mothers unable to support them.

Carmarthen workhouse, developed in 1836, was typical of its kind. Perched at the upper end of Waterloo Terrace, overlooking the centre of town like a bird of prey on a crag, the workhouse was a solid and grimly imposing building of dark grey stone. It could accommodate up to 140 people in the narrow beds of its residential blocks, which were planted within a gated outer courtyard used for exercise and work. Its resemblance to a prison wasn't accidental. Although some, including Carmarthen's, had schoolrooms and infirmaries, workhouses were not meant to be kindly and comfortable providers of charity to the poor. They were there as a deliberate last resort, meant to 'encourage' the unfortunate and destitute to find work, or any other way of supporting themselves, rather than turning to the state for help.

As the name suggested, a stay at a workhouse, whether indefinite or only for a few nights, entailed prison-like hard labour, usually breaking stones or untwisting ropes of oakum. At Llandovery workhouse, one corner of the main floor was occupied by a handmill for grinding corn, at which homeless people who were given a bed for the night had to spend two hours at work before they were allowed to leave the next morning. The infirmary of a workhouse was often the only option for mothers-to-be, like Frances Evans, who could not give birth in the house of their employer and had no family to call upon for help. If both mother and child survived the birth – something not always guaranteed – the women usually left within days, spurred on by the anxiety that, if they lingered, both they and their child would be taken separately into permanent residence and made to earn their keep.

It wasn't only single mothers who had a problem with the workhouse – in fact, most people did. Those who paid the ever-increasing local rates both resented the toll on their income and suspected that, as with the tollgate charges, more money was siphoned off to pay the salaries of officials and middlemen than was spent on the primary object of provisions for the poor. Both radical campaigners and more moderate reformers, meanwhile, were indignant at the harsh treatment of inmates and the separation of families. The Chartists made it a central part of their political platform to oppose the workhouse system across Britain, often labelling the institutions 'modern bastilles' after the forbidding state prison in Paris which had fallen to rioters just over fifty years earlier.

In the aftermath of the events described in this chapter, the Chartist leader Feargus O'Connor visited Wales and tried to get some sense from local farmers of the motivations behind what had taken place. While some protested that they 'did not intend it at all, but were urged forward by the Carmarthen mob', another admitted the validity of complaints about the workhouse: 'the poor of Carmarthen are opposed to the New Poor Law because they are badly used; that they have not enough food; that they are separated from their wives and families, and kept as in a prison.' The same interviewee recalled that, on the day of the demonstration: 'it was the poor farmers, who are grown reckless and can pay nothing, and do not care what they do, led on by the Carmarthen mob, who were ready to pull down the workhouse, or do anything else.'[4]

ON THE MARCH

Like many protests throughout history, the Rebeccaites' march on Carmarthen on Monday 19 June was made up of organisers and their supporters; those encouraged to attend by employers, friends or local influencers; bystanders who found themselves pulled in through agreement with the march's aims; fringe groups hoping to push their own agendas; and those who, sensing an adventure, went along for the ride. Some of those who took part had directly suffered under the weight of road tolls, high taxes, the New Poor Law and the workhouse, while others opposed them on political grounds and argued for a wider programme of reform. There was, then, as now, room for overlap between all these groups.

As Monday dawned, the whole of Carmarthen got itself ready to receive the march. Along the main streets, shops and pubs closed for the day and knots of police were stationed outside the town hall in Guildhall Square from 8 o'clock in the morning. At the town hall itself, the ground floor which usually hosted a bustling indoor market was shadowed and silent, while, in the meeting rooms above, the local magistrates gathered around a table to steady their nerves with a glass of brandy. Outside, the people of Carmarthen lined the streets in their hundreds and loitered on corners or in shop doorways in anticipation of trouble, excitement or the familiar blend of both. The local historian Alcwyn C. Evans later recalled: 'It seemed that every family (including nurselings in arms) had turned out into the main streets to await anxiously and not without fear, for the slightest information of the expected advance of the redoubted "heroine".[5] At 10 o'clock, news reached Carmarthen that the Rebeccaites were assembling outside the Plough and Harrow, around five miles out of town.

Riding up the Cynwyl Road to meet the march was Captain Lewis Evans, an intrepid local magistrate and landowner at Pantykendy Hall, and a Tory radical known for his opposition to the New Poor Law. He was channelling his particular mixture of personal and political interests into a determination to avoid trouble by heading things off at the pass. Halfway through his journey, he met a band of musicians who had been hired to lead the demonstration, and tried to persuade them to turn back – in vain, as they were intent on getting their payment for the day.

Reaching the Plough and Harrow, Evans and a fellow magistrate gave a speech to the crowd assembled outside. With the bloodshed of the Newport Rising on their mind, they implored them not to carry weapons into Carmarthen and not to approach the workhouse when they got there. The speech had some effect, as a pile of guns was left behind outside the pub when the march moved off at 11 a.m.

Just before it set off, Evans took a look at the crowd that stretched into the distance on the sunlit hillside. Massing behind the hired band there must have been several thousand men, women and children, including those he recognised as respectable farmers, who were grouped on horseback at the rear of the crowd. Those in front of them were on foot, and some still armed with staves and walking-staffs despite his exhortations. Some women were brandishing brooms, and, when questioned, explained that they were going 'to sweep the foundations of the tollhouses and the workhouse' – anticipating their total demolition in a manner that left him to guess how literally they meant it. Others held placards and banners emblazoned with the words 'Freedom and better food', and slogans Evans recognised from Chartist pamphlets. At the very front of the procession, he spotted a dark bay horse, its tall and imposing rider dressed in white with a shock of wild horsehair ringlets piled over their shoulders. It could only be Rebecca.

Not staying to see more, Evans galloped back to Carmarthen and relayed what he had seen to the authorities in Guildhall Square. With the requested military assistance nowhere in sight, the local police were sent into the centre of town and stationed near the prison, as well as around corners near the workhouse. At around midday those looking up, shielding their eyes against the summer sun, began to see the demonstration slowly coming into view on the road into Carmarthen from the hills north of the town. The first that could be seen – or heard – of it was the hired band, playing contemporary popular tunes whose jauntiness, the magistrates thought darkly, was an ill fit with the procession's dangerous potential. Behind the band, and just before Rebecca's horse, came a marcher on foot, bearing a bright white banner printed with the words:

Cyfiawnder!
A charwyr cyfiawnder
Ydym ni oll!

Some of the magistrates knew at least a little Welsh, and fearfully translated the slogan to their colleagues as the march approached: *Justice! And lovers of justice are we all!*

REBECCA GOES TO TOWN

Years later, Alcwyn C. Evans would recall the summer's day in 1843 when, aged fifteen and 'urged by a curiosity which was irrepressible', he slipped into the centre of Carmarthen to see Rebecca take the town. Although there had been many claimants in the decades since for the role of Rebecca on that date, he remembered personally identifying her actor as the twenty-four-year-old Michael Bowen, the son of a respectable farming family from the village of Trelech a few miles north of Talog. Alcwyn wrote later of the day's beginning:

> I was anxious to have a peep at 'Rebecca' for the occasion, and soon found her a stalwart young person, adorned with a horsetail beard, and horse-mane wig, and whose bright brown eyes laughed as it were with mischief and fun, one of which winked at me as I stood gazing. I winked back in return, for I recognised her name as Mike Bowen.[6]

Bowen was there, as was Alcwyn, to have a good time. As the clocks in Carmarthen's main streets ticked towards half-past twelve, he shook back his mane of artificial curls, lifted his chin and spurred his horse as it stepped curiously, getting used to the new air of the town, through the ruins of the Water Street gate. Behind him, Rebecca's followers began to flood the narrow streets of the regional capital, their march cascading downhill with the energy and strength of a river bursting its banks.

Breaking out of the long confines of Water Street, the demonstration swept to the right along St Catherine's Street, then back along Lammas Street and Dark Gate. Descending Blue Street towards the banks of the Towy, it spilled left across the quayside where it picked up several of the town's coracle-fishermen, who were quick to make their way into the head of the procession, walking arm in arm. At the end of the quay the marchers swerved left and up, away from the river, climbing the steep turn of Castle Hill and piling onto Spilman Street and Church Street. By this point, it had escaped no one's notice that the marchers had also been joined by the Carmarthen mob, their numbers described later by the press as 'roughs' and 'the rabble of the town'. While some of them might have been looking for trouble, others, having found themselves on the streets under the pressures of poverty, unemployment and the New Poor Law, or driven off the land around the town by enclosure, were merely jubilant, shouting that 'Rebecca had come to save them from the workhouse'.

With the town's own population now swelling their ranks, the march of the hill-dwellers circled back towards Carmarthen's civic centre. It rounded St Peter's Church, curved back along King Street and squeezed through a final few twists of the knot of streets around Guildhall Square until it filled the space in front of the town hall. There the demonstrators slowed to a halt, facing the building. In front of them, stone columns flanked a pair of grand stone staircases leading up to a first-floor balcony, at the top of which, between equally imposing tall arched windows, the magistrates stood massed. Down in the square, three cheers were given, and the crowd did what they had come to do:

> In front of the magistrates, they read a list of their complaints and the changes they wanted, which included, not only the removal of all the turnpike gates in the country, but also the abolition of all tithe and rent charge in lieu of tithes, the alteration of the present poor law, towards which they expressed the most bitter hostility, abolition of church rates, and an equitable adjustment of their landlord's rents.[7]

Looking down at the assembled crowd, the magistrates were at a loss. One of them attempted a confrontational approach, taking a few steps down towards the demonstrators and, pulling open his coat, daring them to shoot an unarmed man – but the absence of guns in the crowd, let alone any desire to use them right now, meant that this challenge was received with some bafflement.

But while those at the front faced the authorities, among a restless contingent at the back of the square a more direct action was being proposed. Somewhere in the pressing and uncertain crowd was Frances Evans, the memory of life inside Carmarthen workhouse still fresh in her mind. This experience might have guided her path as she shouldered her way across the square to the corner of Red Street, from where she led a section of the march out of the square and back uphill, towards the workhouse. Alongside her as she headed with determined steps up Waterloo Terrace was a cross-section of the town's population – tailors, weavers and coracle-men – mingling with the marchers from the hills. Among them, hurrying to keep up, was John Harries, the miller of Talog.

When the breakaway group led by Frances reached the workhouse, they found an equally angry throng from Carmarthen itself had gathered independently outside its gates, waiting for a leader or a signal that would let them vent their anger on the institution. John Harries, forgetting his main objective of recovering his fine from the magistrates, gave it to them. He stepped forward with his fist raised and hammered for admittance on the door of the abandoned porter's lodge. The crowd massing behind him weren't expecting a response, but, with this symbolic gesture of politeness fulfilled, they poured past him under the thick stone walls of the gateway and into the workhouse yard, heading for the main entrance of the building itself.

THE CARMARTHEN BASTILLE

As the multitude of knocks and kicks at the workhouse's exterior door threatened to burst it wide open, the staff inside Carmarthen workhouse steeled themselves. The master of the workhouse had rung the alarm bell, but this did little as the staff were forced to pull the door open and the crowd outside streamed in, quickly making their way through the building's corridors. The workhouse matron, Eliza Evans, thought strategically by starting to lock herself and the children she treated in the pantry with some provisions, but she was soon seized by the intruders. 'Where are the children to go?' she demanded, receiving the retort that 'We will find them a home'.

Elsewhere in the building the workhouse schoolmistress, Sarah Thomas, was also advising the rioters to think of the children and where else they could be taken care of. She collared one man in the doorway of the schoolroom to ask whether he was a father himself. With equal sharpness, he responded that he was indeed a father, that the children could be found homes elsewhere and that 'as he had commenced the work he would finish it, or lose every drop of his blood'.

Abandoning both this line of inquiry and the schoolroom itself, Sarah darted into the corridor outside where she ran into a woman urging the crowd up the narrow stone staircase to the building's upper storey. She recognised Frances Evans from her stay at the workhouse. Hoping perhaps that Frances would be swayed more than the previous man by an appeal to parental instincts, Sarah took her by the arm and asked if she wasn't ashamed to be 'frightening the children' like this. But Frances looked her straight in the eye and stated simply that she 'had seen enough of the workhouse, and was determined to go on', before the two women were pulled apart by the press of the crowd.

As Sarah flattened herself against the wall, Frances plunged on into the chaos of the building's upper floor, where rioters had broken into the locked and empty boardroom where the Poor Law Guardians met. She and others were observed 'dancing on top of the tables, and beating them with their staffs in a furious manner', as well as pulling up the floorboards and throwing bedlinen and entire beds out of the dormitory windows into the courtyard.

Also forcing his way into the workhouse, with different intentions, was James Morse, a Carmarthen stamp-distributor and magistrate. Hoping to calm things a little, he made it to one of the open upstairs windows and leaned out to address the crowd still piling through the gates into the workhouse yard, before a rioter distracted him:

> I endeavoured to persuade them to return, and make known
> their grievances to Parliament ... My address was interrupted
> by a man upsetting the iron bedsteads. On my requesting
> him to desist, he put himself in a fighting attitude.[8]

Outside in the yard, along with two friends of his, was the fifteen-year-old Alcwyn C. Evans. He later recalled that 'The whole of the place was possessed by the rioters ... all the roads leading to the building were thronged with Rebecca's family and their sympathising friends'. From their vantage point, the three teenagers could see the workhouse bedding being thrown out of the windows and other debris raining down into the yard. They rolled their eyes as they listened to the speech from James Morse – until, seeing a disturbance at the foot of the hill below the workhouse, Morse concluded his address to the crowd with the less charitable exclamation: 'There now, you devils! I told you so: the Dragoons are on you.'

Looking downhill with sudden apprehension, Alcwyn and his friends saw 'the flashing of sunlight on a thin line of cavalry forcing their way up the hill and through the crowds. It was the reflection of sunrays from their sabres and epaulets'.[9]

Just after 1 o'clock that afternoon when the workhouse doors were breached, the detachment of dragoons, on their way up from Cardiff, had been breathlessly told that the whole of Carmarthen was occupied by rioters. They galloped the remaining fourteen miles to the town in just over an hour, with two of their horses dropping dead of exhaustion on reaching Carmarthen. On arriving they were instantly directed to the workhouse, and sent riding full-tilt up Waterloo Terrace. The magistrates, descending from their perch on the town hall steps, read the Riot Act to the remaining crowd in Guildhall Square. They then followed the dragoons towards the workhouse, one of them overheard giving permission to the troops to 'cut and slash'.

When the crowd in the courtyard saw the dragoons approaching, covered in the dust of the road but with their drawn swords glinting in the afternoon sun, they tried to scatter. Those who could manage to reach the gates by slipping between the horses and the walls did so, some vaulting onto their own horses outside to escape while others tore uphill on foot through the gardens and fields behind the building. Among the latter were Alcwyn C. Evans and his friends, who, discovering a smaller door at the back of the yard, kicked off its lock and burst through onto Brewery Road where they found a hiding-place beneath a hedge. Others risked fractures and dislocations by scaling the walls around the workhouse yard and dropping from up to fifteen feet before they fled.

The rest, trapped in the workhouse yard and facing armed men under orders to subdue them by any means necessary, fought back with sticks or fists, but, thinking bitterly of having left their more substantial weapons piled up at the Plough and Harrow before setting off for Carmarthen, could otherwise do little to defend themselves. Even the hired band, who had continued playing tunes outside the workhouse throughout proceedings, got involved, with David Thomas, a farmer who was playing bassoon in the band, fighting one magistrate to the ground and clobbering another with his instrument. The day's Rebecca, who had made his way inside the workhouse during the rioting, now took evasive action by crushing his makeshift curls into his hat, before scrambling over the workhouse walls and following scores of his 'daughters' on their retreat towards the hills.

AFTERMATH

Around a hundred men, women and children were taken prisoner at Carmarthen workhouse. Some of them had cuts and broken bones despite assurances, received from the authorities and repeated in the press, that the military had 'behaved with great coolness, and used the flat of their swords only'.[10] The fields outside the town were left full of the demonstrators' horses, while the workhouse yard was scattered with abandoned hats and staffs as well as, in a reminder of the march's cross-class makeup, some 'very genteel walking sticks'. Among the items recovered by the authorities was the pole and placard board that had previously borne the slogan 'Justice and lovers of justice are we all', its paper inscription torn away at some point in the struggle.

Lined up inside the walls of the workhouse yard, many Rebeccaites expected nothing short of instant death – an impression which the dragoons did nothing to discourage, even making jokes about shooting the rioters where they stood. A meeting of the magistrates was held on the spot, and a court set up in the workhouse schoolroom to examine the prisoners. Many of them pleaded that they had been threatened into taking part in the march by others, but several of them were identified as part of the same group that had prevented the police from executing the distress warrants on John Harries at Talog a few days earlier.

As darkness fell on Carmarthen, special constables were put on duty to guard the workhouse until dawn. The magistrates were still going strong, their examination of prisoners lasting until 9 o'clock at night, when they committed six people to the county jail, and three to the borough prison, all to await trial. John Harries was taken into custody, accused of sending threatening letters in Rebecca's name – not the one he had hand-delivered to his local magistrate two days before the riot, but a far more florid one, written in Welsh and English, and received by the master of another workhouse at Newcastle Emlyn:

> REVENGE AND BLOOD. JUNE 19, 1843. As your soul is alive, and we are alive, if you will not come out, with the Poor under your care, before next Wednesday, we are determined to destroy the whole, and woe to any body, because we will take care of thee, so that thou wilt not escape! (Beware!) we cannot trifle any farther. REBECCA[11]

Frances Evans, last sighted dancing on the workhouse's dining-hall table, had been able to slip away with other rioters as they fled the military, but her prominent role in proceedings meant that several of the workhouse staff had been able to identify her to the authorities. She was picked up a few weeks later in her home parish. At her initial examination, conducted in Welsh as Frances spoke almost no English, she was charged with 'having incited and led the mob ... urged on the rabble to proceed upstairs, and otherwise grossly misconducted herself'.[12] On that occasion Frances stood impassively in the dock, saying nothing in her defence, but when her case was put to the next assizes, the press reported that she 'seemed not in the slightest affected by her serious situation – assumed a bold appearance – and said she was glad she had not done sufficient to forfeit her life'.[13]

As with Twm Carnabwth, we find no further mention of Frances in the records, but the dramatic nature of the events in which she took part had gained the movement national attention, including from the Tory government of Robert Peel and *The Times* newspaper, which wrote:

> These outrages, which commenced with the toll-gates, it is now avowed are only the beginning, for the next object of the conspirators (for so I must call them) will be the workhouses; then tithes must be abolished, and afterwards the landlords must be brought to account, none of whom shall be permitted to receive more rent for his land than four farmers shall say is a fair price for it.[14]

The report, although hostile and alarmist, had some accuracy. Looking beyond tollgates to the rural economy in general, and in spite of the defeat at Carmarthen workhouse, it would soon become clear that Rebecca was still in the saddle.

7
REBECCA IN THE SPOTLIGHT

THE JOURNALIST AND THE COLONEL

In the third week of June 1843, two men arrived in Carmarthen, both sent on account of Rebecca's growing fame but with very different intentions towards her.

The first was Thomas Campbell Foster, a reporter for *The Times*, whose editor had dispatched him from their London offices with instructions to find out for the paper's readers – over 20,000 of them at the time – what on earth was going on in this proverbially placid corner of the country. Founded in 1785 by John Walter 'to record the principal occurrences of the times', *The Times* had become London's, and therefore the country's, leading daily newspaper. It wasn't yet, as we might now think of it, the organ of the British establishment – in fact, the English aristocracy preferred to read its rival, the *Morning Post* – but it tended to be critically supportive of the government of the day, and wasn't expecting its reporter to be anything less.

The years before Rebecca, as newspaper printing and publishing became cheaper and more accessible, had seen a huge rise in both the number and variety of papers and their readers. Wales already had a significant weekly press of its own: the *Cambrian* was published at Swansea from 1804 and the *Carmarthen Journal* from 1810, while newer – and more liberal-leaning – papers included the *Welshman* and *Y Diwygiwr* ('The Reformer'). These publications together were read by around 10,000 people each month. Their previous reports on Rebeccaism had been syndicated in the pages of other newspapers, including *The Times*, but there hadn't yet been any direct national coverage. By giving Rebecca a national platform, *The Times'* regular reports on 'The State of South Wales' would gain the movement greater public attention and, eventually, the ear of the government.

Thomas Campbell Foster wasn't an obvious choice to cover a story like this. He had no connection with Wales, but he did have a background in newspapers. He had grown up in Leeds where his father edited the *Leeds Patriot and Yorkshire Advertiser*, and had studied to be a barrister before switching to newspaper sub-editing. In 1843 he had just turned thirty and had yet to make his mark on the world of British journalism – or any other – but his coverage of Rebecca would help him change that. His insistence on scrupulous reporting and journalistic independence, hearing 'all sides of the question', as well as his Yorkshire bluntness, would lead him into conflict with magistrates, military officers, Welsh Dissenters and fellow newspapermen. To the Rebeccaites, he was at first a curiosity but would come to be seen as a benefit, if not automatically an ally.

Before even getting to Carmarthen, Foster had been gathering information and opinions from those he met and forming his own impressions of the situation. His journey into Wales took him through the industrial districts of the south-east, where the 'wretchedness and discontent' caused by the trade depression, he wrote, 'must be seen to be fully appreciated'.[1] Foster was struck, as many reporters and other curious visitors would be, by the contrast between the romantic Welsh scenery and the deprivation and drama that occurred against its backdrop. His path beyond the coalfield, heading west through Glamorganshire to Carmarthen, took him past the ruins of toll-bars, demolished tollhouse walls and the sawn-off stumps of tollgates: Rebeccaism, paying no heed to the tourist guides, was now making its own impression on the landscape.

The second of Rebecca's gentleman callers was a man in uniform. Colonel James Frederick Love was a veteran soldier, who had seen action stretching from the battle of Waterloo in 1815 to the 1831 Canadian Rebellion. Now aged fifty-four, Love had distinguished himself as an enemy of democracy and radicalism. Twelve years earlier, he had successfully put down pro-Reform riots in Bristol and been hailed as a 'saviour' of the city by its gentry and middle classes. He had been stationed in the Welsh coalfield after the Merthyr Rising and most recently at Bradford in 1842, as strikes and riots engulfed the north of England. Now sent in by the national government to take charge of troops in the three counties of Carmarthenshire, Cardiganshire and Pembrokeshire, he may not have been expecting the hill-farmers of south-west Wales to present much of a challenge.

In the early hours of Thursday 22 June, Colonel Love's carriage rolled into Carmarthen, to be followed a few hours later by the 73rd Regiment of Foot. He reported immediately to George Rice Trevor at the Dynevor estate. The forty-eight-year-old Trevor, son of the Lord-Lieutenant of Carmarthenshire, was another recent arrival in the area, having been called back to Wales from London to take over his ailing father's law and order duties. At times of unrest like this, Lords-Lieutenant were in charge of all military forces in the county and formed the main link between central and local government. Proclamations and circulars were sent to them from London, and they in turn passed on resolutions from magistrates and requests for assistance.

Trevor already held the seat of Carmarthenshire as a Tory MP – the same seat held by his father and grandfather before him – and, much to his displeasure, he now needed to fulfil the rest of his family's civic as well as political offices. For now, Trevor acquiesced to Love's decision to place the military around Rebecca's current territory. He sent the yeomanry to Newcastle Emlyn, St Clears and Pembroke, leaving the Royal Marines garrisoning Cardigan and 150 infantry remaining in Carmarthen.

A FISH DINNER

Reaching Carmarthen by public coach a few hours after the military's arrival, an exhausted Thomas Campbell Foster checked in at the Ivy Bush Royal Hotel, a sprawling coaching-inn on Spilman Street. In 1819, during that year's Carmarthen *eisteddfod*, the Ivy Bush's garden had been the site of the first Gorsedd of Bards, a cultural festival of poetry, music and art organised by the poet, antiquary and prankster Iolo Morganwg. Two decades on, the hotel was a favoured stop for higher-class tourists as well as those travelling for business. While *The Times* was clearly sparing no expense for its reporter, Foster was keen to not remain in sheltered isolation in the Ivy Bush's warren of twisting corridors but to embed himself in the community. On his journey into the town, he had already sounded out fellow travellers and locals about the events of three days before:

> Every person I spoke to sympathized with the rioters; and, upon my asking what the attack on Carmarthen Workhouse had to do with the turnpike-gates, the reply was, 'Oh, that is another monstrous oppression – they rob and imprison the poor who are badly fed, and do not even get one-half of what is collected for them.' This was far from being an isolated, but, on the contrary, is the general, opinion.[2]

Surprised by the views he had gathered on the road, Foster began his stay not by soliciting tales of riot and destruction for scandalised London readers, but by investigating conditions at Carmarthen workhouse itself. In an article published a few days later, he interviewed the workhouse matron about the food given to inmates. This, he reported, was mostly barley bread, black, gritty and sour, along with porridge made of one part milk to three parts water, and with meat provided only on Sundays and Wednesdays.

> And on Fridays, the matron concluded, 'we have a fish dinner.'
> 'Oh,' thought I, 'this is kindly intended as a change and luxury, they are near the sea-coast, and cod, and haddock, and mackerel, no doubt are abundant and cheap.'
> 'What fish?' I asked. 'Oh, a salt herring each – and very large ones they are too,' said the matron, qualifying it, as I raised an incredulous look.[3]

Allowing his scepticism to shape his story, Foster invited his readers to compare this diet with the rations provided to inhabitants of the local jails, noting that the bread given out in Carmarthen's prison, which he had also sampled in the interests of investigation, 'was good wheaten brown bread [...] and I have frequently seen such bread from choice eaten in respectable families in England'.[4]

Not only were those committed to the workhouse eating worse than prisoners, but a stay there, in place of financial relief from the parish, often made no economic sense. Foster recorded his argument with a Poor Law official about cases where people were forced into the workhouse for non-payment of rent:

> I have seen a bundle of these orders such as 'Admit John Jones, wife, and three children,' which have been refused, the applicants preferring to starve or live by mendicancy rather than break up their cottage, their only home, and enter the workhouse. I asked what would become of it if he and his family should accept the order and enter the workhouse.
>
> 'Oh,' he answered, 'he would lock it up for a few days till he got work.'
>
> 'Suppose,' said I, 'he should not obtain work for a week, would the Union pay his rent?'
>
> 'Oh, no,' said he, 'the landlord must distrain on his furniture for that.'
>
> Can it be wondered at [that] John Jones should spurn the offer to give him bread on condition that he and his family should become outcasts, by thus consenting to the breaking of the strongest tie to honest industry – his own fireside![5]

Foster was careful to condemn the violence of the workhouse riot itself, but his willingness to consider the causes behind it already set him apart from other mainstream reporters. Settling into Carmarthen, he found a lot of leads to follow, including rumours of a cartload of arms being received in Talog and an offer of paramilitary assistance from the pro-independence 'Repealers in Ireland'. Both stories, Foster went on to reassure the readers of *The Times*, were false alarms – though what was true was that, while farmers had occasionally carried guns for shooting crows or hares, a greater number of them were now doing so in response to the military presence in the area. One farmer who spoke to him also let him know that the firing of blank cartridges was used, along with bugles and flares, as a signal to call Rebeccaites together.

Committed to hearing both sides of the story, Foster tried to gain admission to meetings of the local magistrates, but was informed in a polite but uncompromising note from George Rice Trevor that such meetings were strictly private. This decision to ban the press wasn't the best idea, as people were already anxious and suspicious about what the authorities might be saying behind closed doors. At one such meeting at the Salutation Inn in Pembrokeshire, Trevor made an appeal for calm, but he also said that he would have no hesitation in ordering the military to open fire during any future riots. By the time a version of this speech made its way to a public already inclined to believe the worst, Trevor was rumoured to have said that he would open fire on rioters himself, and 'that he would have all the husbands taken away from their wives if they were not quiet'.[6]

'THEY ONLY WANT THEIR RIGHTS'

George Rice Trevor also urged that an official police force be set up in Carmarthen. This was a debate that would run and run throughout Rebeccaism, as the logic of strengthening the powers of local authority was undercut by unease about the practicalities of doing so. Both the farmers and the gentry opposed the idea of a local police force, the former because they saw no need for it – or were worried about being subject to its attentions themselves – and the latter on grounds of how much it was likely to cost them in rates.

But the switch in the focus of attacks from tollgates to state property marked by the workhouse riot had understandably heightened the fears of landowners. At a magistrates' meeting at Carmarthen town hall in July, there was general agreement that an organised force of some kind was required to deal with the recent outrages. The only dissenting voice was that of William Chambers Junior, who, looking at causes rather than symptoms, argued that 'the only remedy for the existing disturbances was a complete reform of the turnpike trusts'. Inevitably, his point was ignored, and the magistrates instead called for Parliament to increase the financial penalties for destroying trust property, as well as offering higher rewards for information on the movement.

Edward Crompton Lloyd Hall, like Chambers, was in favour of reasoning rather than repression – but, for both men, this had its limits. Following his legal advice to local farmers prior to the Carmarthen demonstration, Hall had been asked to attend a Rebecca action at Blaennant Lane, armed and in disguise. Impatient with waiting for him to sort out the problems with the tollgate trusts through the judicial and legal system, the local farmers wanted him to lend his personal authority to their direct action.

For Hall, this was a ridiculous request, although one that he had good reason to feel nervous about refusing. He needed to tread a fine line between expressing sympathy for the movement – though not so much as to make himself thought of as a dangerous subversive by his fellow gentry – and warning them about the likely repercussions, not to mention retaining his own authority in a community where respect for any kind of authority was rapidly slipping away. His agonising was evident in the open letter he eventually issued, addressed to 'REBECCA AND HER DAUGHTERS, WELSHMEN':

> Do you think I can countenance or join your riotous proceedings? I tell you No ... Enough has been done already to convince the Government of the great and universal discontent which your grievances have caused among you. They have sent down soldiers to keep the peace. I therefore entreat you not to meet together on Wednesday night. I have written for the soldiers to come here and prevent you doing any mischief if you should ... The penalty for pulling down a Turnpike House is TRANSPORTATION FOR LIFE.

What good can you get by running such a risk, when you may attain everything you ought to have, in a peaceable and quiet manner, without running any danger whatever? ... On Thursday morning, let each parish choose two Delegates to come to me ... to make me acquainted with your grievances, and then follow implicitly the advice I shall give them. If you do, peace and prosperity will be sure to return to you. If you do not, I shall leave you to enjoy the results of your ignorance and folly.[7]

George Rice Trevor, meanwhile, may not have wanted the press at the magistrates' sessions, but he was planning his own publicity campaign. At the end of June he issued a public address:

TO THE INHABITANTS OF THE COUNTY OF CARMARTHEN

I feel called upon, at this moment, when so much of illegal and unwarrantable outrage has been committed in some parts of this County, to call your attention to the evil consequences such proceedings are calculated to bring on all those concerned in them. The assemblies that have taken place for the purposes of violence, under the pretence of redressing grievances, are illegal, and though, up to this time, many of those who are concerned in them, have escaped detection, they may be assured that sooner or later the Law will be too strong for them, and make its power to be felt ... For the purpose of restoring order and suppressing tumult, there is a large force of Military placed at my disposal, which I am naturally averse to employ against my fellow-Countrymen; but I beg you to believe me, that if it be necessary, I shall not hesitate one moment to do so.[8]

He then wrote to William Chambers Junior at Llanelli, forwarding his address for circulation there. Although Llanelli was still relatively untroubled, Trevor urged Chambers to hold frequent magistrates' meetings and to contact absentee magistrates and landowners, instructing them to return to their duties and help out – implying that if Chambers wanted to take his place as a genuinely respected member of the Welsh gentry, he could not avoid doing his own duty in this case.

But despite the efforts of magistrates and military to stamp them out, the seeds of Rebeccaism were starting to blossom elsewhere. The rout at the workhouse was not the end but the start of Rebecca's busiest period. A gate at Llanfihangel-ar-arth had been smashed the very evening of the riot at Carmarthen, and in the next few weeks more gates were downed at nearby Pensarn as well as further west at St Clears, Scleddy and Fishguard-Hill. Twenty miles north in Newcastle Emlyn, three gates were attacked in a single night by a crowd who arrived in military formation – and among them, not fully taking part but hanging back to observe, was Edward Crompton Lloyd Hall, obeying his summons from Rebecca after all despite his misgivings.

The authorities and their allies in the local press continued in their failure to grasp both the extent and nature of people's discontent. The *Carmarthen Journal* ran a thundering editorial:

> The war cry against the toll-gates is a mere pretence – it is an eruptive symptom of a deeply-seated and widely diffused spirit of political disaffection – the first development of incipient revolution. Rebel-ca would be a more proper designation for this refractory dame; for we defy any sane man to trace any necessary connection between toll-gates and work-houses to make them indiscriminate objects of hostility to the rural population of this country.[9]

A less radical, but equally obvious explanation remained under the noses of the *Carmarthen Journal*'s editors. The connection between tollgates and workhouses had already been made clear by the Carmarthen marchers themselves: both were symbols of popular discontent at a time of financial crisis. Incomes were falling and outgoings – from fixed rents to the new road taxes – were staying high, and if this wasn't addressed from above, what could people do other than try to address it from below? A farmer interviewed by Thomas Campbell Foster put it plainly:

> The people wish to support the Government, but they are so poor and so oppressed that they cannot pay. How can the farmers pay when butter sold today in Carmarthen market for 6 pence, and new cheese for 1 pence per pound., and yet the rents of the farms are kept up at the same high rate? [...] They do not wish to hurt any one, they only want their rights.[10]

But when Foster asked if the movement would be deterred now that the military had arrived in greater numbers, his interviewee gestured to the dramatic mountain scenery that Foster had previously been admiring, and scoffed at the idea:

> Look at these mountains; of what use would they be here? The people could do them more hurt than they could do the people, and in safety too; for they could come through the country, and if they wished it, shoot them in the groves.[11]

PART THREE:

THE SUMMER OF DISCONTENT

8
A LOSING BATTLE

'DEATH OR GLORY'

As July 1843 began, George Rice Trevor, fed up with the kid-glove treatment of troublemakers he saw around him, tried to put his foot down. Stepping firmly into his new role as acting Lord-Lieutenant of Carmarthenshire, having stationed detachments of Colonel Love's troops around the county, he further ordered that meetings of local magistrates be held as often as possible, that more special constables be sworn in and that 'every effort should be made to keep order'. But Trevor was already fighting a losing battle, both on the ground and in terms of public perception.

By this point, any reader of certain newspapers might have formed the impression that the whole of the country was under the sway of Rebecca, its hillsides littered with the remnants of shattered tollgates and workhouses, and its population, like the *sans-culottes* of revolutionary Paris, ankle-deep in spilled blood. A London newspaper, under the headline RIOTS IN SOUTH WALES, had exaggerated the size and extent of the attack on Carmarthen workhouse, reporting that rioters had occupied the town of Newcastle Emlyn and claiming that placards carried by the Carmarthen marchers had included the slogans 'Death or Glory' and 'Blood and Revenge', as well as the more reasonable-sounding 'Bread to the hungry'.[1]

The Welsh press, while continuing to report on attacks by 'Rebecca', were also at pains to point out the exaggerations and sensationalism of reports beyond Wales. In the *Welshman*, a correspondent from Tenby, perhaps concerned at a potential drop in income from holidaymakers, wrote to reassure the paper's readers that, on the south Pembrokeshire coast at least, both life and the summer tourist trade were continuing as normal:

Our delightful and picturesque little watering-place is rapidly beginning to fill with the elite of England and Wales, in spite of the 'awful' accounts of 'open rebellion', 'fell slaughter of Yeomanry cavalry', 'poor houses', 'Gentleman's Seats' etc being nightly committed to the flames by the Witch of Witches!!! Becca!!! And her ten thousand daughters (ie ten!!! Or thereabouts). These reporters ... deserve the utmost contempt.[2]

During the summer Thomas Cooke, the increasingly put-upon estate manager at Middleton Hall, wrote to assure his mother that despite what she may have read and heard:

We are none of us at all afraid of the disaffected 'Taffies'. The description of our perils must I think be more alarming at the distance of 200 miles than the real facts of the case warrant, for we every one of us eat and drink and sleep well, although every morning does bring news of fresh outrages.[3]

But – as Cooke himself would soon be made aware – there was some truth to the rumours. In the week or so since the storming of Carmarthen workhouse, several more tollgates had been destroyed, and the movement was continuing to grow. From July onwards, attacks exploded across Carmarthenshire, Pembrokeshire and Cardiganshire and beyond, averaging two or three every day. They took place mostly on weeknights, reflecting the rioters' commitment to keeping the Sabbath. Before the year was over, unrest inspired by Rebecca's actions in the three south-western counties would spread to Glamorganshire, Radnorshire, Montgomeryshire, Brecknockshire and even Anglesey in the country's north-west corner. And these actions would not simply be confined to tollgates.

DRAG VS DRAGOONS

After Wellington's triumph at the battle of Waterloo in 1815, some British army officers, like Colonel Love, continued in illustrious careers. But many ordinary soldiers on their return to Britain fell back into the same hard times they had been trying to escape by joining up. Griffith Bowen had been a labourer before enlisting at the age of seventeen, seeking better prospects than could be found in his village just off the coach-road from Llanelli to Carmarthen. He had committed himself for unlimited service, but, after seeing action with the Grenadier Guards in Spain at the battle of Barrosa, and later at Waterloo, Bowen was discharged. By June 1843 he was back in Wales on an army pension, living with his wife in Meinciau, only two miles south of the church where he'd been christened.

Like many former soldiers, Bowen had taken what work he could get after arriving back in the country. One of his jobs was as keeper of the Pen-y-garn tollgate on the road from Carmarthen to London. The tollhouse he lived in had been standing for around fifteen years and was an unusually imposing example: two storeys high with a slate roof and stone walls twenty-two inches thick, adjoining a gate with posts of solid oak measuring four feet around. But, one night towards the end of June, Rebecca made short work of it all. When Thomas Campbell Foster arrived at dawn, notebook and pencil at the ready to report on news of yet another outrage, he found the tollhouse and gate reduced to rubble and 'the poor man and his family sitting houseless by the wayside'.[4]

Bowen's gate was meant to be under the watch of the dragoons now stationed around Carmarthen, but its destruction proved that the military's presence was no guarantee of safety. The Welsh landscape had become a contested arena, with the occupying troops facing a local population ready to adopt guerrilla tactics. Across the stretch of countryside between the town of Carmarthen and the county border, Foster reported:

Dragoons are seen lounging about, and standing in the doorways of the different cottages where they are lodged and billeted, in strange contrast with the poverty-stricken inhabitants and the apparent quiet of the place ... It is difficult to fight against a united people. They are all spies upon the soldiery, and warn each other of their approach.[5]

One immediate problem was that the dragoons might have had a certain style, but subtlety was a foreign concept to them. Their uniforms, with tall, plumed helmets, thick braided epaulettes and blindingly polished shoulder-belts, made them objects of curiosity in the places they were stationed, as their horses clattered down narrow country lanes and picked their way through market squares. It also made them highly noticeable when mounting patrols at night or when attempting to make a clandestine counter-attack on Rebeccaites destroying a gate.

Often, the military's presence was simply ignored, or openly defied; groups of Rebeccaites were seen 'parading' on main roads or through town squares as though they were an occupying army themselves. On other occasions, the military were outmanoeuvred or outwitted. It had become common knowledge, for instance, that a frequent signal for Rebeccaites to gather was the sound of a horn being blown. But when the military tried to make use of this intelligence by rushing to defend any location where they picked up this signal, horns began to be sounded in ever more misleading directions, none of them near the scene of an attack. On 26 July a gate at Croeslwyd was being guarded by dragoons when they were decoyed up the road to St Clears by the sound of horns. They left two police constables watching the gate, who were startled a short time later by the sound of not a horn, but a whistle. The signal brought thirty Rebeccaites out from the adjoining hedges where they had been lying in wait to demolish the gate, which they had fully accomplished by the time the dragoons returned.

It was becoming clear that these actions weren't the spontaneous work of a loose handful of troublemakers; they were well-organised and coordinated operations. In addition to strategies for misinforming the authorities or distracting the military, the parties of men who destroyed the gates, walls, bars and tollhouses had worked out the most efficient ways to dismantle them so as not to waste time and to make their escape before the authorities arrived, and sometimes before they were even alerted.

As shown by actions like that at Croeslwyd, Rebeccaites' knowledge of their local country and the quickest ways around it, plus the already established networks of communication between farms and cottages a few miles apart, allowed them to convey information about the actions of authorities and the movement of troops. Thomas Campbell Foster, among others, was impressed by the speed and effectiveness of this:

> A note is sent to the nearest farmhouse addressed to some distant destination. The farmers know what it means, and are instructed what to do, and some man or boy on the farm is immediately sent off with it as fast as he can run to the next farm in the line, and the farmer there pounces on it in like manner, so that you have in reality information going almost any distance and across any sort of country at about the rate of eight miles an hour. No wonder that the authorities, without almost any plan or organization, find themselves baffled by organization like this. The Dragoons with military tramp and parade travel along the road, confident they shall at last pounce on the Rebeccaites, whilst some ragged urchin takes the shortest cut over hedge and ditch, with a letter in his breast, to be passed on from farm to farm to the scene of action, and the Dragoons find they are just too late.[6]

News of impending actions was also made known to local people in advance, and when they happened they could involve up to several hundred people, and sometimes more, who turned out to lend encouragement and support or simply to watch. A report in the *Swansea Journal* showed how the formula had been perfected in Cardiganshire, with information, coordination and communication coming together in the space of a few hours:

It was rumoured throughout this place last week that Rebecca and her daughters would pay us a visit on Friday night. About ten o'clock that night, the town was in a state of excitement, the inhabitants going towards the Common by hundreds, not only from Cardigan, but from Saint Dogmell's, Kilgerran, and the neighbourhood. About half-past eleven, the ground in the neighbourhood of the toll-house was covered with people, and hundreds were on the Common road up to the milestone. A few minutes before twelve the report of a gun was heard between us and the Warren banks, and immediately after the crowd came running down the road, shouting She is coming! In a few minutes a party of 12 men, mounted on horseback, some of them wearing feathers in their caps, and having their faces blacked, and otherwise disguised, made their appearance. They were followed by about 150 men on foot, armed with guns, pickaxes, hatchets, pitch forks, clubs, etc, most of whom were disguised. On arriving at the gate they demanded that it should be instantly opened. This was immediately complied with, and about one half of the force marched through, when they fired off their guns, and commenced the work of destruction. They appeared to be well organised; for although they commenced their work almost immediately, there was no confusion, each person apparently taking a portion of labour allotted to him. Some with hatchets commenced to break down the gate and other woodwork, others got on the roof, while a large party proceeded to break down the wall which reaches from the toll-house to the hedge at Pensarn field, about 90 feet in length. The toll-house was a firm and compact building, erected two years ago, at a cost of nearly £100. It was so strongly built that for a long time it resisted the efforts of the rioters. One of the men on the roof, after toiling a considerable time exclaimed 'Damn me, mammy, it's hard work, send more hands up here'. More hands were sent, and after an hour and a half of hard working, they succeeded in levelling the house. The 'Rebecca' for this night was a tall man, dressed in white, with a very large bonnet.[7]

HOUSES OF OPPRESSION

The military's only relative success was in making sure the attack on Carmarthen workhouse wasn't repeated a few hours' ride west, in Narberth. Rebeccaites had already visited this town three times, destroying several gates, and a few days later had called at an abandoned tollgate where the tollkeeper still lived, warning him not to set up a functioning tollgate again. The tollkeeper, like his counterpart at the Water Street gate, had had a worrying conversation with 'Rebecca', who told him ominously 'that there were larger houses than this should come down'.[8] Given recent events at Carmarthen, this could only have meant the local workhouse.

On 29 June Thomas Campbell Foster, hearing of the threatened attack, rode immediately out of Carmarthen to get ahead of the story. On his late-night journey to Narberth he was accompanied by a local guide, who, as they passed the workhouse – 'the most substantial and best-built house in the Neighbourhood' as Foster noted dryly – gave vent to his feelings on it:

> Ah! Sir, there's the house of oppression, 'them whom God hath joined together let no man put asunder'. Do you, Sir, think it right that they should, because we are poor, take our children from their mother, and me from my wife? And do you think it right that if a poor girl has been led astray, she should be obliged to pay all for the child?[9]

Foster marked this down as another example of what he was coming to call the 'religious fanaticism' of the Welsh people he encountered, which led them to give scriptural, as well as political reasons for their subversive actions and ideas. The words of his guide showed, however, that the Rebecca movement's particular strength was its ability to channel both religious and secular feelings of injustice into seeking material changes.

Reaching Narberth in the early hours of the morning, Foster found it already in a state of somewhat panicky preparedness: the local magistrates were still up at an all-night session, and the town's workhouse was surrounded by a handful of the Castlemartin yeomanry, with hastily sworn-in special constables sent out into the countryside to keep watch. Just after midnight, one special rushed back into town with a report of what he described as between 500 and 1,000 people marching on the road from Cardigan, on horseback and on foot, with Rebecca at their head. They had, he said, come within half a mile of entering Narberth when one of their group met them with information that the military were stationed at the workhouse. The crowd had stopped to hold a hurried conference before, perhaps also remembering the dragoons at Carmarthen, they decided to disperse into the night.

With this news allowing the authorities of Narberth to breathe slightly more easily, Foster found a bed for the night before staying to report on the next day's county fair. Usually crowded and raucous, the event passed off quietly and sedately under the eyes of the military. Foster observed, however, that despite the large number of livestock available for sale, for what his English readers would find startlingly low prices, no one seemed to have the money to make a single purchase.

The local constables and specials weren't faring any better than the soldiers, and weren't given a pass for being Welsh. It was difficult to see the magistrates' logic in stationing a small number of police at likely sites of attack; if one happened, they weren't provided with either rockets to fire a distress signal or horses to carry the news elsewhere for reinforcements, and they were clearly incapable of holding off an armed crowd who outnumbered as well as outgunned them. Their presence completely failed to deter the rioters, who seemed mostly to regard the police with contempt and sometimes as sources of amusement, as on one occasion early in July, where three parish constables guarding a tollhouse found themselves surrounded by Rebeccaites, and were made to help in demolishing the place.

Even with more troops sent in and stationed within communities at local pubs and coaching-inns, the success of local intelligence on one side and the failures of incompetence on another allowed attacks to continue, often audaciously. At Llandeilo in early August, the local carpenter Thomas Jenkins, whose father was an associate of the radical lawyer Hugh Williams, recorded in his diary with a note of satisfaction: 'The Walk Gate and house was taken down to the ground by the Rebeccaites with soldiers billeted at The White Hart and Walk on both sides, so much for soldier vigilance.'[10]

9
ALL BUT OPEN REBELLION

AN ANGRY SUMMER

For the increasingly anxious authorities in south-west Wales, there was still a worrying silence from the Home Office in London. Its chief minister, Sir James Graham, had enough to contend with in the summer of 1843. Robert Peel's government was only just catching its breath after the previous year's general strike, in which half a million workers in mines, mills and factories had protested at cuts to their wages, long working hours and high rents. Beginning among the miners of Staffordshire in the Midlands, and with Chartism fanning the flames, the strike had spread across Britain – up to Yorkshire and Lancashire and as far as Dundee, as well as down to south Wales and Cornwall. The government had responded by sending the military into the streets, resulting in deaths and injuries of protestors in the northern towns of Halifax and Preston, while 400 people had been arrested at a 5,000-strong Chartist demonstration in Nottingham.

The year 1842 had also seen two separate efforts to assassinate the young Queen Victoria, attempts on whose life were becoming so frequent that she had been issued with a bulletproof parasol. By 1843 thousands of strikers and rioters, along with leading Chartists including Feargus O'Connor, were still being hauled through the courts for their part in the general strike. Meanwhile, Daniel O'Connell's campaign for independence from Britain was sweeping across Ireland, and in January Peel's private secretary had been shot dead on Whitehall by an allegedly insane Scotsman who thought he was shooting the Prime Minister himself. The Home Secretary wasn't certain he could make room for Wales on his list of current constitutional anxieties.

But the government couldn't claim that it knew nothing about the urgency of matters in Wales. In addition to the news now carried in the London papers, including Thomas Campbell Foster's in-depth dispatches for *The Times*, and the equally regular calls for help from magistrates, the Home Secretary was being deluged with letters from one magistrate in particular – Edward Crompton Lloyd Hall. He sometimes fired off more than one letter each day, and when he got no response, he simply wrote again, offering to send copies of the letters he had sent already: 'I have received no acknowledgements of the receipts of my several letters to you of the 22nd, 23rd, 25th and 26th instant. Should they not duly have come to hand I will send you duplicates.'[1]

These letters hadn't been acknowledged not because they hadn't been received, but because the Home Office wasn't quite sure what to make of Hall. Though he was clearly keen to offer information, he also turned up in other people's reports from Wales, where he seemed to be appeasing the Rebeccaites: while he urged them to follow legal means to address their problems, he didn't deny that they were right to want the problems addressed. To an overworked and paranoid Home Office, which saw potential subversion and radical plots around every corner, this even-handedness was too close to sympathy for those breaking the law.

In one of his letters, Hall suggested that insurgents from the Welsh coalfield, and even from rebellious districts in England and Ireland, were flooding into Carmarthenshire – not to offer to teach the farmers their own methods of resistance, but to learn from Rebecca's own success. This anxiety – justified or not – about a crossover in unrest wasn't confined to Hall: in July in Glamorganshire, Bridgend's chief constable wrote to the Marquis of Bute to caution him that although locally things were quiet, 'Becca has sent her agents into this county with tenders of service.'[2] In Carmarthen, Colonel Love was also worried about overlap and crossover between agitators, but he blamed migrant workers, returning to their home farms and cottages from the riotous coalfields, for the increase in disturbances in the countryside. Love, too, wrote to the Home Office with worries about Chartists infiltrating Rebeccaism, as well as with an astute enough assessment of the 'great maladministration' taking place under the turnpike trusts.[3] His authority meant that he met with greater success than Hall, getting 150 more Met officers dispatched to Carmarthenshire as well as – with some doubt from the Home Office about their necessity – two pieces of field artillery and ammunition.

AN INSIDE JOB

Although many a newspaper would claim otherwise, the organisation and operation of Rebecca's summer of discontent in 1843 was almost entirely an inside job. Actions were planned by small committees that met in farm outbuildings, around pub tables or on lonely spots on the hillside, with information passed between neighbouring groups and timings for attacks coordinated. Large farming families, who were already seen as community leaders in the absence of the gentry, often moved into leading the coordination of local actions. They might not all be willing or able to carry out attacks themselves, but they had access to labourers and servants who, if they weren't already willing to help bring down the hated tollgates, were willing to do so for a top-up to their wages or merely being treated to food and drink afterwards. This money 'for the cause' was collected from locals, with farmers often asked to bring 'subscriptions' to a particular meeting. Cash was then gathered by the Rebecca of the night and distributed to those who took part in the attacks – along with guns, bonnets and petticoats for those who couldn't supply their own. It was estimated that the average pay for casual rioting was two shillings and sixpence – not a bad rate when a farm labourer's earnings could be as little as a shilling a day.

At these meetings and outside them, intelligence was routinely gathered and shared on the movement of troops and police and the opinions of local magistrates and landowners. Sometimes this information came from those on the inside, perhaps from workers on large estates, like a young coachman who worked for the Vaughan family at Golden Grove estate and was suspected of passing information to local Rebeccaites. Pub landlords became a notably useful resource as, used to handling relatively large sums of money, they could act as treasurer and accountant for a particular group, as well as providing a place to meet. Publicans could also provide intelligence on the movements – and the often low morale – of the military who were billeted in their establishments, in addition to passing on any drunken indiscretion or useful piece of gossip they might hear from their patrons.

Once a target had been identified, intentions were posted up on notices or spread by letter or public criers. While the attacks themselves were planned and timed clandestinely, the intentions were often a public matter, giving the authorities the opportunity to offer concessions over a particular gate, though very few did. Those who took part in attacks were both the willing and sometimes those pressured or bribed into willingness. Their leader, Rebecca, was often a local community figurehead but, as Twm Carnabwth showed, could be anyone, however humble, who was suited to the part – and who was granted, as in the 'world turned upside down' of festivals and carnivals, a temporary freedom and authority that might not have been available to them in 'normal' life.

Rebecca and her daughters were ordinary men who became extraordinary through taking action. Outside of attacks, they existed as regular members of the community, but during them they materialised as something different, putting on their 'Rebeccaite' persona through their costume and their actions. Similarly, the clothing they wore and the implements they used in protest became, when out of action, ordinary household objects, which couldn't constitute evidence if the police turned them up when searching a cottage or farmhouse – there was no reason a petticoat, axe, bonnet or gun shouldn't be in the normal possession of a farmer's or labourer's family. All this, plus the level of community support for Rebeccaism, made the movement particularly resistant to investigation.

BEYOND THE TOLLGATES

The tyranny of the tollgates was now being challenged even in daylight – and by those not even bothering to wear Rebecca's uniform to do so. In early August, the Plain-Dealing gate at Narberth was approached by seven farm-carts whose drivers demanded free passage. When the toll-collector refused to let them through without payment, one of the drivers unfastened his horse from the cart and yoked it to the bar across the road, proceeding to drag it off its hinges before declaring 'that was the way to pay the toll'.[4] The disturbance attracted the attention of a policeman, who ran to the nearby hotel where both a local magistrate and the yeomanry were stationed, giving them the news and then returning with three other constables to arrest the cart-driver. But the other drivers held them off, surrendering to custody only when the yeomanry were sent out as back-up.

The troubles of the Plain-Dealing gate didn't end there. The following morning, with the toll-bar hastily repaired, a farmer on horseback also refused to pay before riding his horse directly into the beleaguered bar, snapping it in half. He too resisted arrest, threatening 'to take the life of anybody who attempted to apprehend him'.[5] After fending off six or seven constables by himself, he eventually surrendered to the yeomanry, and was fined twenty shillings and discharged. Resistance to the toll system, it seemed, was now widespread, commonplace and even expected by those who used the gates.

But the targets of Rebecca were evolving to encompass more than tollgates. They now included the enclosure system: near Ammanford, a newly built wall that cut off a section of formerly common land to form a private field, held to be 'an encroachment on the common rights of the villagers',[6] was torn down and the field thrown back open to public use. Meanwhile, a vicar at Penbryn received a threatening letter for having forced local Nonconformists to donate to the cost of a Church school. These incidents reflected longstanding and deeply felt social issues, now breaking to the surface in the volatile times Rebecca had brought on.

121

And the ripples were spreading as far the estates of the gentry. At Middleton Hall in late July, Thomas Cooke was recovering from the previous evening's visit by a mob of Rebeccaites. The target of their ire hadn't been Cooke but, for reasons Cooke couldn't quite make out, the butler. The man had fled the manor house as the crowd approached and spent the following two hours hiding in the bushes, until they left without doing any damage beyond shouting at the mansion's impervious walls. However, it couldn't have calmed Cooke's nerves when a few days later he was handed a letter delivered to the mansion and signed by 'Rachael and Paul for Rebecca'. It referred to Cooke himself as 'the fat Steward', but he brushed this disrespect aside and worked out that the reason for complaint was his having sent a bailiff to collect overdue rent from his employer's tenants.

Cooke, in his own opinion, was just doing his job, and whether tenants could afford to pay their rent or not was hardly his problem. It also wasn't his problem when, three days later, the bailiff in question had every window in his house smashed. But that same night, Cooke, up late again in an attempt to disentangle the estate's accounts, heard the sudden blast of a horn outside his own window, followed by a gunshot.

He peered cautiously between the curtains and looked down to see around forty armed men, dressed in white and riding behind a tall and stout figure, who was fully committing to his role as Rebecca by riding his horse side-saddle like a woman. Cooke watched as, firing off guns at the houses they passed, the column quickly covered the distance to the tollhouse at Llanddarog. Watching the gate go down in the distance without the slightest interference from anyone, Cooke pushed the account-books to one side and sat down to compose a report of the excitement for his mother. His letter concluded that the nearby village looked 'as tho' it had been taken by an enemy'.

A few days later, it was the turn of local landowner and magistrate Rees Goring Thomas. Returning through the village of Llanon between 2 and 3 o'clock in the morning after demolishing a nearby gate and burning the tollhouse, some of Rebecca's followers began stoning the windows of Goring Thomas's mansion. They were called off by the night's Rebecca who, in a line that might not have particularly reassured Goring Thomas, declared 'Now girls, if you are my daughters, leave that house alone, until I shall command you another time'.[7]

The group then moved off to knock up the landlord of the Kings' Arms, on this occasion paying for their beer. All in all it was a relatively law-abiding excursion, but this didn't deter Cooke from writing:

> It is difficult to guess where all this will end – the country is in a state of all but open rebellion – the country people frightened out of their senses, and well they may, for the noise they make in their night doings, is sufficiently alarming to awe stronger nerves than the generality of them can boast of.[8]

Even the Chartists, for all the caveats and concerns they would go on to raise as the movement grew, couldn't help but find Rebecca impressive. At the end of July, the *Northern Star* syndicated one of Thomas Campbell Foster's reports 'from the seat of Rebecca's warfare'. The paper's editors added: 'The state of Wales is most critical. An organised opposition to "constituted" authority is there systematically at work, and it has hitherto baffled all the efforts made to put it down.'[9]

The same matters were being discussed, with unamused alarm, at the highest levels of the British state. In June 1843 a letter to the Queen from her friend and adviser, Viscount Melbourne, noted his concern that her government seemed:

> to have permitted these lawless riotings in South Wales to go on with success and impunity a great deal too long. When such things begin nobody can say how far they will go or how much they will spread. There are many who

123

expect and predict a general rising against property, and this is invariably the way in which such things begin.[10]

Victoria firmly agreed. From Buckingham Palace, she passed on Melbourne's sentiments to Sir James Graham at the Home Office, and noted that any action taken against the 'very unpleasant' Rebeccaites would serve as an example to other restless territories:

> The Queen trusts that measures of the greatest severity will be taken, as well to suppress the revolutionary spirit as to bring the culprits to immediate trial and punishment. The Queen thinks this of the greatest importance with respect to the effect it may have in Ireland, likewise as proving that the Government is willing to show great forbearance, and to trust to the good sense of the people; but that if outrages are committed and it is called upon to act, it is not to be trifled with, but will visit wrong-doers with the utmost severity.[11]

The Home Secretary, despite everything else on his plate, couldn't ignore an intervention from the Queen herself. With a sigh, he moved the need to deal with Rebecca much higher up the government's list of priorities.

10
REBECCA GOES SOUTH

A GOLDEN COUPLE

Elizabeth Davies of Ystomenlle farm was doing her best to stay out of the Rebecca riots. She was the eldest and much-admired daughter of a respectable family at Hendy, a village on Carmarthenshire's border with Glamorganshire, but it wasn't personal disapproval of the movement that stopped her. Nor was it the fact that she was a woman – although most women would have struggled on their own to destroy the heavyweight gates and bars, there were plenty who joined in the action, either acting as sentinels for the approach of police or soldiers, or shouting encouragement as the men did the heavy lifting, or simply standing by as witnesses to the sanction given by the local community.

As the child of a law-abiding farmer, however, Elizabeth didn't want to risk her family's reputation by being arrested or even spotted at the scene of one of Rebecca's attacks. But on the night of 6 July Elizabeth, accompanied by her maid, managed to slip out of her family's farmhouse and away down the Bolgoed road. The two girls' destination was the Fountain Inn, less than a mile away, where they made their way inside, grabbed a drink and settled nervously at a window on the upper storey. As Elizabeth looked out over the darkened road in front of the pub, and the tollgate that barred it, she clutched the hand of her companion as though they were occupying a box at the theatre. She was looking forward to seeing the man she loved playing a leading role in the drama to come.

Elizabeth's suitor, Daniel Lewis, lived with his parents in a cottage beside Pontarddulais' Goppa Chapel, and worked as a weaver of wool at a local mill. He was known for his cheerful and jokey disposition. As Twm Carnabwth had combined pugilism with chanting the *pwnc* at chapel, Daniel was given equally to highbrow poetry, which he wrote under the bardic name Petrys Bach, and to playing pranks. While this irrepressible young man had captured Elizabeth Davies's heart, none of his qualities endeared him to her father, who insisted to Elizabeth that she would marry a stolid and respectable farmer or not at all.

When, a few weeks earlier, Daniel Lewis had begun asking around to acquire a white dress, the neighbourhood might have assumed he was orchestrating another of his practical jokes. But it was for the serious business of joining the Rebeccaites, and as their leader at that. Elizabeth was the first person Daniel told of his upcoming adventure, and the couple's excitement meant they were unable to keep it to themselves.

By midnight on 6 July, the whole community knew the identity of the man they saw mounted on a white horse, disguised under a white dress – he had eventually borrowed one from his mother – as well as a white cap and bonnet. He rode at the head of a column of hundreds of Rebeccaites as they streamed down from the lower slopes of Goppa mountain, down the Bolgoed road and past the Fountain Inn towards the tollgate. The audience, not least Elizabeth, watched raptly as 'Rebecca' gave a short speech before directing the crowd to get to work – including telling them to carry the tollkeeper's possessions to the side of the road and keep them safe while the tollhouse and gate were demolished.

Such was the success of Daniel Lewis's performance that he was asked to reprise the role some days later, when the Rebeccaites attacked another gate at Rhydypandy. Playing Rebecca was becoming an almost aspirational position – even disapproving press reports could betray a grudging admiration for the commanding style of the leadership figure – and Daniel might even have hoped that it would give him a greater community standing in the eyes of Elizabeth's father. But letting your role as Rebecca become public knowledge wasn't helpful for the movement's need for secrecy and anonymity.

With Carmarthenshire now largely under Rebecca's control, it wasn't surprising that the movement should have spilled over the county's south-eastern border into Glamorganshire. Daniel's debut at Bolgoed had also been Rebecca's first appearance in the county, and his performance had drawn the attention of Captain Charles Napier, a former soldier and now Chief Constable of the newly established Glamorgan Constabulary. The morning after the Bolgoed attack, Napier arrived in Pontarddulais and went door to door, asking questions that, as in his previous inquiries into Rebeccaism, got him no useful answers. He then issued a substantial reward for information, hoping this might be more effective. What he didn't realise was that love could prove an even more effective motivation than money.

THE SIEGE OF CWM CILE

John Jones, a jobbing labourer of Llangyfelach, a parish some miles south of Hendy towards Swansea, might have had no political objection to the tollgate riots – indeed, he happened to have been part of the crowd at both the Bolgoed and Rhydypandy attacks. But he did have a personal objection to Elizabeth Davies, a former object of his affections, choosing to court Daniel Lewis over him. He also had a longer-standing grudge against the Morgans, a local family of tenant-farmers who had been seen at the destruction of the Rhydypandy gate and who had previously participated in destroying John's *tŷ unnos* on Llangyfelach common, because the dwelling interfered with the grazing of their livestock.

While drinking with a local policeman at a pub in Swansea, John had let slip that he had been present at the scene at Bolgoed and Rhydypandy. Thinking fast, he turned this accidental confession to his advantage by offering to identify the leaders and organisers on both occasions. Napier's offer of a reward for information seemed like the perfect opportunity for John to exact revenge and get his love rival out of the picture, as well as earning some much-needed cash in hand. But when he walked into Swansea police station and offered up several names – for Bolgoed, Daniel Lewis and the landlord at the Red Lion Hotel, Griffith Vaughan, as well as Matthew and Henry Morgan for Rhydypandy – he had unwittingly set in motion something much bigger.

Arrests began in the early hours of Sunday 23 July. The fact that the attacks had taken place at tollgates near the county borders of Carmarthenshire and Glamorganshire initially posed an administrative problem, but Napier wanted to act without delay. His superintendents quickly nabbed Griffith Vaughan at the Red Lion, just inside the boundary of Carmarthenshire, before heading back over the border to arrest Daniel Lewis.

With the police knocking at the door of his parents' cottage, Daniel, rather than argue the finer points of county jurisdiction, reached for his knowledge of other legal niceties and insisted that to arrest him, the police wagon needed, by law, to be brought right up to his door. After observing the officers struggling to guide the wagon through the narrow winding lanes, providing amusement to his neighbours one more time, Daniel held out his hands for the cuffs and calmly stepped inside.

The Morgan family, by contrast, had no intention of coming quietly. Having travelled overnight from Swansea into the hills, Napier and his men arrested one of the sons, Matthew Morgan, at his cottage at daybreak on Sunday, before Napier and a single inspector headed on horseback towards the Morgans' farm at Cwm Cile. On arrival they found Matthew's brother Henry in the farmhouse kitchen surrounded by his parents, two brothers and his sister Margaret, all ready to defend him with whatever they had to hand, and particularly indignant that the arrest was taking place on the Sabbath.

As the police moved forward, attempting to grab Henry and drag him into the yard outside, the family struck back. The three men brought the inspector to the floor while the women rushed Napier – Margaret brandishing the kitchen's gridiron and the elderly Mrs Morgan flinging a saucepan of boiling water she had snatched up from the stove, before beating Napier around the head with the emptied pan. As the struggle spilled out of the house into the farmyard, the Morgans continued to hold off the police by grabbing improvised weapons from around their dwelling, including a reaping hook, a fishing-spear, a hammer and a wooden crutch.

In the chaos Napier, pinned to the ground and finding a gun being held to his head, managed to draw his own pistol and fired wildly, wounding Henry's brother John in the stomach. The sound of the pistol-shots brought the rest of Napier's detachment running from Matthew Morgan's cottage and, faced with both police guns and cutlasses, the family retreated indoors. As the police made their escape, Margaret Morgan tossed the abandoned hats of Napier and the inspector into the yard after them with a few choice words of contempt.

Later the same day, a force of over thirty policemen and soldiers arrived to bring in the whole Morgan clan, who this time, recognising the odds were against them, did not resist. Their arrival at Swansea, along with Daniel Lewis, brought the town to a standstill as huge crowds filled the streets, held back by the military.

At the initial examination of the prisoners at Swansea town hall, John Jones was called to describe his first encounter on Goppa mountain with the Bolgoed gate attackers. In his detailed account, he walked a fine line between acknowledging his own involvement in the event and making sure he emphasised that of Daniel Lewis, as well as stressing Daniel's recklessness in letting the community know about his role in advance:

> They sat down on the mountain, and others came from all parts to join them ... I had my coat turned inside out. I also put a handkerchief about my face. I did it for the purpose of being like the others ... I remained there for about half an hour. During that time the numbers increased. Becca was calling upon them, throughout all the neighbourhood. When they left the mountain, they amounted to some hundreds; I was then in the midst of them.
>
> One rose upon his feet, and said to me, 'You know where we are going – it is to break down the Bolgoed gate.' It was Becca that said that. I knew who Becca then was, but not so exact as afterwards. I suspected it was Daniel Lewis; I knew him by his voice, but at the gate I saw his face. I had heard

129

all the neighbourhood say that Daniel Lewis was to act Rebecca's character. I had not heard that he was generally Rebecca, but that he was to be so on that night. I heard that a week or a fortnight before ... from a great number of persons.[1]

None of the arrestees made a statement of their own, and a subsequent meeting of the magistrates set their trial for four months' time.

REBECCA MANIA

As Daniel Lewis and the Morgan family were carted off to Swansea prison, attacks continued to spread south, deeper into the scoop of Wales that lay between Carmarthenshire and the turbulent south-eastern coalfield. The significance of Rebecca's move into Glamorganshire was not lost on Thomas Campbell Foster, who reported from the scene, with some sensationalism, that the industrial population there were very different from the farmers and labourers he had met so far in the western districts:

> There they are a simple agricultural people, while here the great majority of the population are violent Chartist politicians. In the Merthyr district I learn from undoubted authority that secret political meetings are held weekly, and oftener, and that there are secret arms distribution clubs, to which the men subscribe, and by which they are supplied with a musket, bayonet, cross-belts, etc. ... Threatening notices have been served upon some of the workhouses [and] Captain Napier tells me, that they heard the bugle of 'Rebecca' in the hills more than once during the night.[2]

In view of this, plus the mobbing of the town's courthouse after the Morgan family and Daniel Lewis were brought in, the authorities in Swansea were understandably jumpy. They grew more so in the next few days, on hearing that a gate and tollhouse just outside town on the road to Carmarthen had been demolished, and that police had seized a box of guns and ammunition which had been headed for Pontarddulais. When Swansea's mayor, on the lookout for signs of trouble as darkness fell, saw a large crowd advancing across the fields just outside town, he suspected the worst. His fears were confirmed as the shadowy crowd drew nearer. Not only could he see a figure hoisted on other men's shoulders, their white head-covering picked out in the twilight, but among the jubilant shouting he could make out the cry 'Rebecca for ever!'

What the mayor had seen was William Williams, a local mason, with his work-apron tied over a straw hat to look like Rebecca's customary white bonnet and veil. The crowd surrounding him were not about to ransack Swansea but merely playing a prank on the panicky authorities, which had succeeded rather too well. Williams was dragged before the magistrates and charged with 'exciting a tumult', despite expressing regret over what he explained had been merely 'a hay-field lark'.[3] The case was eventually dismissed, but it showed how quickly anxiety was growing over any glimpse of possible Rebeccaism, even if made in jest.

By this point in the summer of 1843, the movement was becoming so widespread, and even more widely well known, that one newspaper referred to 'Rebecca mania'. The *Welshman* reported the destruction of a tollgate, far away in Mark and Wedmore parish, under the headline REBECCA IN SOMERSET.[4] The *Swansea Journal* reported that travel to the June fair at Cardigan would be toll-free, with a nudge and wink as to the cause of this being 'circumstances of a local nature, which our readers in this town will fully understand and appreciate'.[5]

The press, and the crowd at Swansea hayfield, might have been finding things amusing, but for the magistrates and military things were looking ever more serious. The spread of attacks from Carmarthenshire into neighbouring counties, and their increasing frequency in places often miles apart, were taking their toll on troops already overstretched by dealing with strikes and unrest in the coalfield. The soldiers were exhausted by false alarms that brought them out to a deserted stretch of hillside for nothing, and were demoralised by being fragmented into small detachments when they had been trained to fight as a body.

In an attempt to combat this, Colonel Love marched in more troops, billeting them in temporary barracks all over the three counties, often in pubs where they carved graffiti, drank and got into fights with the locals and even the police. This development particularly alarmed Edward Crompton Lloyd Hall, who worried that Rebeccaites would attempt, under the guise of being harmless ordinary pub-goers, to overpower the troops and steal their weapons. While nothing of the sort was tried, the more strategically minded of the soldiers tried to cultivate local informants or infiltrate meetings. They met with a predictable lack of success, and the occupied areas began to settle into a tense state of stalemate.

11
ORGANISED CHAOS

FROM CARMARTHEN WITH LOVE

From his base in the Ivy Bush Hotel, Thomas Campbell Foster was able to interview a wide selection of Carmarthenshire's population, from farmers and cottage-dwellers in the hills to the commercial classes in town, as well as – when they deigned to speak to him – the local magistrates and police. He also rode all over the country to visit the scene of destroyed tollgates and other attacks, to report on public meetings of the magistrates, or simply to chase leads and rumours. He picked up information where he could, from gossip in shop doorways to shadowy conversations in pubs, but many people who had come to recognise him as a journalist were happy to openly seek him out and offer their own opinions and experiences.

When he called in one day at a watchmaker's shop in Carmarthen, the shopkeeper regaled him with tales of farmers and their wives begging him to purchase their watches and clocks – items of high value at the time and often cherished family heirlooms – so that they could make up their rent and bills. In one strikingly Dickensian scene, Foster wrote:

> He then showed me a wedding ring, which had been brought him by a farmer's wife, who declared, with tears in her eyes, that she was obliged to part with it, as her corn had not sold for sufficient to make up her rates. I took the ring in my hand – it was a very substantial one, weighing upwards of two pennyweights, although it had the appearance of having been worn for years, and bearing inside of it as a motto the words 'No riches like content.'[1]

Another farmer's wife, whose mountainside cottage was near the site of a large public meeting which had attracted press attention, found herself playing host to not only Foster but two other London reporters, all of whom had sought shelter with her from a sudden downpour of rain. Having offered the men crowded into her home a meal of bread and cheese, she reminded them as they ate that this was the good bread, kept for guests and chance callers, and not the gritty barley bread her family usually lived on. Warming to her theme, she explained her family's situation and how it might lead them to look sympathetically upon Rebecca's activities:

> We have tried as hard as anybody to save a little against the time we get old and helpless to keep us from poverty, but we can only just make a living, we cannot save, and it grieves us we cannot give a little to start the children. We have tried to get the rent lowered, but there were plenty to take the farm at the same rent if we would not give it.[2]

Her words made an impression on Foster, who had heard similar stories throughout the three counties. In his subsequent reports, he explained that the system of 'small farms and rack rents' in south Wales was comparable to that of Ireland, where it was also causing despair and unrest on a far wider scale. He earnestly invited the largely comfortable readers of *The Times* to empathise with those whose income was immediately swallowed up by outgoings and who, under the New Poor Law, could expect no safety-net other than the workhouse when they became unemployed, ill or too old for labour:

> I can conceive nothing more sickening to a reflecting man – nothing more paralysing to effort, than the thought that his daily labour but gets him his daily bread. With an oppressed heart he dreads sickness and misfortune, and dares not contemplate the feebleness of age.[3]

At other times, Carmarthenshire's population was less forthcoming. When Foster wanted to send his editors some examples of notices showing the practice of farms being let to the highest bidder rather than on the basis of need – a system which he found outrageous – he met opposition from people suspicious of what he wanted them for, and ended up surreptitiously paying the local bellman to peel the notices off the walls for him.

GOING UNDERGROUND

At the end of July, Foster persuaded Colonel Love and George Rice Trevor to let him accompany them as they led a detachment of dragoons on patrol around the outskirts of Carmarthen, in response to information they had received on a threat to several tollgates in the area. After fruitlessly traversing the roads on horseback with them until 11 o'clock that night, he noted that their progress was clearly being watched from the hills, with guns fired off in the distance to signal a warning of their approach.

Assuming the intelligence they'd received was another false alarm, the authorities gave up for the night and the soldiers retired to barracks, but Foster remained on the road. After less than an hour, his persistence paid off. He recorded the Rebeccaite spectacular he witnessed in a report for *The Times* that was shaped more by awed admiration than alarm:

> A sky-rocket was sent up from one of the hills in the neighbourhood, and in a few minutes, several large bonfires were lit on the various hills around, as answers to the signal given by the firing of the rocket. The consequence of these signals soon manifested themselves to the inhabitants of the surrounding country by the almost instantaneous appearance of about 1,000 men, colliers and others, who appeared to be in a well-organized condition. They commenced their operations by attacking and completely demolishing the Bethania-gate, compelling the toll-collector

to seek safety by flight; they then walked in procession by Cwm-mawr, through the village of Drefach, and, in fact, through the entire neighbourhood, being accompanied in their procession by a species of 'rough music', consisting of a number of horns and drums, and continually firing shots as tokens of triumph. They then proceeded to demolish two tollbars on the road from Carmarthen to Llanelly, which exploit they accomplished in a very short time. The scene throughout the whole affair was remarkably striking; the bonfires burning on the hills, the firing of the rockets; the explosions from the guns the mob carried, the beating of drums and the blowing of horns, the surrounding country in the meantime being beautifully illuminated by the light of the young moon, were striking and lovely in the extreme.[4]

The appearance of colliers in the attack on the Bethania gate was significant, and would become more so. In the semi-industrialised south of Carmarthenshire, miners had been subject to the same lay-offs and pay cuts that were affecting the coalfield further east. Colliers might earn higher wages than farm labourers, but this didn't mean much when they were out of work, and had to deal with the same burdens of fixed rents and tithes, plus the same threat of committal to the workhouse if they couldn't make ends meet. Why shouldn't they join in the protests that were calling attention to these problems?

The end of Foster's report included a near-comic description of the advantages the colliers had in finding ways to disappear from the scene of an attack:

The Rebeccaites continued their procession and depredations to the terror of the inhabitants until near midnight; they then disappeared with the same astonishing alacrity that they first of all displayed in appearing. Numbers of them, being colliers, precipitated themselves recklessly down the different shafts of the collieries, which are so plentiful in the neighbourhood; others took refuge in the cottages on the road side.[5]

The colliers, it seemed, were joining in not just with the destruction of gates but also with menacing their opponents in the gentry. On their patrol's way to the threatened gates, George Rice Trevor and the dragoons had had to be given directions. They called at the house of John Thomas, a landlord and magistrate who also owned several of the local collieries, and his son accompanied them to the gates as a guide. A few days later, Thomas received an anonymous letter reprimanding him for his son's actions. He dismissed this as 'an idle threat'. But in the early hours of the following morning he found his isolated country house surrounded by 'colliers and peasants', blowing horns and firing guns. Departing after half an hour of this, they left another note pinned to the door, not only instructing Thomas to prevent his family from publicly disparaging the movement and helping the authorities, but also demanding that he dismiss one of his colliery overseers. The letter was signed, in 'a good bold hand', *Rebecca Talog*.[6]

QUOITS AND COPPERMEN

Visitors to Wales during Rebecca's reign were often surprised by how quiet things usually seemed. Curious tourists and reporters found that they could travel in perfect peace and security, with nothing more disturbing to witness than the ruins where tollgates once stood. It made the increasingly visible presence of the military seem even more incongruous, but troops still continued to pour in. At the end of July four more companies of infantry arrived in Swansea and three at Carmarthen, while the whole regiment of the 4th Dragoons was stationed across south Wales – keeping an eye on both the countryside and the coalfield – and a detachment of artillery was heading towards Carmarthenshire from Brecon.

Relations between troops and townspeople were usually cool, but could flare up at the slightest provocation. While their officers received invitations to the houses of the gentry to dine and drink, entertaining and perhaps reassuring them with their tales of previous military triumphs, the ordinary soldiers had nothing to occupy them other than fruitlessly chasing phantom Rebeccaites down moonlit roads and across empty hillsides. They grew bored and restless.

The inhabitants of Llandovery, on their sober and respectful way to chapel one Sunday morning, were scandalised to see their local detachment of dragoons playing a raucous game of quoits in the middle of town, where they were later joined by some of the sons of the gentry who brought along quantities of gin. A local policeman confiscated the quoits, though not the gin, and reported the whole affair to the magistrates, who refused to interfere. Matters were only settled when the local vicar called on the dragoons' officers to explain the degree of offence occasioned on the Sabbath by this clash of cultures.

Meanwhile, in Swansea, Daniel Lewis and the Morgan family were still awaiting trial, but out on bail. The magistrates were making plans to try them at a Special Commission, and had invited a government official, the Solicitor to the Treasury, to offer them legal advice. Public hostility to the arrests was still running high, and rumours had reached the magistrates from the hills around the town that the defendants, when they returned to town for trial, would do so in Rebeccaite splendour, in a coach-and-four surrounded by hundreds of supporters on horseback. While possibly another of Daniel Lewis's pranks, this mooted mock-triumphal procession had obvious echoes of the Rebeccaite march into Carmarthen, and the Swansea authorities added it to their ever-lengthening list of things to worry about.

Higher up on the list was an imminent strike by the town's coppermen, in protest at wage cuts in response to the depressed copper trade. Employing around 4,000 people, the huge copper works at Swansea had existed for around a century, processing ore from Cornwall, Liverpool and Ireland, and trading as far afield as South America. While the wages the copper workers received were relatively high, the work was intense and exhausting, and wore out many men by early middle age. The strike of 1843 was the first for twenty-five years and involved the entire workforce across nine sites, who made their intentions known to their employers in an open letter signed 'One and all'. At a mass demonstration in Swansea, met and addressed by the local MP, one workman argued, with a touch of proto-marxist analysis:

> Masters pretended to feel for the poor while they stored themselves upon thousands, and the workmen who enabled them to procure those riches, and who were pining and working themselves to death with hard labour, could not earn sufficient to maintain themselves.[7]

Another workman declared: 'We would rather starve idle than starve while working hard, and that's an end of it.'[8]

While the magistrates and employers were contemplating their next move, the local Chartists added to their woes, plastering the town with notices announcing a meeting at Swansea Trade Hall to be addressed by a speaker from Glasgow. His lecture was entitled 'The People's Charter and No Surrender: Britain's wrongs, and the way to redress them'. This was one potential headache too many, and the Trade Hall's owners refused to sanction the meeting, forcing the Chartists to pull it.

MOCKERY AND MYSTERY

Across Carmarthenshire, the presence of the military was still proving no deterrent to Rebecca, and her existence was now also firmly established in Cardiganshire, the neighbouring county to the north. At Lampeter in early August, six gates were destroyed in one night by a crowd accompanied with music and banners. A few days earlier at Cardigan itself, a gate was taken down by a group of almost 200 people. In formerly sedate Aberystwyth, a spate of Rebecca letters to the local gentry, threatening their homes and property, prompted them to call in the Castlemartin yeomanry and a company of infantry. The troops had a fruitless few days' stay, which saw the poorer population of the hills flooding into town to gaze in curiosity at their brightly uniformed visitors and shout mockingly about their chances of 'Going to catch Becky!' More substantially, the town was suffering financially from a drop in tourism, as rumours of Rebeccaism encouraged the usual summer trade to find calmer watering-holes.

Elsewhere, during an attack at New Inn, shots were fired at a tollkeeper and his wife, and the latter was wounded. The tollkeeper was then accompanied by Rebeccaites to a nearby chapel, where they requisitioned a bottle of communion wine to treat his wife's wounds. Later in August the town of Llanon, although garrisoned by troops and police, was occupied by a crowd of hundreds. The Rebecca on this occasion came equipped with a horse-drawn carriage, which got stuck for several hours on a bridge over the river Morlais before the crowd moved on to attack the home of local rent and debt collector John Edwards. The carriage wasn't a one-off; while most Rebeccaites adopted the bonnets and shawls of working women, some appeared with coaches and servants, and accessorised with parasols and elaborate jewellery or hairpieces, as though making a point of mocking the luxurious dress of the gentry.

While events like the above could contain surreal or comic moments in between the violence and threats, other occasions seemed to have an almost supernatural quality. The destruction of gates miles apart on a single night led people to speculate that 'Rebecca may be in several places at one time', before rationalising that it was more likely 'that there are several Rebeccas'.[9] And the press described Rebeccaites as able 'to cast a spell or illusion over those who might naturally be expected to hear and witness them at their work of destruction'.[10] A writer to the *Welshman* even pastiched Shakespeare in a passage comparing Rebecca to Queen Mab, and her actions to the nightly pranks of the fairy realm.[11]

Witnesses to attacks were often drunkenly making their way home from a pub, or just awakened from sleep, and their confused state of mind only reinforced the indistinct impression of nightmare or hallucination. John Davies, a shoemaker, testified that he had spent the evening of 25 August at a pub on the Fishguard road where he saw – or thought he saw – a few men lurking outside in the shadows with 'sprays of trees about their hats'. On leaving for home, he came across another twenty or thirty ethereal figures, beckoning to him like sirens: 'One of them said, I must come to join Becca, or would I join Becca?'[12] Other witnesses reported seeing spectral figures dressed in white, faces mysteriously veiled, with 'feathers in their caps', 'branches of trees about their heads', their leader 'seeming to have a shawl on, and a low crowned hat'. Their uncertain appearance could resolve into terrible clarity when witnesses heard the words 'Here's Becca come', or simply 'Forward!'

In early August, Thomas Cooke was riding back to Middleton Hall around midnight, and guiding his horse down a narrow lane, when he had a similarly uncanny encounter with several dozen Rebeccaites who seemed to materialise before him:

> they were all dressed in white, had veils before their faces and long poles, or guns, in their hands; they stood as motionless as so many statues, not a word was spoken by either them or me; and I was suffered to pass through the crowd untouched. I had a desperate fight with my horse only which shied and would not face them, but I forced him through. Several of them were so near me, that I could have struck them with my stick, but I thought it more prudent to thrash my horse instead of them, and was glad to get off so cheaply.[13]

After Cooke's escape, the group was joined by dozens more and they moved on to attack the last tollgate left standing in the area, at Porthyrhyd. Cooke had ridden past this gate as he fled, and shouted a warning to the tollkeeper and his wife, who quickly made themselves scarce. They left the gate guarded by several police constables, who also bolted when the Rebeccaites appeared. This was an unusually destructive attack in which the crowd demolished not only the tollgate but also the tollkeeper's property, smashing furniture inside the tollhouse and destroying the wheels of a newly built cart, as well as committing several truckles of cheese to the flames. The tollkeeper's wife later recalled hearing one of the attackers saying 'the law is now nearly all in the hands of Rebecca and her daughters'.[14]

Cooke himself, having safely reached home, extinguished all the lights in the place and sat up on guard until dawn. Although Middleton Hall remained untroubled that night, a short while later another Rebecca letter was pushed under Cooke's door. As he reported to his mother:

> I received a notice to quit the country, commencing with 'Imp? what do you want here?' charging me with advising Mr Adams to keep up his rents, and ordering me to leave the country for that I should experience neither peace nor happiness in it again from this time forth etc ... I am wondering where all this is to end. Mr A threatens to become an absentee, which I am not surprised at for it is by no means pleasant not to be able to sleep in peace and safety. It is a new state of things to us.[15]

Perhaps taking his cue from his employer's faith in firearms, Cooke took to sleeping with no less than three loaded pistols next to his bed.

A GENERAL SENSATION

In the face of all this, the region's civic powers seemed as helpless as the military – but they didn't help themselves by continuing to prioritise the repression of disorder, rather than trying to understand and tackle what lay behind it. In late June, Pembrokeshire magistrates crowded into the Castle Inn in Haverfordwest to hear the reading of a letter from the Home Office on 'the present disturbed state of the county'. In his missive, Sir James Graham directed them to shore up Colonel Love's efforts by offering rewards for information on the movement.[16]

After agreeing to have further troops stationed at Narberth, the meeting, just about to break up, was shocked by the intervention of one magistrate, his name sadly not recorded, who said:

> Gentlemen, a number of remedies has been suggested, but I have not heard one observation made as to the real evil, which is the poverty and distress of the country, and which has arisen from high rents, increased and increasing tithes, exorbitant poor and highway rates, and extensive taxation; while the depression upon agricultural produce is such as to put it totally out of the power of any man to meet their demands.[17]

This humble enough call to look at the causes of unrest, rather than attacking its symptoms, 'caused a general sensation', but, like William Chambers's earlier advice to focus on the tollgate trusts, it was not taken up, and largely forgotten as the meeting's attendees dispersed in search of lunch.

Other directions to magistrates from those above them, like that of the Radnorshire MP John Walsh, made it clear that, in the absence of any intervention by the national government, the hands of local authorities were tied:

> The course pursued by the magistrates in another part of the county has been to support the law, and to protect the property of the Turnpike Trusts. The magistrates have nothing to do with the question of grievances, and alleged abuses under the existing law. Their duty is to maintain it, until it be altered by legal means.[18]

The lack of interest in any response, other than increasing the military and police presence in south Wales, meant that the authorities' efforts continued to meet a dead end. Magistrates regularly met to swear in more special constables, but of those summoned, few appeared in fear of reprisals. At Bethania chapel in Talog, the town crier read out a warning from 'Rebecca' not to be sworn in as a special. Meanwhile, few people could be induced to take on the job of tollkeeper either.

Rebecca's stated intention – to make the system of tolls itself untenable – seemed to be working. And to make matters worse, the movement's attention was now increasingly turning beyond the economic problems of tollgates and even workhouses to matters of wider social justice – including the operation of the New Poor Law itself.

12
LADIES OF LETTERS

A PREMIUM ON IMMODESTY

As the riot at Carmarthen workhouse had made clear, the changes that had taken place under the New Poor Law were the subject of open complaint in Rebecca's country about not only the harshness of the workhouse itself, but the reasons that people were sent there – particularly unmarried mothers and their children. The new bastardy clauses were strongly criticised, not only by the single mothers subject to their strictures, but by workers and farmers who now had to pay collectively to support women in workhouses rather than having them receive support from their children's fathers as previously. One farmer joked grimly to Thomas Campbell Foster that 'I pay more under the new law for the support of bastards than ever I did before'.[1]

Others pointed out in more earnest terms that, in these days before paternity testing, judgements about paternal responsibility now relied upon the authorities believing a woman's word against a man's – or upon the testimony of a third party. This was hardly ever the case, particularly if a woman was unwilling to offer up to a panel of local dignitaries the details of her sex life and the circumstances of her child's conception to prove the identity of the father. As another farmer explained:

> for though the parishes very well knew who the fathers of bastard children were, they could not prove it; and the result was, that the parish officers starved the mother and child. The bastardy law was against humanity. It required corroborative proof of a fact of which there could be no proof, if the mother were a modest woman. It was a premium on immodesty.[2]

145

But Rebeccaism was making it possible to assert the continuation of older traditions when it came to tollgates and the common use of land – so why shouldn't this be extended to correcting injustices under new laws in the private as well as the public sphere? As the movement took both a firmer and a wider grasp on life in the late summer of 1843, Rebeccaites took action to reassert the older Welsh custom which saw children born both in and out of wedlock as equally legitimate and worthy of support. To begin with, they tried to encourage or enforce a marriage between a pregnant woman and the child's father. If this was refused – or if the mother preferred to remain independent – 'Rebecca' visited the fathers in question and demanded either financial support or for them to take the child in.

Edward Crompton Lloyd Hall reported the local case of a servant girl who – like Frances Evans – had given birth in the local workhouse after being impregnated and then sacked by her employer. The father was woken at midnight by a knock at his door, and opened it to find Rebecca and around 200 daughters, who instructed him to take in and raise the child under her 'sharp eye'. David Morris, a blacksmith who was identified locally as having fathered the child of Jane Jones, received a similar visit:

> Last night about 12 o'clock, Rebecca elegantly attired in female clothes, and three of her companions ... awoke the smith, and jocosely asked him if he knew her. The smith replied 'no.' She turned herself round to enable him a fair view of her person, then put the cap on the gun she carried, and desired the girl to be called. Jane Jones came, and was told to lay her right hand on the lock of the gun, and make her oath most solemnly as to the father of her child. She did so ... and was then told to hold herself ready to accompany them on a future night for the purpose of conveying the child to its father. She wanted to excuse herself and said she could not walk so far; but they told her they would find a cart to convey her, that there were plenty of them in the village, and if any owner showed an unwillingness, they would make him

come and be the driver of his cart. The girl said she would go with pleasure. Rebecca then left and proceeded on the road towards Llandeilo, and fired two shots off. The smith was so frightened that he was unable to work today.[3]

These actions could extend to other unorthodox marital arrangements – and the idea of the sanctity of marriage, like the need for a child to be supported by two parents, could sometimes override the feelings of the individuals involved. In Cardiganshire, the Revd William Walters was forcibly reunited with his estranged wife by around fifty Rebeccaites, who, bringing her to his door at midnight, 'ordered him to love and cherish her' and further instructed Mrs Walters to 'stay with him and behave like a good and dutiful wife'.[4]

Rebeccaites also lent their support to Harriet Devonald, a young widow who was evicted from her home in Pembrokeshire by John Partridge, a coach-builder who had been conducting an on-off affair with her for over a year. Informed by a servant that 'Mrs Devonald intended attacking the house by bringing Rebecca'[5] to demand the return of her clothes and furniture, Partridge sent for two policemen and made an unsuccessful attempt to call in the military from Cardigan, before leaving his employee James Francis to guard the house.

This might have seemed like an overreaction to a spurned lover coming to pick up her stuff, but what was notable in James Francis' account of what happened next is how Harriet Devonald not only called upon Rebecca's aid, but seemed to take upon herself the commanding position usually reserved for men playing Rebecca's role. When she arrived at the head of a hundred-strong mob, an armed siege commenced in which Harriet and another woman, Mary Griffiths, took the leading part:

After ten o'clock an assembly came and knocked at the front door. I asked who was there, and was answered, Mrs. Devonald, and that she wanted her clothes. I said she could have them in the morning if she wanted them; she said she would have them then, and insisted on coming in; I told her if she came in, I must give her in charge of the police; she said she was determined to come in. She then went up to the front parlour window and I heard a pane of glass break, and a number of footsteps, then the mob came and broke the whole ... Told them that if they did not go we must fire on them; that I had the London police with me and that we were armed. Was very much afraid ... Mrs. Devonald and Mary Griffiths came into the room shortly after. Mrs. D. told me if Mr. Partridge had not gone home in time both he and his horse would have been shot dead. I retreated to the landing-place, and Mrs. D. followed the men out, and said, 'Do not fire again, for if you do, murder will be committed.' Mrs. D. took hold of a policeman and struggled with him but nothing particular happened.[6]

Harriet and Mary then offered the terrified Francis safe passage, ushering him through the crowd and out of the house, before they returned for Harriet's possessions. The redoubtable Mrs Devonald subsequently appeared in court with her face – like that of many 'Rebeccas' in action – covered by a veil. She was found not guilty of riot by the jury while John Partridge's ungentlemanly treatment of her was criticised.

YOUR BELOVED FRIEND, REBECKA

The rise and spread of Rebeccaism saw not only men acting on behalf of women against the New Poor Law's injustices, but an increasing number of women acting on their own behalf under the auspices of Rebecca. Martha John, another single mother, also had the option of calling on Rebecca for help. She did so through writing a letter to the child's father, Evan Protheroe, a Narberth farmer whose service she had left while pregnant. After he had faced down a previous attempt by Martha before the local magistrates to get him to support the child, Protheroe received a threatening letter from 'Rebecca', stating that 'unless he would contribute towards the maintenance of the child of Martha John, that she, "Becca", with "Nelly" her eldest daughter, would visit him, and set on fire himself and all his possessions; that he should be like Martha John, without bread and cheese'.[7]

Many more 'Rebecca letters' like this were sent in the summer of 1843. They were not the usual kind of letter, neatly handwritten, sharply folded or tightly scrolled up and sealed with wax and signet-ring, that were sent by mail-coach to London, distributed by rural and town letter-carriers, or conveyed between the houses of the gentry by errand-boys or servants. Rebecca's letters sometimes arrived by post, but more often they were delivered in the dead of night, pinned to a house door or slipped underneath it by unseen hands.

The letters were signed under a number of inventive pseudonyms, identifying the writer either as Rebecca herself or as a daughter or sister, members of her ever-growing 'family'. Some writers picked other feminine handles, as did some of Rebecca's followers during attacks; a popular choice was 'Charlotte' – incidentally the name of Lady Guest, wife of the prominent Dowlais ironmaster John Guest. Others took the names 'Nelly', 'Eliza', 'Lydia' and 'Rachel', sometimes signing on behalf of their 'respected mother'.

Rebecca letters were scrawled on scraps of rough paper, the spelling often phonetic or, when complex words, just guesswork, by those more used to speaking their minds than writing them down – or by those trying to imitate the kind of official language they had previously heard used to them by employers, landlords, magistrates or their agents. They could echo the style of formal public addresses – beginning with 'Take notice, Sir' – or polite social intercourse – 'I take my pleasure to write you these few lines' – but they could then descend into the characteristic Rebeccaite blend of Biblical cadence, black humour and bloodcurdling threats:

> Sir – for as much as I have heard your career in this neighbourhood, I therefore take my pleasure to write you

these few lines hoping that it will have some effect on you; as you are an agent under Mr Yelverton, you thought you were a most in parish, but I mean to reduce you little. Hearing that the poor and hungry are turn away like dogs, without having nothing; and therefore you are a hard gentleman to be amongst us Welshmen, for we usually gave to the poor … In a word that you are to quit the neighbourhood within four days after this note at your own peril … I do not care to call three hundred of my children at the same time to level the place in less than an hours time, either by powder, or digging, or shotting, or putting the place to fire …

Youngest Rebecca

In correspondent with the old one.[8]

Take notice Sir, in consequence that you quite an high farmer, retaining three farms in your hands. You have heard the law, Sir, towards such a persons. I may quash a person that disobeys the laws of Rebecca, because she want very much to Reform things that are out of the way. You are to fall into the laws of Rebecca immediately, within four days after this note, at your peril of losing your goods.

Rebecca is here learning you.[9]

I hear that you will not leave my children alone. Rebecca is very particular about her children. Rebecca does not like to see them abused or injured. You have many years abusing them, and I will pay you a visit with some of them on Saturday night, and fire some of the corn and hay that you have taken fraudulently out of the country … I, Rebecca, am determined to put a stop to your proceedings … So now take warning, that I may not come to bring you to rights.

REBECCA.[10]

There had always been letters like this, written by the desperate or resentful with no other recourse under existing law than pouring out vitriol and threats against those who had wronged them. Under Rebeccaism, however, these missives increased and were now written specifically to associate the writer with Rebecca and with the urgency, confidence and collective strength that her name now carried. While previously such victims of injustice had had little or no hope of redress, now they had at least the promise of it. Their letters' often ironic imitation of legal notices combined with this impetus to show that the writers meant to demonstrate that there were now 'laws of Rebecca' – a new power and authority – under which ordinary people could act and expect to be heard and obeyed.

The elderly Bridget Williams of Cenarth in Carmarthenshire wrote a note to Benjamin Evans after her poor relief had been stopped, in which 'Rebecca' threatened to pull down his house. At her trial she was given three months' imprisonment, despite the jury's recommendation of mercy on account of her advanced age and poverty. The judge at her trial observed: 'It was a shocking state of things when a poor woman like this could put a man in bodily fear through the instrumentality of a gang of persons calling themselves Rebecca's children.'[11]

This was, of course, precisely the point. Under this 'shocking state of things', anyone could now step into the role of 'Rebecca', and even the most abject and marginalised felt that they could call on the figure of Rebecca for help or protection. Edward Crompton Lloyd Hall, again seeking the attention of the Home Office, told them that 'a poor idiotic girl' had come to his door at Emlyn Cottage to beg for support. When he told her to go instead to the local Poor Law guardians, he wrote, 'Her only reply was murmured out (in Welsh) "I'll tell 'Becca".'[12]

In both word and deed, the power and influence of Rebecca now seemed unstoppable. She was taking on the nature of other celebrated folk outlaws like Robin Hood, and she was thought of as having supernatural or superheroic qualities, ready to use her powers on behalf of the oppressed who had only to use her name to invoke these abilities themselves. Alcwyn C. Evans recorded a long poem on Rebecca's mysterious nature, which compared her – with the poet's tongue mostly in his (or her) cheek – to both mythological and more solidly historic figures, as well as reflecting on her liminal gender identity:

> Where is Rebecca? – that daughter of mystery?
> Where is her dwelling? Oh, where is her haunt?
> Her name and exploits will be coupled in History
> With famed Amazonians, and great John of Gaunt ...
> Who is Rebecca? – She seems Hydra-headed
> Or Argus-like, more than two eyes at command
> The mother of hundreds – the Great Unknown – dreaded
> By peaceloving subjects in Cambria's land
> Unknown her sex too – she may be discovered
> To all our bewildered astonishments soon,
> to be Mother Hubbard, who lived in a cup-board
> Great Joan of Arc's ghost or the Man in the Moon.
> 'twould puzzle the brains of a Newton or Secker
> To trace out thy epicene nature, Rebecca![13]

The same poem referred to how difficult it was to nail down Rebecca and her movement's political beliefs or ideas, beyond their disruptive and threatening nature:

> What are your politics? Some people say for you –
> The Levelling System you always will aid;
> And 'twould appear the far happiest day for you
> Throwing wide open the road to Free Trade ...
> The state is in danger, and nothing can check her
> From ruin, with politics like yours, Rebecca![14]

More strategically minded voices would endlessly debate whether 'Rebecca' was of any particular political persuasion, and whether this was – or should be – the paternalist conservatism of the Tories, the new free trade arguments of the Whigs, or the tradition of radical democracy that stretched from the Levellers to the Chartists. Meanwhile, many of Rebecca's individual followers and adherents simply embarked on autonomous action, with a spirit of unbridled anarchy whose only politics was a sense of popular justice.

The tollgates had been the first domino to fall. After spending so long in a sense of unrelenting crisis and stasis in which having to know one's place was paramount, the lifting of these social controls, and the demonstration of an ability – real or imagined – to at least challenge, if not change your circumstances, was a heady feeling for many. Letters written in Rebecca's name began to display a dizzying sense of sudden empowerment, and an ambition that was impatient to combat not simply local but universal wrongs:

> Sir, I am known by the name of Rebecka. I have purpose to visit many places and persons, wherever or with whoever there is injustice, until we shall have all the world plain ... You do not consider that the times has been so bad and low prises for everything that the poor people could not make up the money which they promise ... I shall in a few nights come to Visit you and you may depend that the best way for you to take notice of this,
> Because it is not words only but the standing truth,
> Because I have got the world in my Hand to do Justice Justice Justice
> Your beloved friend
> Rebecka[15]

13
OUT OF THE SHADOWS

REBECCA'S CONVENTIONS

By the middle of August 1843, there were so many dragoons stationed in Carmarthenshire that every bed in every pub and guesthouse was full, as were those in Carmarthen workhouse. Newly arrived troops had to be awkwardly lodged in town halls, jails and vicarages. The debates over establishing a rural police force had resolved themselves in favour of the enterprise, although with no less grumbling about the cost, and a police chief, Captain Richard Andrew Scott, had been appointed with the sanction of the Home Office. Most significantly, the government, acting on the advice of George Rice Trevor that public attention to the operations of the turnpike trusts might cool things down, had dispatched a Bow Street magistrate to the area to make preliminary investigations into how the trusts were run. This combination of concession and repression would see order restored – or this, at least, was the plan.

Sir John Walsh, MP and Lord-Lieutenant for Radnorshire where he owned over 12,000 acres of land, had been so relaxed about Rebeccaism that he remained out of the country for much of 1843. In his previous dealings with farmers and shopkeepers in his constituency, he had noted in his personal journal that 'Money Money Money is never out of the minds of these people ... the farmers are all ruined, totally apathetic and reckless'[1] – and despite being a landowner, landlord and parliamentary representative, Walsh didn't feel he could do much to intervene in their misfortune. On 18 August, Walsh was unwinding onboard a steam-packet ferrying him from a trip to Ostend back to Ramsgate on the Kent coast. The ship's captain came to offer some news he thought might interest him – apparently, he reported, 'the Rebeccaites had broken out' in Radnorshire's neighbouring county of Shropshire. Once on shore, Walsh picked up the day's newspapers with some haste, but could find nothing to alarm him. On the contrary, as he wrote in that day's journal, the Rebeccaites 'seemed to be taking to meetings and complaints, instead of outrages'.[2]

Walsh's impression was broadly correct. In the summer and autumn of 1843, almost a hundred public meetings were held in Rebecca's country, attended by men and women in their thousands. They marked a change from previous secretive gatherings: they took place on the hillside in daylight and were planned and advertised weeks in advance, with official speakers invited along with the press. For some in the audience, it was the first political meeting they had ever attended, while others had been present at too many to count. Unlike meetings restricted to pub back-rooms or town halls, they could not be 'packed' by supporters of a particular faction; they were open discussions, not political rallies. Everyone who turned up was able to speak – including Tory and anti-Reform voices – even if this meant some debates lasted for up to four hours. They usually ended with the setting down of written resolutions – including demands for lower tolls and rents, an end to the New Poor Law, and representation in Parliament for ordinary people. Those who took part weren't just complaining about the state of things, but offering their own solutions.

The first 'Rebecca meeting' of this kind was held in late July at the Carmarthenshire village of Cwmifor. The crowd was small enough to fit inside a schoolhouse, but attendance would soon grow. Other meetings sprang up in barns, fields and chapels, where audiences that brought together farmers, labourers, craftsmen, industrial workers and servants openly discussed their grievances, drew up petitions to Parliament and the Queen, and chose individuals as delegates to convey their opinions to larger meetings. These gatherings showed, if further evidence were needed, that the Welsh 'peasantry' were not apathetic, ignorant or inarticulate about politics. They did not need to be manipulated by outsiders to recognise unfairness in their daily lives and to ask each other what could be done about it.

Even some of the local gentry, from the arriviste William Chambers Junior to the dynastic George Rice Trevor, attended and spoke at these meetings. Other landowners begged the authorities to ban them, or cautiously went along to attend before making a swift exit at the nature of some of the speeches they heard. Edward Crompton Lloyd Hall was typically twitchy about the situation, noting that 'one injudicious remark may act like the spark to a barrel of gunpowder and then there will be no answering for the consequences'.[3] In fact, the meetings were free of any violence beyond the occasional bit of fiery rhetoric – even though, when Edward Adams of Middleton Hall went along to a meeting at Porthyrhyd, he dragged along both Thomas Cooke and his butler for protection and ensured, as Cooke later told his mother, that all three of them were 'armed to the teeth ... our pockets literally crammed with hostile weapons'.[4]

THE FARMERS' UNION

Around 300 people attended the first of 'Rebecca's Conventions', and among them was Thomas Campbell Foster, although as an outsider, he had to bargain for admission by promising that he would give a fair account of the proceedings in any report he made. A few days later, acting on a tip-off about a similar meeting taking place at Penlan, he turned up on a gloomy and rainswept night at an isolated farmstead, accompanied by a local man as a guide. When neither his face nor his name were recognised at the gate to the farmyard, Foster reached into his pocket and offered a rain-sodden circular from *The Times* to prove who he was. His guide, hustled to one side of the yard and questioned, also vouched for him, but even this did not completely allay suspicion.

As they were reluctantly ushered out of the rain into a dimly lit barn, Foster made out around seventy farmers arrayed on stools or benches or on bundles of straw in the shadowy reaches of the barn, all of them regarding him with 'caution and distrust'. After sitting in strained silence for several minutes, it occurred to Foster to introduce himself and assure his audience that any report he might make of the meeting would not identify anyone there. This also had no effect, until his guide repeated it in Welsh, after which his presence was grudgingly accepted. With the guide translating for Foster, the meeting began. It soon became clear why secrecy was paramount: the farmers had decided to form a union.

Trade unionism in the 1840s, technically legalised after its banning by the 1799 'Combination Acts', was mainly associated with Britain's growing class of industrial workers. But a decade before Rebecca, a group of agricultural workers in Tolpuddle, Dorset, had notoriously been harshly punished with penal transportation for their attempt to organise a union in protest at low wages. Known as the Tolpuddle Martyrs, their plight became a *cause célèbre* for the movement for workers' rights and 800,000 people signed petitions for their pardon and release. Even after this had been achieved in 1836, trade unions still had a precarious and restricted status in Britain. So the farmers at Penlan could be forgiven for wanting to proceed carefully, particularly with a reporter in the room.

After declaring that the union was 'for the purpose of taking into consideration all grievances that shall affect the agriculturalists and the country in general',[5] the meeting's chair produced a constitution, complete with clauses on the re-election of officers every six months and penalties for drunkenness or swearing at meetings. With the bureaucracy out of the way, a heartfelt discussion began among the farmers on the need for the union:

'This union among us is a very excellent thing if all join. When they elect members of Parliament they do just as they please, and we have no voice, but here we have. There is no way of putting things to rights till we get this union, and then we can do as we please and think best.'

'Our grievances are too numerous to mention, but here we can talk to each other, and make known to each other things as they really stand.'[6]

It further emerged that more unions of the same kind were being formed in neighbouring parishes that same night, and that they intended to collectively take up their grievances with landlords and magistrates. A while later at the close of the meeting, still rather disturbed by his difficult reception, Foster made his escape in search of a drink to settle his nerves:

> I then scrambled my way back across the miry fields in the dark till I reached the lane. All was darkness and silence. I reached the roadside inn in about 10 minutes, and found it to be past 11 o'clock. The landlady said, the Dragoons from Llandilo were expected every minute to patrol past. I ask, of what use in such a country, and with a people like this, are Dragoons?[7]

After this less than auspicious start, Foster persevered, reporting frankly for *The Times* on the meetings he attended, while preserving the anonymity of attendees and gradually gaining their trust. He was present at over fifty meetings in August and September, and he also made himself useful to several groups of farmers who were unimpressed with their ability to put their grievances before the government commission which had recently been sent to the area.

The earliest commission on the operations of the tollgate trusts had travelled through south Wales in a hurried and secretive manner, meeting in private and taking cursory statements only from those who had enough notice, time, status and self-confidence to appear before them. The *Welshman* newspaper was particularly contemptuous of the government's attempted use of a commissioner 'to pacify a people whose grievances he did not enquire into, with whose habits he was not familiar, whose language he did not understand, to whom he presented himself in the mere aspect of an upper constable police magistrate'.[8] The local farmers, like many after them who felt they were unable to get a fair hearing from official channels, decided instead to go to the press.

In mid-August, a deputation of around a hundred farmers packed into the top floor of the Blue Bell Inn at Llanidloes to meet with Foster. They had brought along their own legal adviser, an attorney from Carmarthen. The pub landlord, who was also a farmer himself, acted as Foster's interpreter as they outlined their grievances. These went deeper than superficial references to the general unfairness of tollgates: the farmers specified having been told that the tolls taken locally were intended to pay for the building of a new road – but this promise had been made thirty-five years ago with nothing yet to show for it. They identified actions by tollkeepers and magistrates that contravened both the letter and spirit of the Turnpike Act – charging farmers for cartloads of lime for personal use, charging twice for a return journey at the same tollgate, charging for horses carrying no greater load than a sack of potatoes.

Another group of farmers at Newcastle Emlyn then got in touch with Foster, asking him to accompany them to a meeting of local magistrates and landowners at the Salutation Inn, where they put forward four hours' worth of complaints on the tollgates, the workhouse system and the New Poor Law. Perhaps mindful of the press presence, the authorities took a conciliatory tone, and suggested that they would agree to not put up any new toll-bars. The *Swansea Journal*, reporting on what it called a 'Curious Welsh Tribunal', emphasised the novelty of ordinary people making use of their access to the national press in this way: 'This is the first time that a newspaper has thus formally been acknowledged as a tribunal for investigation, and its reporter something like a public Commissioner of Inquiry.'[9]

HAND IN HAND?

At a Rebeccaite meeting in August, Thomas Campbell Foster spotted another reporter – not from the London press, but from the Chartist newspaper the *Northern Star*. To see them reporting directly on Rebeccaism might have come as a surprise, given that a few weeks earlier in the same paper, the Chartist leader Feargus O'Connor had come out strongly against the movement on the basis of its class composition. He had warned his readers that the farmers' struggle seemed to have a similar dynamic to the earlier

Reform campaign, with middle-class campaigners using the threat of working-class unrest to achieve their demands, then leaving them to take the blame and punishment from the state when they tried to take things further in their own interests. He urged his readers not to make the same mistake this time around:

> To the working people we have one word to say in reference to these Rebecca riots. Let them alone. Have nothing to do with them. Let the middle class men fight their own battles and take their own risk. Those farmers who now feel 'the pressure of the times' are the very fellows who would have ridden down, trodden down, and sabred down, you all at any moment, in any effort for your own rights. They now seek to involve you in the meshes of this lawless struggle merely to make 'cat's paws' of you. They will use you to work their mischievous purposes; and then, whether their project hit or miss, they will lend themselves to Government for your destruction.[10]

At a Chartist meeting in Newcastle, Samuel Kydd, devoting an entire lecture to Rebeccaism, had taken a similar tone towards the movement's concentration on 'sectional grievances'. Examining clause by clause the resolutions passed at a Rebeccaite meeting, he concluded that 'no benefit would accrue to the labouring classes, if Lady Rebecca was to get all she wanted in her Charter ... It was true [that] Mrs Rebecca wanted a change in the Poor Law Amendment Act; but that change was expressed with great ambiguity.'[11]

Even without the leadership's concerns about political strategy, some ordinary Chartists treated Rebeccaism with suspicion or contempt because the movement seemed old-hat, and even reactionary to them. Its costumes and symbols came from an older culture which had grown out of rural festivals and carnival, and which had little relevance to modern working life in factories and mines. And its localised way of taking action could seem sluggish and short-sighted when compared with the Chartists' demands to solve a wide range of problems all at once by getting the People's Charter adopted and giving the vote to all working men (and even, as some fringe elements continued to advocate, to working women).

This wariness went both ways. Many Rebeccaite farmers regarded Chartists as dangerous radicals and outsiders, who should stay out of their business and not bring grand ideas about national democracy into what was a limited dispute about living costs. Wages, rents, tithes and tolls might have been common concerns across the country, but to many Rebeccaites they were local problems to be solved locally – and, ideally, solved by a return to the kind of benevolent paternalism they had previously been comfortable with, before the changes of industrialisation and the New Poor Law. Despite their issues with the current system, they worried that Chartists wanted to overthrow it for something wholly new and untested – or, worse, for what already had been tried in France and ended in bloodshed and war. The Rebeccaites tolerated the *Northern Star* reporter's presence at their August meeting, but Foster noted, with a touch of professional rivalry, that the man looked 'sadly frightened, for the farmers would have nothing to do with him'.[12]

But even if the national Chartist leadership and the more respectable Rebeccaites weren't keen on alliances, there were individuals and groups on both sides who recognised their common interests and were willing to make personal links and draw political connections between their problems. Indeed, after Hugh Williams had founded the first Welsh branch of the Chartist Working Men's Association in Carmarthen in 1836, hundreds of Welsh men and women had enrolled as Chartists in towns and villages across the country, including in rural areas, and although their numbers and energy had begun to fade after the Newport Rising, their spirit and the desire for political change remained. Many Welsh villages still had their 'Old Chartist' who could be relied upon to tell stories over a pint of past glorious struggle. After 1842 when the Chartists' second petition, bearing over three million signatures from across the country, was presented to Parliament and rejected, interest in the movement's ideas – both moral and physical force – had, once again, gained ground. On the other side, at a meeting of Chartists in Bolton in August 1843 Robert Peddie, a popular speaker from Edinburgh, gave a two-hour address which included a cautious shout-out to the actions of 'Mrs Rebecca'. She was, he said, 'a curious lady', and he wished 'her heart were in the right place'. Nonetheless, he praised the unity of the movement and its good showing against the inept forces of the state.[13]

As the summer of discontent rolled on, different theories and arguments around the same central dissatisfaction with the status quo infiltrated each other – and this was what increasingly worried the authorities. In early August, a Carmarthenshire magistrate intercepted a communication from the mining districts around Merthyr, where many migrant workers had ties to or roots in south-west Wales. It offered a pledge of mutual support: 'that if the Rebeccaites will join the Chartists of Merthyr and advocate the five points of the Charter, the Chartists will aid and go hand in hand with the Rebeccaites.'[14]

CHAMBERS GOES ROGUE

At Llannon, one of Rebecca's Conventions was so well attended that the crowd spilled out of the schoolroom where it was being held into the open air. At the meeting's close, the farmers there handed the local landowner and magistrate Rees Goring Thomas an open letter to him and his fellow authority figures, imploring them to remove the tollgates, lower rents and tithes, oppose the establishment of a rural police force and simplify the Poor Law. Also present in the audience was William Chambers, who responded immediately that he was personally willing to lower his rents by 15 per cent. By contrast, Goring Thomas havered, claiming that he needed more information before he could make any decision.

While ordinary people were putting forward offers for solutions, this bickering and intransigence among magistrates got in the way of any attempt at peacefully resolving things, and Chambers tried to make this impasse clear to his colleagues. After attending another meeting of his parishioners at Llanelli, which had resolved that they were paying tithes at an unaffordably high rate, he sent a copy of the resolution to Goring Thomas, adding a note of apology for having attended such a meeting of agitators but emphasising that he endorsed their demand. The note was dismissed, which was particularly frustrating when Chambers had made a point of being more open than many magistrates to the problems of his local community, and was making efforts to see things from their point of view. He was also putting his money where his mouth was by offering concessions over the level of his own rents – but this could only be a limited solution unless other landowners did the same. In his precarious position between the people and the more established gentry, Chambers was finding his sympathies increasingly swayed to the side of the former.

Towards the end of August, with these issues still unresolved, plans were being made for a huge public meeting on the mountainside at Llanelli. George Rice Trevor, in recognition that this was Chambers's turf, wrote a high-handed note to him with some anxiety about what might happen there:

> Pray let me know what is this meeting I hear about as likely to take place at or near Mynydd Sylen on Friday. I am told notices have been put on to the Chapel doors to the people to attend at 10 or 11 that morning. I wish to have also, if you please, some idea of what is felt by the magistrates as to allowing the meeting to take place or not. I think if it is to petition, that they must, and it is attended by the Farmers and there are no arms, I would allow it, but I would also have persons there to find out the feelings shewn, and to report their observations for our future guidance.[15]

Trevor's apprehension would have only grown when he discovered that not only was Chambers going to allow the meeting to go ahead – he was also going to chair it.

14

'MORE THAN ONE HUNDRED THOUSAND STRONG'

THE REBECCA GOVERNMENT

The 'Great Meeting' on the slopes of Mynydd Sylen on Friday 25 August brought together several thousand farmers, labourers, industrial workers and servants, some of whom had given up their day's wages to attend. At mid-morning, shops and market stalls in Carmarthen and Llanelli stood empty, and, in the hills around the towns, ploughs, anvils and looms stood abandoned as farmhands, craftsmen and labourers trooped up the country lanes and hillside paths behind a cavalcade of farmers. With them came middle-class teachers, clergy, shopkeepers and even a handful of the local gentry. Carts were driven into the mud to serve as platforms for speakers so that they could be heard and seen above the heads of the crowd. Thomas Campbell Foster was there, busily scribbling shorthand notes for *The Times* and giving a cordial nod to other men of the press, who had travelled in from London and further afield in recognition of Rebecca's growing fame. These included William James Linton of the *Illustrated London News* who, having been visiting his friend and fellow radical Hugh Williams, had been invited along and was now at work on a lithograph of the event. In the meeting's chair, placed unsteadily on top of another cart, William Chambers Junior dutifully recorded the meeting's resolutions, which included demands for toll, rent and tithe reductions and a full publication of the accounts of the tollgate trusts.

Although on one level a collective show of strength, the meeting reflected unresolved divisions within the movement. In exchange for getting their demands met, the offer made by many who attended was to cease the more subversive meetings by night at which direct action was planned. Taking his place with dozens of other speakers, Hugh Williams called for universal suffrage, read out a petition of grievances and called for the government to be removed if they failed to address them. But in a direct reference to the debates within Chartism, another speaker, Revd Rees, said he 'wanted to see men in Parliament who would take into consideration the interests of all classes' but then warned that the meeting's grievances 'could not be removed by "physical force", but by moral force, by peaceable agitation, and above all, by discontinuing their nightly meetings'.[1]

A few days after the Great Meeting the *Northern Star*'s correspondent, having improved his relations with the farmers, was able to attend a night meeting at another dimly lit barn in the hills. The speakers he heard there discoursed on rapacious landlords, church tithes and the Poor Law, and directly challenged the discouragement of night meetings in uncompromising terms that made clear the movement's continued sense of strength and solidarity:

> 'The great men are wanting us to hold no more midnight meetings, but to meet openly in the eye of day. We will meet by day, and by night also! They are fearing for their rents, when they want us to give up our meetings at night. They feel our force, and they fear us; but they shall fear us yet more before our bond is dissolved. What are we striving for? We wish only to live. We cannot live as things are at present.'

> 'Let our children be educated, and our poor be fed; let the tenth of our produce no longer be given to a lazy and indolent priest or prelate; let us ourselves choose our referees and magistrates, and Wales will again become what she once was, the quietest portion of the dominions of our queen. But if these our just demands are refused, she shall never know peace or quietness again.'[2]

A later meeting at Llandeilo resolved not just to demand reduced tithes, but to refuse to pay them at all. Thomas Cooke wrote:

> At the moment I am writing the curved horns are sounding in every direction, announcing a meeting somewhere for the committal of some outrage or other. They are not satisfied now with tollgates, but they hold large meetings frequently in the daytime, and demand that rents shall be lowered at least a third – the tithes they say shall be lowered 50 per cent ... the payment of tithes is to be resisted, it seems, by the Rebecca government, and they also say there shall be no English stewards and no distraints ... 'or else' these two last words close all their threats, leaving the poor wight to guess the rest.[3]

Hugh Williams, taking a stroll with William James Linton on the day after the Mynydd Sylen meeting, confessed his worry that the increasing police presence in the three counties meant that 'the Rebecca movement, so far unobstructed, was at an end'.[4] But the regular public meetings illustrated that although the more respectable element now felt both cautious enough about the police and confident enough in the movement's strength to put forward an effective bargain with the authorities over attacks on tollgates, others wanted wider demands to be met or favoured more direct action, and felt strong enough to argue for it. Williams himself told Linton that the tollgate campaign had always been, for him, 'a preparation for farther political action'.[5]

'PREPARE THEE A PLACE FOR THY SOUL'

William Chambers Junior had returned from taking the chair at Mynydd Sylen to the relative sanctuary of Llanelly House, brushing the mud of the hillside off his boots with some nervousness about what the response of his fellow gentry would be. A letter from George Rice Trevor was mildly reassuring; after the opening reprimand that by attending such a meeting Chambers might have found himself 'seriously compromised', Trevor added that he thought his motives were good, and so acquitted him of any blame.[6] Chambers, still intent on getting his fellow magistrates to see sense, sent another note to Rees Goring Thomas, laying out the resolutions made at Mynydd Sylen. This time Chambers did not mince his words, writing that Goring Thomas 'must see as a matter of common justice ... how much the people had been imposed upon by his agents'.[7] Perhaps inspired by Chambers's example, Edward Adams of Middleton Hall, who was a **trustee** of the Kidwelly and Three Commotts Trust, convinced them to lower their tolls and to reduce the number of side-bars.

While conciliatory actions like this were often noted with thanks at public meetings, it wasn't enough to diminish the general hostility towards the gentry that Rebeccaism had now transformed from passive attitude into action. The day after the Mynydd Sylen meeting, Chambers himself received another letter, signed with the pseudonym 'the night worker' and instructing him to pay fortnightly rather than monthly wages to his staff and the workers at his potteries. Although a relatively mild demand by Rebecca's current standards, it reminded Chambers that for all his concessions to the people, he remained a landowner and an employer, subject to the same dislike and objections as the rest of his class:

> Sir, Owing to a General Complaint having been made by your worker slaves against your monthly payments this is to give you three dais notis only, that you are to aquint them that you will pay them every fortnight from hence forthe and acording to your own promise made to them on the first of January last not taking it unto Cosnaidiartion to keep a penny from each man or other waise to suffer a visit from us on the night of the 30th instant with out any further notice.[8]

From Newcastle Emlyn, Edward Crompton Lloyd Hall wrote, yet again, to the Home Office to report that a stone had been thrown at Captain Lloyd of Dolhaidd estate, in broad daylight and, what was more, outside a church. Walter Jones of Lancych estate, who had publicly urged that tolls continue to be paid, and also voiced his opinion that many of the people he saw in his capacity as a Poor Law Guardian would not need to ask for help if they spent less of their wages on drink, was awakened one night at midnight by the crash of his downstairs windows being broken in. Shots were then fired from outside at the upstairs window, one bullet narrowly missing Jones as he grabbed his own pistol and leaned out of the window to fire back at the scattering crowd below.

Threats of further attacks were made to the Vaughan family's estate at Golden Grove, and to Rees Goring Thomas, who at the end of August begged William Chambers to dispatch some of the local military from Llanelli to defend his property. Despite his differences with Goring Thomas, Chambers dutifully journeyed there himself along with some soldiers, although no attack took place. A few nights later at around 1 o'clock in the morning, however, the mansion of John Williams at Bettws was surrounded by Rebeccaites blowing horns and firing guns. They left a letter by the drawing-room window that read: 'Prepare thee a place for thy soul. We will find a place for thy body, even if it was as big as a great mountain.'[9]

As the movement grew large and confident enough to shift its attention from physical symbols of injustice to the system's personal representatives, even the ancient Dynevor dynasty found itself threatened by Rebecca's uprising. Fields of wheat on the family's estate were set on fire on two occasions and George Rice Trevor discovered, in the grounds within sight of his windows, a hole dug to the approximate dimensions of a grave. A letter received shortly afterwards predicted that his own body would fill it before October.

QUESTIONS AND ANSWERS

As September began, magistrates continued to attend public meetings and discuss the shortcomings of the tollgate system, motivated by a combination of increased threats from Rebecca and, for some, belated recognition of their civic duty. At a meeting at Aberystwyth, the 'toll-farmer' Thomas Bullin was finally called to account as farmers charged him with illegally taking tolls for cartloads of lime. While the magistrates agreed that the tolls should be reduced, Bullin, with his usual audacity, requested compensation from them for his loss of income.

As for the operation of the New Poor Law, a meeting at Kidwelly was addressed by a former Poor Law Guardian, who harshly criticised its workings and blasted his former colleagues for the lack of attention and care he had seen them display towards the cases brought before them:

> The desire of the guardians was to get over the business as quickly as possible. They might have read a line in the poems of Pope:
> > 'And wretches hang that jurymen may dine.'
> This was very applicable to the guardians of the poor. The poor might starve if only the guardians could get to dinner. The meeting could not conceive how the rapidity with which they got through business increased as they became hungry.[10]

He was far from the only insider inspired to become a whistleblower. Matters were now being made unavoidably public about the flawed operations of the tollgate trusts and the workhouses, the inadequacies and incompetencies of those who ran them, and the part they had played in worsening a general social and economic crisis for the area, which partly and sometimes wholly justified the popular complaints about them. It was becoming impossible to deny that destroying tollgates and attacking workhouses were not the actions of an irrational mob, but a reasonable attempt to call attention to an intolerable financial burden and social injustice.

But the authorities still seemed at a loss as to what to do about these revelations. At Rebeccaite meetings, by contrast, political and economic alternatives were being proposed – some of them wide-ranging, ambitious and often uncomfortably democratic in the eyes of some in the movement. At a meeting in Newcastle Emlyn, a Mr Smith attributed the New Poor Law to 'improper' representation in parliament, and urged the meeting to advocate for vote by secret ballot and for 'every landlord to give his tenants liberty to vote as they thought right'. A carpenter speaking at a Lampeter meeting went further: 'The working classes gathered the wealth of the nation, and it was but fair play that the working classes wanted. All those who had to obey the laws should have a voice in making them.'[11]

At another meeting, a shoemaker from Carmarthen advocated uniting class interests:

> One thing he considered very essential for the improvement of the country – that the middle and the lower classes should unite together. The separation of these two classes had been the cause of much grief and vexation, and almost the total destruction of the land they lived in ... He wanted every working man to be defended, and the farmer made secure – one link should be joined in the other.[12]

Another speaker, the radical David Gravelle of Cwmfelin, offered support for Irish independence: 'This country and the sister island were at present in a deplorable state, but that Ireland was in a worse condition than Wales. Was it, therefore, surprising they should exert themselves for the repeal of the Union?'[13]

In the parish of Penboyr, a notice was stuck up in which 'Rebecca' urged farmers to collectively petition their landlords for rent reductions, pointing out that if farmers' rents were lowered, farmers would be able to use the money saved to employ more labourers and offer higher wages. Again, this proposal argued for the common benefit of both 'respectable' middle-class farmers and poorer labourers and farm servants:

> in case the prices of your land were lowered, you would have twice as much spirit to work and to give work to the poor labourer, instead of being low-spirited and broken-hearted as of late, not knowing what to do, whether carry lime or not, sow seed or not, raise hedges, etc, or not, so that the poor labourer who wished to get work could not have a day's work, at the price of his own meat, without talking of his family. But were the rents lowered, there is plenty of work about your farms (they have been so long neglected and left untidy) for the poor labourer, and you would have sufficient spirit to call him to work, and once the poor man gets work there will be an end of the workhouse.[14]

After these reasonable arguments, however, 'Rebecca' backed them up by reverting to threatening rhetoric:

> ...in desiring your landlord to lower in your rents therefore I will take your part, were we forced to burn the bodies of those that dare try to take your land ... As notice, if you will not endeavour to retake your farms, as the Lord God knoweth, you shall see more fire than you have ever seen in your lives.[15]

The movement was finely balanced between the acceptance of a limited victory on the issue of tollgates, and the urge to go on pushing for a wider economic and political reshaping. It was understandable that the better-off farmers, whose financial situation would be improved merely by lowering tolls and tithes, stood to gain less from more radical demands than did their labourers and servants and the poorer farmers of the area. Meanwhile the colliers and other industrial workers who made up an increasingly significant part of the movement, many of them influenced by Chartism, were also growing more militant.

From the perspective of the authorities, these internal differences were less significant than the wholesale threat posed by Rebeccaism to their own status and the social order they were trying – and largely failing – to uphold. Was 'Rebecca' really capable of overthrowing the current system and imposing her own?

Some of her followers certainly thought so. In a letter printed in both the *Welshman* and *The Times* at the start of September, 'Rebecca' looked forward to certain victory with a force that encompassed as many as possible:

> [W]e don't care a straw for all the soldiers, rural police and special constables, for Rebecca can bring into the field a better force and a much more numerous one. Rebecca is more than ONE HUNDRED THOUSAND strong. The people, the masses to a man throughout the three counties of Carmarthen, Cardigan and Pembroke, are with me. Oh yes – they are all my children – when I meet the lime-men on the road covered with sweat and dust, I know these are Rebeccaites – when I see the coalmen coming to town clothed in rags, hard worked and hard fed, I know these are mine – these are Rebecca's children – when I see the farmers' wives carrying loaded baskets to market, bending under their weight, I know well that these are my daughters. If I turn into a farmer's house and see them eating barley bread and drinking whey, surely, say I, these are the members of my family – these are the oppressed sons and daughters of Rebecca [...] My children are simple without information and politics. They shall not always be thus [...] We MUST be free – REBECCA.[16]

Above: Photograph by Francis Bedford of 'Llanberis, Group of Three Welsh Peasants', c. 1860 (Heritage Image Partnership Ltd / Alamy Stock Photo)

Left: Painting by George Childs of Dowlais ironworks in 1840 (Art Collection 3 / Alamy Stock Photo)

Below left: Engraving by John George Wood of Penydarren ironworks in 1811 (Historic Images / Alamy Stock Photo)

Bottom: Postcard of Dynevor Castle, 1936 (Public domain, via https://www.tuckdbpostcards.org)

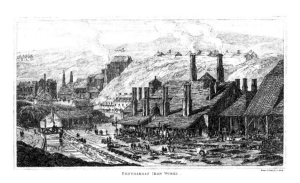

PENYDARRAN IRON WORK .

Copyright. LLO. 45   DYNEVOR CASTLE, LLANDILO.   Raphael Tuck & So London.

Left: 'Welsh Fashions. Taken on a market day in Wales', drawing by R. Griffiths, 1851

(Logic Images / Alamy Stock Photo)

Below left: Photograph by Frederic Evans showing the Mari Lwyd at Llangynwyd in Glamorgan, taken between 1904 and 1910

(Public domain)

Bottom: Postcard of Cyfarthfa Castle, 1903

(Public domain, via https://www. tuckdbpostcards.org)

CYFARTHFA CASTLE.

Drawn by J.P.Neale.
Engraved by T.C.Varral

MIDDLETON HALL,
CAERMARTHENSHIRE

Above: Engraving of Middleton Hall, 1818 (Historic Images / Alamy Stock Photo)

Below: Coracle fishermen and children on the bank of the Towy circa 1908, by John Roberts (Public domain, via People's Collection Wales)

CARMARTHEN BRIDGE AND CORACLE MEN.

Left: A depiction of 'Carmarthen peasantry' from the *Illustrated London News*, c. 1843 (Public domain, via https://welshhat.wordpress.com)

Below: Carmarthen workhouse gate approached from Penlan Hill (Photo by the author)

Bottom: Carmarthen workhouse approached from Waterloo Terrace. (Photo by the author)

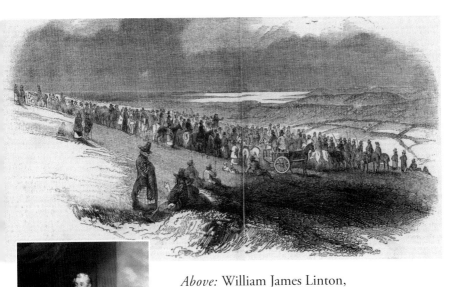

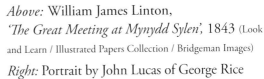

Above: William James Linton,
'The Great Meeting at Mynydd Sylen', 1843 (Look
and Learn / Illustrated Papers Collection / Bridgeman Images)

Right: Portrait by John Lucas of George Rice
Trevor, 1841 (Public domain)

Below: Drawing of Carmarthen Town Hall,
1853 (Historic Collection / Alamy Stock Photo)

REBECCA AND HER DAUGHTERS.

Tolltaker . . Sir R. P—l.   Irish Rebecca . , D—l. O'C—l.   Rebecca's Daughters by Members of the Repeal Ass—n.

Left: Image from *Punch,* 1843 (Punch Cartoon Library / TopFoto)

Below left: Photograph of the Stag and Pheasant inn, 2007. (Lyn John via Llanelli Community Heritage)

Bottom left: Image from the *Illustrated London News,* November 1843, captioned *Rebecca Rioters, or 'Becas* (Chronicle / Alamy Stock Photo)

Bottom right: Plaque marking the destruction of Efail-wen tollgate. (Aled Hughes - The Photolibrary Wales / Alamy Stock Photo)

PART FOUR:

AT THE POINT OF A
BAYONET IF NECESSARY

15
REBECCA RULES

REBECCA TAKES THE THRONE

In the autumn of 1843, after months of frantic missives from magistrates, landowners and the military, the Home Secretary was finally forced to respond with something of substance. By this point Rebecca's followers controlled 2,000 square miles of territory across Pembrokeshire, Carmarthenshire and Cardiganshire, the muzzle of south-west Wales. On a hilltop in Carmarthenshire between the villages of Llandeilo and Llangadog, three stone pillars almost thirty feet high had been raised in a single night, ready to function as markers for a meeting-place or as beacons for signalling. Thomas Campbell Foster, who had been taken to see the stones, reported that two of them were referred to as 'Rebecca and her daughter', while the third, a short distance away, had been dubbed 'Miss Cromwell'. A few weeks later, in the centre of the pillars, a flagstaff was added, as if to mark that this was now officially Rebecca's country.

At the end of August, it was possible to ride from Carmarthen to Aberystwyth – almost fifty miles – and have to pay at only two tollgates, one at either end of the journey and both heavily guarded by the military. The rest were now reduced to ruins, their gates downed, the posts that had once held a bar or chain sawn through, and their adjoining tollhouses demolished, burnt or both. When the trusts and magistrates sent off for timber, bricks and slate, and for builders to rebuild the tollgates, they found that no one local could be employed to help, and contracted builders from outside the area found no one willing to sell them materials for reconstruction. Nor could anyone be found to take up the increasingly dangerous job of toll-collector. Farmers, carters and drovers were ferrying their cargo through the wreckage with abandon, and lime, once again, flowed freely on its journey from the coastal kilns to the hillside farms inland.

Thanks to the press reports from Foster and others, people outside Wales were hearing about the success of direct action and raising the issue of what they thought to be extortionate tolls on road travel in their own localities. On the letters page of *The Times*, a debate raged after a letter written from Ilfracombe on the Devon coast suggested 'that the riots going on under the title of "Rebecca" would be advantageously introduced into this county'.[1] More law-abiding correspondents argued for the logic behind taxes on road travel to pay for upkeep and repair, while others pointed out the unrepaired and dangerous state of many roads in Britain despite the taxes. A reader from Surrey even wrote: 'I trust the stir in Wales touching tolls will lead to an investigation of the accounts of the trustees, and to the relief of the public, in the neighbourhood of London'.[2]

But it was also becoming clear that 'the stir in Wales' had spread beyond a single-issue protest, becoming a new kind of authority that had overturned not only the operation of local administration but the concept of law and order itself. Several landlords were now returning between 5 and 20 per cent of their rents, on receipt of letters from 'Rebecca' demanding that their tenants be reimbursed. Rebecca was also preventing the execution of debt collections, arrest warrants and evictions of tenants. She disrupted visits by bailiffs and stopped auctions of the property they seized. She threatened people out of signing up as special constables: in September, out of 250 summonses issued by magistrates to farmers requesting they be sworn in as specials, only two had been responded to. One man explained to Rees Goring Thomas, in tears, that if he remained a special he feared 'he should be burnt out and murdered. Terror had got possession of his mind'.[3]

More widely, Rebecca defied the New Poor Law by continuing to collect child support for unmarried mothers, keeping them and their children out of the workhouse. In some places she had stopped the collection of poor rates and tithes, forcing Poor Law officials to take a cut in salary and sending Poor Law unions in the areas into arrears – one Cardiganshire union was over £1,000 in debt. Rebecca was making this not just a problem for south-west Wales, but one which threatened to throw a spanner into the machinery of national government.

And even – perhaps especially – now, hardly anyone would inform on anyone connected with the movement. Even when arrested, Rebeccaites were frequently discharged by sympathetic local juries and received a hero's welcome when released. After an acquittal of prisoners for riot at Haverfordwest, the defendants were carried shoulder-high in a triumphal procession to the Prendergast tollgate, before being 'lifted on top of it and swung backwards and forwards for about ten minutes, during which the country people gave full vent to their powers of cheering'.[4] The Swansea magistrate Lewis Weston Dillwyn reported to the Home Office the case of another man who had been granted bail after his arrest:

> I am sorry to tell you ... that on being discharged he was accompanied for a mile homewards by the cheers of a vast body of the tradesmen and other inhabitants of Swansea and the neighbourhood ... the Mayor is generally censured for allowing the town police at all to interfere with Rebecca.[5]

Dillwyn's report ended with something that seemed even more disturbing:

> About a week ago Feargus O'Connor came from Merthyr to Swansea and after lurking for three or four days about the neighbourhood he is supposed to have gone on to Carmarthenshire with the hope of becoming Rebecca's Prime Minister.[6]

The analogy, which reflected the local authorities' paranoia more than any change in O'Connor's feelings about Rebeccaism, was with O'Connor as Prime Minister and Rebecca as Queen. As the movement's figurehead, 'she' had already been compared with Victoria, in both playful and insulting terms – referred to as 'Her most graceless majesty' and 'Rebecca Regina, Rent Reducer' – but could Rebecca seriously become an alternative ruler in Wales, at the head of a government of Chartists? This was unthinkable stuff, and the local authorities were also preparing to think the unthinkable in terms of their response.

On 11 September, William Chambers Junior feared that Llanelli was about to come under attack from a Rebeccaite mob. He wrote to George Rice Trevor who, having consulted Colonel Love, replied that armed force could be used, with the backing of the Home Secretary, if necessary to stop any entry to the town. In Pembrokeshire, a meeting of magistrates called for a central military force to be set up, while others wanted punishments simply for mass gatherings. The Deputy Lieutenant of Cardiganshire called for magistrates to be supplied with hand grenades. And back in London the Home Secretary, particularly troubled by the threatened boycott of rents and Poor Law rates, considered that the insurrectionary 'infection from Ireland has spread to [South] Wales in its worst form'. He wrote to the Welsh magistrates to say that money must continue to be collected, 'at the point of a bayonet if necessary'.[7]

DOWN A DIFFERENT RIVER

The life of a salmon in the river Teifi, which snaked along the border of Carmarthenshire and Cardiganshire, normally saw little excitement. Even with all the drama happening on land during Rebecca's reign, a salmon was mostly concerned with avoiding the fishing-spears of local poachers and the nets regularly dragged downriver between two coracles by the cottagers who lived on the river's banks. But there had been less of these particular perils in recent years, due to the building of a weir at Llechrhyd by the local landowner, which trapped the salmon in the river's lower reaches and left them prey only to the gentry.

As with many other instances of the privatisation of common land and resources, the weir fell to Rebecca in early autumn 1843, demolished by a crowd of around 400 people armed with crowbars and pickaxes. The salmon were now free, leaping upriver as far as Lampeter, thirty miles away, and, once again, able to be picked off by the poor as well as the rich. It all made little difference in the end to the salmon, but their situation made it into threatening letters to the gentry of the three counties, as an example to warn them, along with attacks on gamekeepers and the throwing down of walls and fences, that all game now belonged to Rebecca – and thereby to everyone.

Along with the game laws, another cornerstone of the rural economy was the bailiff, and they, too, were now held at bay by Rebecca. The impending arrival of bailiffs at a cottage or farmhouse was noted by neighbours, and a signal sent up – usually a blown horn – to summon Rebecca and her children as they approached. Goods were sometimes taken from the house and hidden before the bailiffs could get there, or seized back when they attempted to take them. If the goods were taken away before Rebecca could intervene, the subsequent distraint sales were disrupted and potential buyers of the goods threatened out of taking part.

On one of these occasions at the end of August, the land agent of the Baron de Rutzen's Slebech estate in Haverfordwest sent a bailiff to seize cattle and horses from a tenant as payment for overdue rent. The animals were successfully taken, with no interference from Rebecca, and stationed in the area's pound. But at around midnight that night, the pound was visited by Rebecca and her daughters, who attacked Rutzen's gamekeeper with sticks and knocked him unconscious into a hedge. The gamekeeper blearily came to as one of the impounded colts, now released, jumped to freedom over his head. Struggling to his feet, he heard the cheering of a gathered crowd and saw the pound had been emptied of all animals, its gate swinging open with 'Rebecca' standing mockingly on the other side of it. At Brechfa in Carmarthenshire, another bailiff who had seized the goods of a farmer was himself seized by Rebeccaites, before being bound hand and foot and carried to the local pound. In an illustration of Rebecca's grim sense of humour, he was released the following morning only on his employer's payment of the customary fourpence for collection of stray animals.

Meanwhile, Rebeccaites had begun to more stringently police their own community as well as the conduct of the gentry. On the nights following the Mynydd Sylen meeting, groups of Rebeccaites visited farmers in Carmarthenshire and Pembrokeshire who had been found to be hoarding quantities of corn, waiting for its price to rise before taking it to market. 'Rebecca' instructed them instead to sell it at once at an affordable price. In the following weeks shopkeepers were given warnings for selling underweight produce, and further threats were made to farmers who were stockpiling food and grain. These actions might be compared with the commissions of subsistence in revolutionary France, which requisitioned food from the countryside and punished hoarding and speculation – but these were actions within local communities themselves, not between rural and urban areas. Like the support offered to unmarried mothers, they reflected the movement's growing determination to enforce economic fairness and social justice among themselves as much as from the ruling classes. A similar impulse could be seen at Abergwili fair in October, when Rebeccaites stopped ale being brought in from outside the area to protect the interests of local producers.

From the perspective of both the Welsh authorities and the Home Office, however, the whole scene in south-west Wales was deeply unsettling. This disorderly domain – one where tenants served notices on their landlords, bailiffs instead of possessions were seized and impounded, and poverty-stricken women could issue demands to rich men – was now a permanent example of the 'world turned upside-down' that Rebecca's carnivalesque costume had threatened, or promised, from her first appearance.

SOLDIERS OF FORTUNE

Almost unnoticed in the chaos engulfing south-west Wales at this time was an incident in New Inn, Pontyberem, a village halfway between Carmarthen and Llanelli, on a night in early September. It concerned a tall and bearded man who was heavily drunk in the middle of town, dressed in a white gown, plaid cloak and straw bonnet. As he staggered along the darkened street, he fired a gun through the windows of shops and houses seemingly at random. Witnesses heard him shout, when challenged: 'By god, I am Rebecca, and I will have justice done.'[8]

This man was John Jones, who would become better known to history and legend as Shoni Sguborfawr. He had started life outside Rebecca's country, on Sgubor-fawr farm in the parish of Penderyn in Glamorganshire's Cynon Valley, where – the records, and the rumours, were unclear – either he or his father had worked as a labourer. As Thomas Rees was dubbed Twm Carnabwth after the cottage where he lived, so Shoni was known by 'Sguborfawr'. Similar in age to Twm, Shoni was also a Baptist by persuasion and also known as a prize-fighter, but had come to value his physical strength above any more spiritual qualities.

Shoni had grown up in the riotous iron town of Merthyr Tydfil, where he seemed to have absorbed the place's reputation for toughness and trouble. He had made his name as a pugilist in 1840, when the opening of the Taff Vale Railway at Merthyr was celebrated with festivities that included a bare-knuckle contest between Shoni and John Nash, the boxing champion of Crawshay's fiefdom of Cyfarthfa. Shoni could also read and write, and had worked as a shaft-sinker in the coalfield. There he displayed a perhaps surprising fondness for animals, taking hauliers to task verbally and sometimes physically for mistreating their horses.

1843 was a pivotal year for Shoni, who was dragged before the Merthyr magistrates in March, charged with being drunk and disorderly. He was discharged on vowing 'to lead another life', but only two months later he appeared before magistrates in Swansea on an almost identical charge. As Rebeccaism spread in the summer of that year, Shoni moved further afield to find work in the mines of Pontyberem, where he made the acquaintance of the man who would become his brother in arms and partner in crime.

David Davies was, like Shoni, in his early thirties and from the south-east, with a similar history of moving from farm labouring to work in mines and quarries. At Pontyberem in the summer of 1843, he had worked his way up to a foreman's post, where he mediated between employers and the mineworkers – one of whom was Shoni, who caught David's eye. While Shoni fought with his fists, David had a more refined way of competing, with music and words. His poetry and harp-playing had won him prizes at *eisteddfodau* and he had also been a lay preacher, teaching choral singing and gaining the nickname Dai'r Cantwr – Dai the Singer.

Shoni and Dai also shared a background in the industrial unrest of the previous years – though sometimes on the side of the state. Shoni had spent some time in the 98th Foot infantry in Monmouthshire, during which period he also served as an informer on the Scotch Cattle's attempts at industrial organisation. The Brecknockshire MP Thomas Wood, who would later appeal to the judiciary for mercy on Shoni's behalf, remembered swearing him in as a special constable at Brecon to keep the peace during an election.

Together, Shoni and Dai seized the opportunities for self-interest offered by the tumult of Rebeccaism. They set up headquarters at the Stag and Pheasant, an inn a short way outside Llanelli, from where they could meet, gossip and strategise with local activists over a round of drinks. They joined in with the prevailing work of destruction and intimidation and, with Shoni able to indulge his flair for physical violence, they quickly established themselves as local leaders. Although they began as the usual hired muscle, offering farmers their help in attacking gates, Shoni and Dai were soon in wider demand with their readiness to use guns and even accept contracts to settle personal grievances. They did business not just with those looking to demolish a tollgate but with anyone who had a complaint or dispute or a grudge against their neighbour – as long as they also had the money for their services.

As they were shrewd enough to see that farmers who had paid for their help with Rebeccaite attacks had thereby left themselves open to being identified to the authorities, Shoni and Dai's activity soon expanded into a kind of protection racket. Shoni in particular began to live off the farmers who asked him for help. William Chambers Junior later described his methods:

> The influence that such men [as Shoni] got over the minds of the farmers arose from him having been employed by them in that way; and, being rather a sharper fellow, the others all felt that they were in his power, and then he ran riot ... He would go to a farmer's house, lived there as long as he pleased, and paid nothing for it; and then to the next.[9]

Like many other inns, the Stag and Pheasant rented rooms to labourers, farm servants and travellers. One of its lodgers was a farm servant who went one evening to another local pub, the Farmers Arms, in search of his master. He found him huddled in the pub's parlour with a group of men including Dai, who he recognised from the Stag and Pheasant. Spotted by his master, he was press-ganged into putting on a blue dress and joining in the group's attack on a nearby tollgate. The action included Shoni as Rebecca, riding a dark horse in a gown and bonnet and brandishing a gun. Shedding their disguises on the way back, they crowded into the pub's back-room again and were handed half a crown each by the landlord, the money having come from local farmers. Money for the cause was often requisitioned and produced to be shared among those joining in an action, but Shoni, as the servant noted on this occasion, often pocketed more than his fair share.

DEMANDS AND DIVISIONS

In the autumn of 1843 many things were reaching a turning-point. Some of the turnpike trusts were beginning to offer concessions, particularly as the facts divulged at public meetings forced them to acknowledge that some aspects of toll collecting were contravening both the Turnpike Act and general principles of justice. At a meeting of trustees at Haverfordwest in early September, local farmers demanded to know how the money collected from tolls for the past fifty years had been spent. The trustees, protesting that they couldn't answer for what had been done so long ago, nonetheless saw the farmers' point of view and agreed to look at lowering the tolls.

But this wasn't enough to satisfy or pacify the movement. The Radnorshire MP John Walsh, now back in Wales after a long absence and struggling to adjust to the changes that had come over his constituency, found to his confusion and dismay that 'all the people were friendly to the Rebeccaites' and that 'even fair Mrs Meddings, the pretty landlady' of his local pub, was a supporter of demolishing the tollgates and more. Writing in his journal, Walsh confessed himself at a loss:

> I did not know at all what to do – I felt quite sure that nothing I did would be supported by any vigour ... And after all, what was to be done? The gates were down, and I knew all the facts – a dozen magistrats could not make the thing better ... these people are all paralysed, or disaffected.[10]

Back in Carmarthenshire, the vicar Eleazar Evans, who had made a point of publicly denouncing Rebecca, was now sleeping with a wardrobe jammed against his window in fear of a spray of bullets at midnight. He had good reason to worry: another vicar at Llansadwrn had been visited by a figure claiming to be Rebecca's sister Charlotte, and told that the clergy owning land was 'contrary to Becca's law'.[11] He was given the choice of either giving up his leasehold of some fields next to the vicarage and turning them back to common use, or moving his furniture out of the house before her children set it on fire. Like most recipients of Rebecca's ultimatums, he chose the safer option. Meanwhile, at the Carmarthenshire estate of Towy Castle, a bailiff had been spending the night at a repossessed farmhouse when Rebecca's children arrived, led by a figure in a horse-mane wig and feathered cap. They dragged him from his hiding-place under a bed and chased him back to Carmarthen. And throughout all this, more and more 'Rebecca letters' were appearing, settling like an early snowdrift on not only the desks of the gentry but even the kitchen tables of some wealthier farmers. The letters reflected discontents and grudges from labourers and servants, which they now felt confident enough to voice under Rebecca's name.

This confidence further reflected a growing division within Rebeccaism. On 1 September, the *Welshman* published an editorial on what it saw as the state of the movement:

> Rebeccaism, we are sorry to see, in several cases is getting worse and a different class of persons with different objects has taken the field. Malice and personal spite, wanton outrage and unreasoning riot have in these cases made head. But on the other hand public meetings have been held, in which thousands in the face of day have fairly made known all their wrongs, real and unreal. Such meetings are the safety-valves of popular effervescence, and they ought to be encouraged by every friend to peace and prosperity. Besides being the media of redress ... the very fact of their being held shows that the people are beginning (however awkwardly) to get their right foot foremost.[12]

This was a fair assessment: as the focus of the movement broadened, its aims became diffused, giving opportunities for individual vengeance and petty crime in the gaps between more organised opposition to collectively agreed injustice. This was where Shoni and Dai found an opening, arriving as they did at the tail-end of a movement whose solidarity was already threatening to splinter.

16
RAISING THE STAKES

'GOING A LITTLE TOO FAR'

Beyond the diffusion into gangsterism and personal score-settling at its fringes, elsewhere in the movement more political developments were happening. In the autumn of 1843, Chartist lecturers from Merthyr arrived in Carmarthenshire. They met and debated with local groups of Rebeccaites, advocating, as usual, campaigning for universal suffrage to solve their problems. The national Chartist leadership remained reluctant to fully engage with the movement, still questioning why the labourers and farm servants weren't going it alone. In a series of editorials in the *Poor Man's Guardian*, Bronterre O'Brien called for Welsh labourers to separate from the farmers and set up 'a Rebecca of their own'.[1] But individual Chartists who connected with Rebeccaites on the ground found them impressive enough to support, including with donations of money. The *Northern Star*'s correspondent in south Wales praised the Rebecca meetings he had been to:

> I have attended many Chartist meetings, and have ofttimes been pleased with the zeal and determination which were manifested by the people to work out their own political salvation, but I never, in the whole course of my life, was a witness to such a degree of determination and energy as that manifested by the individuals who were present at this midnight scene.[2]

In August 1843, Peel's government was facing the challenges of the pro-free-trade Anti-Corn Law League and Ireland's independence campaign as well as the unrest in Wales. An effervescent poem in the *Northern Star* by the Midlands activist E. P. Mead depicted Rebecca

185

as part of a rising popular front alongside Daniel O'Connell, the Radical MP Richard Cobden and the Chartist movement, their combined forces ready to overwhelm the British ship of state and steer it to the calmer waters of an idyllic 'Freedom's Bay'.[3]

On other pages of the *Northern Star*, however, Feargus O'Connor was quoting Thomas Campbell Foster's sympathetic reports on Rebeccaism as reason enough for Chartists to treat it with caution. Shouldn't any radical with their wits about them be suspicious of a movement that was receiving praise like this from the mainstream liberal press? Far from wanting to be 'Rebecca's Prime Minister', O'Connor claimed that his own conversations when visiting Wales had been with Chartists who didn't even have land to pay rent on, or horses to drive through tollgates – so what stake did they have in this struggle over farm-rents and tolls? He denied that the *Northern Star* reporter who attended the Rebeccaite meeting back in August had been sent there with his knowledge, let alone his approval.

Nonetheless, the social composition of the Rebecca movement was widening, with farm labourers and coalminers now forming a significant part of those who showed up at meetings and took part in actions. This only heightened the mixed feelings that some of the more respectable farmers were developing. It was one thing to remove road tolls and demand lower rents, but the farmers were now themselves, they realised, in a position to be asked to lower the prices they charged for their produce, and to raise the wages they paid to their farm labourers. What if the labourers realised this, too?

And by the autumn of 1843, it seemed that some of them had. In early September, farm labourers and servants began to hold their own meetings and to organise separately from the farmers who employed them. These meetings were held openly and with no attempt to keep them secret. Thomas Campbell Foster recorded, with both alarm and curiosity, that the labourers were:

> holding meetings every night on the hills in [Carmarthen-shire] and Cardiganshire. They complain that the farmers pay them ill and treat them badly ... They say to the farmers

'We have heard your grievances and helped you to get them redressed, and now we will tell you ours.'[4]

Meanwhile, a meeting of around 250 'collier Rebeccaites' took place one evening in a field outside Carmarthen. Sitting calmly in a circle under the shade of the trees, they discussed 'existing hardships' and the need for farmers and shopkeepers to lower their prices to more affordable levels. As the meeting saw it, this was a fair exchange for their participation in anti-tollgate action: 'Inasmuch as they had assisted the farmers in the reduction of rents and turnpike tolls, they should now call on them to reduce the price of butter and other agricultural produce, and insist on the publicans reducing the price of beer.'[5]

That servants, labourers and industrial workers were now meeting and organising independently, and articulating their own demands, was a development that would no doubt have pleased the Chartists. It certainly worried the Tory *Carmarthen Journal*, which noted in early September that 'the labourers and farm servants have discovered that they have class interests distinct from their employers'.[6] As would soon become apparent, this discovery unsettled not only some better-off farmers but also some middle-class radicals who supported the movement.

While the labourers, colliers and farmers were considering their options, the Swansea magistrate John Dillwyn Llewelyn's quiet evening at home at his Penllergare estate was interrupted by one of his regular attacks of gout. For the squirearchy of the era, this affliction was as much of an occupational hazard as fending off Rebeccaites was becoming. At around 11 o'clock, Dillwyn Llewelyn was upstairs in his dressing room and had half-undressed to bathe his inflamed foot in hot water, when a sudden pounding at his front door caused him even greater inconvenience. As he recorded later:

The gout for the moment was forgot. I dressed hastily and went downstairs – the knocking was from a party of policemen who were in a state of great trepidation – they told me that they had met a party of Rebeccas marching on the road between us and Felindre.[7]

It was a measure of the movement's power at this point that the police weren't looking to confront the Rebeccaite party, who outnumbered them, but only seeking sanctuary at the magistrate's house. Nonetheless, he directed them to move cautiously along the road while he rode to fetch reinforcements from Swansea.

On his way back, with a handful of troops behind him, Dillwyn Llewelyn's night took another twist. His horse was overtaken by a rider who he recognised not only as a Swansea tradesman, but also as 'a very advanced radical in his politics' and a supporter of Rebeccaism. When the magistrate expressed his surprise at seeing him willing to join them, the tradesman confessed that he was having a change of heart about the movement, which he felt was now 'going a little too far':

At first I thought they had some real grievances to complain of and sympathized with them, but now I find that they are levying black mail – and a bad set of fellows are joining their ranks – men coming from a distance in the hope of disturbance and plunder. They are going too far, and talking about division of property – and as I have a shop full of goods I don't approve of that.[8]

This nervous agreement between authority figures and the commercial middle classes that Rebeccaism had gone too far, its upheaval not only generating more militant demands but also attracting mercenary opportunists like Shoni and Dai, seemed to bear out Feargus O'Connor's warning that a split among better-off Rebeccaites and the rest of the movement was inevitable. While wealthier farmers were appeased by the reduction of tolls, many of those below them remained determined to push for what greater changes might be possible. Events in the autumn of 1843, as solidarity began to fracture and many rioters risked arrest and imprisonment, would make it clear how severe the stakes were becoming.

THE BATTLE OF PONTARDDULAIS

On the morning of Wednesday 6 September 1843, a letter was handed to William Chambers Junior at Llanelly House. It contained information from a farmer – one of Chambers's own tenants, who were still willing to offer him intelligence – that Rebeccaites planned to attack tollgates at both Pontarddulais and Hendy that same night. Chambers wrote immediately to relay this both to Colonel Love and to the local chief of police, Captain Napier – the latter still smarting from his fight with the saucepan-wielding matriarch of the Morgan family some weeks earlier.

Rather than rushing into action, Chambers and Napier sat down and thought more strategically about this opportunity than any opponents of Rebecca had previously done. The tollgates at Hendy and Pontarddulais lay on opposite banks of the river Loughor, and they reasoned that Rebecca, contrary to public rumours about her supernatural abilities, could not be in two places at once. The plan therefore was for Napier, along with a handful of police and magistrates, to arrive at Pontarddulais and wait to catch the rioters in the act of destroying the tollgate, while, on the other side of the river, troops led by Chambers would protect the Hendy gate.

As midnight fell on the Carmarthenshire–Glamorganshire border, anyone looking down from above at the wooden bridge over the river would have seen two detachments of armed men making their separate ways towards it. While one party, under Chambers's direction, rode directly to Hendy, the other, led by Napier, took a more covert route across the surrounding fields, keeping off the main roads, eventually stopping to tether their horses in a field a few hundred yards from the Pontarddulais tollgate. The same observer, had they waited a while, would then have seen the night sky suddenly lit up by rockets and flares, their explosions interleaved with the blowing of horns and gunfire. After this, a third group could be seen converging and beginning their own march towards the bridge – not in military formation but with a similar determination and purpose, and in a uniform of their own devising.

The attack on the Pontarddulais gate was led by John Hughes, who was known as Jac Ty Isha from the name of his family's farm. He was twenty-four years old and the eldest son of a well-respected farming family in Llannon, a few miles from Hendy, where around 150 Rebeccaites had assembled that night at around half-past eleven. Described as 'hale, powerful and good-looking',[9] and dressed suitably dashingly that night in a long white cloak with a scarlet handkerchief tied around his neck, Jac took the head of the procession as it moved off.

The Rebeccaites were on horseback – most horses carrying two people – and clad in white flannel dresses and shawls, coats turned inside-out, and bonnets or straw hats stuck with ferns and feathers, an affect which, to several onlookers, gave the effect of plumed helmets. Their faces were painted in red and black, and, in addition to guns, they carried axes, saws and sledgehammers. Some members of the procession – or so they later claimed – had been pressed into joining by Rebeccaites who had arrived at their door on previous nights, offering both money and threats, while others were joining as curious observers.

The unusually bright moonlight that September night illuminated the procession, making them visible from some distance away, but the Rebeccaites could be heard even before they were seen – not only their hoofbeats, horns and guns, but put-on voices that, to some observers, sounded like both 'the mewing of cats' and 'a host of old market-women'.[10] Reaching the top of Fforest Hill on the Hendy side of the river shortly after midnight, the crowd halted at the Red Lion Inn, cheering loudly and firing off their guns, before they lowered their heads and charged across the bridge towards the Pontarddulais gate.

At Pontarddulais, the toll-collector had already made a quick exit after dragging his possessions out of the tollhouse into the garden. Still stationed in the field nearby, Captain Napier heard the destruction of the tollgate begin and sprang into action. Reaching the gate, he directed his men to form a line across the road before calling on the rioters to halt. He was answered by three of the crowd, so intent on the work of demolition that they had been taken by surprise, swiftly turning their horses and readying them to charge the police line. One of the three drew a pistol from under his cloak and levelled it at Napier. The shot narrowly missed, and, at almost the same instant, Napier shouted his own command to fire.

What followed was later described by the police as 'a regular scramble'.[11] In the space of less than ten minutes, sixty or seventy shots were exchanged. The police discharged two rounds of bullets at the crowd around the gate before they returned fire, then panic set in and many Rebeccaites turned to escape back up the hill or, standing their ground, began to grapple hand to hand with the police. Napier himself, marking the man who had shot at him by the red handkerchief he wore around his neck, fired at the man's horse. The shot caused the animal to wheel and throw its rider, who vaulted off onto his feet and launched himself at Napier.

In the ensuing struggle, Napier was hit from behind and lost sight of his assailant. Another rioter, David Jones, fled into the tollhouse where he was pursued by a constable, and the two exchanged blows with an iron bar and a cutlass. Jones, bleeding from the cutlass wounds he had sustained, was taken into custody along with another man, John Hugh, who had been pulled from his horse. The third prisoner taken that night was Jac Ty Isha, finally subdued and with his arm shattered by a police bullet.

Over at the Hendy gate, William Chambers could make out the sound of gunfire from across the river, but was too far away to decide if this was a genuine pitched battle or simply the customary discharge of guns when a tollgate was being demolished. But then, seeing a man walking speedily from the direction of the bridge,

Chambers moved to confront him. On drawing closer, he saw that his face was smeared in red and black and that he was surreptitiously stuffing something under his coat. Chambers stopped him and grabbed the item he was trying to hide: it was a white bonnet.

Chambers took the man prisoner, and then, leaving half his men where they were, led the other half towards the bridge. On the way they passed other escapees and, noting their painted faces, straw hats and other giveaways, also took them in. Reaching the Pontarddulais side of the river, Chambers found the gate and tollhouse destroyed and the three prisoners lying handcuffed on the floor. He and Napier began to drag them into the remains of the tollhouse. Several of the Rebeccaites, refusing to abandon their comrades, returned to make an attempt at rescuing them, but the arrival of more of the military, summoned from Swansea, forced them to retreat back up the hill towards Llannon.

Jac Ty Isha and David Jones, both badly wounded, were taken to Swansea jail along with John Hugh. There, the three had their clothing searched and the police made an exhaustive list of their costumes and accessories: a woman's cap, a white dress, a hat covered with white canvas, a plaid cloak, three straw hats, a black hat, two tin horns, three cow's or bullock's horns, one coat with the sleeves turned inside-out and one flannel apron. More damningly, their pockets were found to contain gunpowder, percussion caps and shot, and knives in the case of Hugh and Jones. In Jac's pockets were receipts for Rebeccaite subscriptions from farmers and, written in Welsh, a typical Rebecca business note, instructing the recipient: 'Come with your armour to Lanbystia, to assist us, on Wednesday night next, or else you shall not have another notice. BECCA.'[12] It seemed like a fair cop.

DUST FAILS TO SETTLE

As Thursday dawned, news of the clash and arrests had spread quickly, and huge crowds were already surrounding Swansea police station. The town's mayor acted quickly after the prisoners were brought in, ordering that they be taken by stretcher to the prison infirmary. There, Jac had the police bullet extracted from his arm, but less could be done for David Jones who appeared to be in a state of shock, not yet near death but with his cutlass wounds still bleeding and his back riddled with pistol-shot. Later that day the police, followed by a crowd of hundreds, brought down the third prisoner, John Hugh, who was still wearing his Rebeccaite accessory, a battered straw bonnet trimmed with ferns and red ribbons.

For Rebecca's opponents, the battle of Pontarddulais seemed at first like an unquestionable victory. The arrests, and the capture of at least one 'Rebecca', made national headlines and notes of mutual congratulation made the rounds between local magistrates, police chiefs and the gentry. Napier wrote triumphantly to local landowners to assure them that the outcome of the 'scuffle' would now put a stop to Rebeccaism in Glamorganshire.[13]

But a few days later, when the Pontarddulais Three were questioned at Swansea town hall, the place rapidly filled up with both curious and angry spectators. The press reported that John Hugh – still wearing his Rebecca bonnet – seemed 'alarmed and apprehensive', while Jac Ty Isha, with his injured arm in a sling, was 'pale and thoughtful'.[14] David Jones, having seemed to be 'in a dying state' after his arrest, now appeared to be recovering. The prisoners were still in no condition to be at the bar for long, and the examination was soon adjourned for a few days' time, but not before the police gave evidence that the first shots at Pontarddulais had been fired not by them but by the crowd around the tollgate.

This didn't make much difference to those packing the streets outside the courtroom, who were protesting at not only the conduct of the police but also the actions of William Chambers's men in capturing four other members of the crowd as they fled the shoot-out at the tollgate. These four, all young farm servants, had now been charged with riot and were being held at Swansea jail. Meanwhile, accounts and rumours had emerged from local witnesses that contradicted the police's version of events: they claimed they had heard Napier give the command to fire before any shot had been discharged by the Rebeccaites; they had seen the police firing off their pistols before even reaching the gate; they had been told that people in the crowd had been wounded with hunting-knives in addition to gunfire. Police were continuing to scour the nearby towns and hillsides for men who had escaped from Pontarddulais, some of them wounded, and whose whereabouts were still unknown even to their families.

For days, crowds of almost a thousand people surrounded the courthouse and police station, prompting Swansea's mayor to read the Riot Act and place soldiers on the streets. Threats were made to storm the town's jail and liberate the Rebeccaite prisoners. Thomas Campbell Foster, struggling to reconcile his liberal sensibilities with what he saw around him, reported that:

> The Welsh are a peculiar people, and they have become completely exasperated in consequence of their countrymen having been shot, as they say, by a villainous body of police ... The multitude declare that they will have a deep revenge.[15]

Foster also picked up on rumours circulating about mineworkers at nearby Pontyberem – the haunt of Shoni Sguborfawr and Dai'r Cantwr – pledging support to the arrested Rebeccaites. This was expressed in eyebrow-raising terms as the colliers threatened to turn the skills they had developed in the service of industrial expansion towards resisting the forces of the state:

> The miners and colliers near Pontyberem have declared that they will resist the soldiers, and that they will undermine and blow up the road; and they threaten that, as the Glamorganshire police laid in wait for them, they will have an ambush for the police some day ... But all kinds of rumours are afloat.[16]

Far from dealing a decisive blow to the movement and subduing public support for it, the dramatic events at Pontarddulais were having precisely the opposite effect. Edward Crompton Lloyd Hall, always given to excitable alarm but now with what seemed to him increasing justification for it, wrote to the Home Office that, if things went much further 'all the soldiering you have at your disposal will be insufficient to prevent the occurrence of the scenes of the French Revolution'.[17]

17
DEATH AT HENDY

SARAH WILLIAMS

The Welsh landscape's traditional power to seduce the unwary traveller was still in evidence in September 1843, when Joseph Downes arrived in Hendy. Like Thomas Campbell Foster before him, he had been dispatched to report on the state of south Wales, this time by *Blackwood's Edinburgh Magazine*, a Tory journal that blended political coverage with cultural reviews and satire. After his early life in London and Edinburgh, Downes had settled in Builth in Breconshire, from where he wrote freelance essays, stories and nature poems for periodicals like *Blackwood's*. In 1836 he had published *The Mountain Decameron*, a collection of Welsh folktales. An altogether gentler soul than Foster, in his own current attempt at reportage, Downes, accompanied on his journey by his teenage son, was finding his naturist's eye drawn less to matters of economic and political analysis and more to the sweeping romantic scenery of the places they passed through. But as the pair approached what Downes described as the recent 'battle-field' of Pontarddulais, he was already troubled by having his rural tranquillity interrupted by encounters with 'some hurrying dragoon, some eager gossiping group, or fresh "news" of some farm "burned last night", or rumours of "martial law" being actually impending.'[1]

When Downes came upon a picturesque whitewashed cottage surrounded by a small and solemn crowd, with a few items of furniture scattered on the road outside and a burnt-out tollhouse standing opposite, it was his efforts to cultivate a reporter's instinct as well as a tourist's curiosity that drove him to investigate. Having negotiated entry to the cottage, he found the traditional chance of stumbling into horror beneath the scenic beauty of Wales was still in operation. This time it was not the emergence of beggars from the ruins of Neath Abbey that had so disturbed Armand Bon Maudet, but the body of a woman, laid out on a low bench and barely covered by a rug. Drawing closer, Downes could see that her clothing was stiffened and dark with dried blood. Propped against the wall nearby was a coffin, its nameplate – 'Sarah Williams, age 75 – already prepared'.

Less than three days earlier in the same cottage, at 11 o'clock on a Saturday night, Margaret Thomas had been preparing for bed. The recent clash at Pontarddulais was on her mind and she took a moment to check for any signs of trouble closer to home. The Hendy tollgate, just across the road from Margaret's cottage, had a new keeper, who had moved in a week ago, but Sarah Williams was known to have collected tolls for years, at gates all over the country, and so could surely look after herself. As midnight approached, Margaret could see the tollhouse and gate in the near distance were still standing and in the darkness all was quiet, so she settled to sleep next to her husband – but no sooner had she closed her eyes than they were both jolted awake by what sounded like the firing of five or six guns in the street outside. In the sudden quiet that followed, the voice of the Hendy tollkeeper could be heard outside their window, calling for help to put out a fire at her tollhouse.

After a moment where the couple stared wide-eyed at each other, in silent agreement that they couldn't do much to help without calling Rebecca's attention to them, too, Margaret shuffled her way to the door and tried to do what she could. She whispered urgently to Sarah to bring her possessions from the tollhouse to Margaret's own dwelling, and then come in herself for shelter. In the light of the burgeoning flames across the street, she watched as Sarah began to pull items of furniture onto the road, but then lost sight of her in the smoke-filled darkness. The night became wrapped in an eerie silence, with none of the blown horns or shouting of directions that she had come to expect when Rebecca was at work.

For over half an hour, Margaret waited in her open doorway, before she heard a cry of 'I know who you are!' The sudden shout in the darkness was answered by another burst of gunfire. Then she

197

saw Sarah emerge from the smoke and shadows, dragging herself along the street using the housefront walls for support. Margaret rushed forward and caught the old woman around the waist as she sank down on the doorstep. With her husband at last out of bed, Margaret hauled Sarah inside and tried to sit her up, but in a matter of minutes the couple knew their efforts to save her were in vain. As they drew closer together in the early-hours chill, it dawned on them that, for the first time since Rebecca's reign began, a life had been lost at the hands of her children.

At the moment of death, Sarah Williams seemed to have so little blood on her that Margaret Thomas thought she might have died of fright. By the time Joseph Downes had stumbled upon her corpse, it had been examined by two surgeons summoned from Llanelli. At the inquest into Sarah's death held a few days later at the Black Horse Inn, both surgeons agreed that the cause of death was loss of blood, and that the cause of that had been the gunshot wounds found on the left side of her body, which had penetrated her armpit, her breast, her lungs, her throat and her forehead.

The case seemed clear-cut, but the jury at the inquest, composed of local men, took a surprisingly long time to consider it. The verdict they eventually returned was even more surprising: they concluded that Sarah Williams had died 'from the effusion of blood into the chest, which occasioned suffocation, but from what cause is to the jury unknown'.[2] In other words, they agreed her death had happened, but they had no idea what had prompted it. The jury's decision rendered the presiding coroner speechless, while one of the surgeons got to his feet and walked out of the room in disgust.

UNDER FIRE

For the local authorities, the death of Sarah Williams was a straightforward case of murder, committed by reckless or outright villainous Rebeccaites and outrageously excused by a jury of sympathisers. There was little they could do to change the inquest's verdict, but George Rice Trevor wasted no time in plastering the county with placards offering a cash reward for information on the perpetrators. The actions of the Hendy jury also meant that the decision was taken to hold the trial of the three Pontarddulais rioters, as well as those of Daniel Lewis and the Morgan family, in Cardiff, lessening the potential for their juries to be similarly influenced by local support for the movement.

The authorities were taking things increasingly seriously, but there was also still serious public anger in the aftermath of Pontarddulais, on which the death of a tollkeeper had little impact. While there was natural sympathy expressed for 'the poor old woman', there was also the assumption that Sarah's death had been accidental – a mistake in the heat of the moment, a shot fired in confusion during a hurried and volatile attack on the tollgate. It was said, with a sad shrug, that she had been given several previous warnings not to continue collecting tolls at the Hendy gate, and that, by trying to interfere with the dismantling of the tollhouse instead of getting well out of the way, as other tollkeepers had done before her, she had brought this tragedy upon herself. Joseph Downes was shocked by some of the casual responses he got when speaking to local people about the death:

> 'Didn't she die in a fit; or of fright; or something?' was a frequent question, even from those near the scene of this tragedy. 'What did ail the old creature to go near 'em? Name of goodness! Didn't they order her not?' Even from her own sex, a disgusting lack of warm-hearted pity and indignation was most palpable.[3]

Some even argued that Sarah's alleged warning to her attackers that she recognised them had been an implicit threat to identify them to the authorities, which could only be dealt with by ensuring that she would be in no fit state to report anyone. And even sympathetic people were less angry about this unfortunate death than about what they still saw as the deliberate actions of the police in firing upon the crowd at Pontarddulais.

The actions of William Chambers Junior at Pontarddulais were still coming in for criticism, too. Scant weeks after he had been given pride of place at the Mynydd Sylen meeting, his involvement in the capture of Jac Ty Isha and the other prisoners had made him the villain of the piece – even more so than Captain Napier, who at least had never given the impression of being sympathetic to Rebeccaism and so could not be accused of betraying the cause. Some of the men who had taken part in the Pontarddulais battle were still missing from their homes, and lurid rumours began to spread that, in the confusion following the clash, Chambers had dragged one of the injured rioters around a corner and shot him in cold blood. When stacks of corn were set on fire in a field he owned in the very centre of Llanelli, those watching were heard to mutter that 'Becca has put Mr Chambers' field of corn on fire, and let it burn to the Devil'.[4]

Chambers was now alone at Llanelly House, having sent his wife and children to safety in England and ignored their pleas for him to accompany them. The rumours about his actions reached him via local gossip and warnings from his fellow gentry, and he began an open letter to protest his innocence:

> The lie of my having shot the man round the corner of the Inn at Pontardulais arises probably from my having performed the only act of kindness I could to the unfortunate men whom I first saw wounded in the gate house by getting them water. Once established this lie was, I have no doubt, sedulously retailed by persons who were anxious to sever the good understanding that had existed always between me, and the Farmers of this neighbourhood. How well they succeeded I need not tell you.[5]

But while Chambers was putting pen to paper, the gossip about him was being carried further by word of mouth, and it soon reached the ears of Shoni and Dai's gang at the Stag and Pheasant. Their organisation was now attracting – or sometimes press-ganging – a wide cross-section of men in the area, drawing in publicans from the Star and the Farmers Arms, colliers and workmen as well as farmers. At his later confession, Shoni identified his and Dai's eclectic associates as including 'Jack of the Star, William the Clerk to Colebrook Works, Farmer Stone, Jones Bryngorse and all the people about there'.[6]

Shoni also later insisted that topics of conversation at the Stag and Pheasant were limited to 'tithes, taxes, rent, and rates'. But at one particular drinking session before the group were due to attend a public meeting at Pembrey mountain, the 'shocking thing' of the Pontarddulais arrests was raised. 'Suppose,' mused Thomas Philips, a workman from Topsail, 'if we were to offer a sum of money for shooting Chambers?'

This idea met with general approval around the pub table. Dai Thomas of Cilverry launched into a fiery speech, lasting ten minutes, arguing that Chambers ought indeed to be shot in return for shooting men at Pontarddulais, and calling on God to assist them in bringing this about.

As they left the Stag and Pheasant, the group were joined by others heading to the mountainside meeting. They proposed anti-enclosure actions and discussed passwords, before their talk returned to more particular matters. According to Shoni, there were so many supporters of the idea of shooting Chambers that a fund was set up to raise money for anyone willing to do it. The price on his head was first of all set at ten pounds – at least eight times what many labourers earned in a week – and then, when the subscribers protested that this was beyond what they could afford, reduced to half that amount.

In turn, rumours of these developments got back to Chambers almost immediately. The news of his proposed assassination, with its cut-price reward adding insult to injury, reached him at the same time as an invitation to again attend a public meeting in his neighbourhood to discuss popular complaints. The latter request had come at precisely the wrong moment, and an infuriated Chambers took the opportunity to unburden himself about the whole situation. He wrote back in high dudgeon, with a touch of his youthful temper, and with his own request that his letter be read to the meeting when it took place:

> Sir, I think it right to inform you why I do not attend your meeting today. Having taken the chair at Mynydd Sylen, I should again have attended, but the manner in which I have been treated by parties whose cause I have always done my best to support fills me with surprize and disgust ... I was one of the first to lower the rents to, and to pay the police rate for, my tenants ... Ask them, if there are any from the town of Llanelly, whether I have not lent many a poor man money to carry on his buildings or to carry on his business, they can acknowledge this.
>
> I think I have answered every lying report. I have gone thus far into explanation, as it is a duty I owe to myself, not to the cowardly miscreants who fired my houses, my corn, my hay ... I have my life (devoted for these twelve years to the expenditure of my Father's ample fortune in this County) threatened, but the coward who did this had better mind that the sacrifice of his own is not the reward of his temerity when he thinks proper to attempt mine.[7]

THE FALL OF MIDDLETON HALL

The evening before Chambers finally set down his exasperation in words, Joseph Downes had been strolling the banks of the Towy, lost in admiration of what seemed to him a placid twilight landscape straight out of the tourist guides. It took him some time to realise, at around 10 o'clock, that the prospect before him was being lit so pleasantly not merely by the moon but by a huge fire beginning to rage on the other side of the river, in the fields surrounding Middleton Hall.

An hour or so later Edward Adams, riding home from his magistrates' duties at a Quarter Session, also caught sight of this conflagration at his estate, and quickly dug his heels in to speed up his journey. He galloped through the gates of Middleton Hall to find the fire reaching its height, his hayricks on fire and the plugs in the nearby fishponds removed, which also removed any chance of finding water to quickly extinguish the blaze. In the woods surrounding the mansion, he could make out shadowy figures looking on in the light of the flames. Barely stopping to dismount before he charged into the manor house, Adams dashed off a note to George Rice Trevor demanding military assistance, thrusting the letter into the hands of a servant while he gathered up his papers and other valuables in case the fire should reach the house itself.

Galloping eight miles west to Carmarthen, the request for help reached town at around 1 o'clock in the morning. The cavalry, however, were nearly fifteen miles away in Llanelli and no spare carriages could be found to transport the infantry. Back at Middleton Hall, Adams raged at the authorities' incompetence while the gathered crowd outside warmed their hands around the blaze until two in the morning.

The following day, with the remains of the hayricks still smouldering, Thomas Cooke was trying to placate his still-furious employer when rumours reached them of another impending attack on the estate. This time Adams's request for soldiers from Carmarthen was granted, and for a few hours they stood guard around the house, but no attack materialised. When George Rice Trevor, arguing that there was no immediate threat to Adams's property, ordered the troops back to Carmarthen, Adams could take no more. As Cooke later recorded:

> He says a magistrate is not sufficiently protected in the execution of his duty, appears disgusted with what he calls the neglect of the Government in not putting down these outrageous doings, has packed off all his plate and his Title Deeds to a place of greater security and (I believe) is going off to France in course of a day or two quite disgusted.[8]

Reflecting on the past few days, including the death at Hendy, Cooke wrote with palpable weariness: 'I think the whole country is gone quite mad.'

At the end of September, Adams and his family did indeed depart for France, but not before he fired some parting shots at a meeting of 150 of his estate's tenants. For an hour and a half, pacing up and down and using 'intemperate language', Adams loudly berated them for seeking to tell him how to run his estate, certain that those responsible for burning his hayricks a few days ago were in the crowd before him, and that also present was the writer of a Rebecca letter to him, which he proceeded to read aloud.

The letter demanded, among other things, that Adams dismiss the 'thick-headed' Thomas Cooke from his staff. Cooke, who was dutifully present in the audience, was unsure where to look as Adams roared, at a pitch that Cooke recalled as probably audible a quarter of a mile away, that Cooke, however thick-headed he might be, 'suited him' and that he would not be threatened into sacking anyone.[9] It was perhaps the closest his boss had ever come to paying him a compliment.

Adams finished by blaming the tenants themselves for his imminent transformation into an absentee landlord, and warned them that he might no longer be investing his money locally but he would certainly still be collecting his rent. After a final discourse on what they could expect to suffer under impending martial law, he told his audience they were dismissed, and left to pack his bags. The crowd, who had received him with a blend of shock and bewilderment throughout, trooped out silently, along with Cooke, into a lordless manor.

18
ARE THE GOVERNMENT MAD ENOUGH?

DAGGERS DRAWN

At the end of September 1843, following the injuries and arrests at Pontarddulais, the death of Sarah Williams at Hendy and the flight from the country by several of the gentry, the Home Secretary gently suggested to the Prime Minister that a general military officer should be put in charge of Wales. The Queen herself had written to both men, expressing concern that her government had underestimated Rebecca, and in a speech to Parliament she had lamented the outbreak of 'insubordination and violence in a part of the country usually distinguished for good order and willing obedience to the law'.[1] Although some in Peel's cabinet called to send into Wales a figure of no less illustrious brutality than the Duke of Wellington, the government settled for the unassuming George Brown, a former soldier and now a civil servant. More troops scattered around the country were rounded up and sent to Carmarthenshire, where it was rumoured that martial law – direct control by the military rather than the civic authorities – was now imminent, to the open contempt of many of the country's inhabitants. Thomas Campbell Foster reported:

> Nothing can exceed the exasperation expressed by all classes of the people as this idea gains ground. 'Are the government mad enough', they say, 'instead of boldly redressing the grievances, to seek to proclaim martial law, and hang up Welshmen at the behest or on the evidence of a soldier or so? If they do they will have the whole country in a flame, and must proclaim martial law everywhere.'[2]

The prospect of martial law concentrated the minds of many in the movement, whether they wished to respond by challenging it head on or by seeking to calm things down. As the conflicted reactions to the idea of military rule further splintered the movement, George Rice Trevor wrote to William Chambers Junior rejoicing in the rumours of 'anything like a schism amongst the Rebeccas. I believe with you some of the farmers would wish now to get out of the scrape they are in'.[3]

The letter reflected the fact that Chambers was now back in his fellow lawkeepers' good books. George Rice Trevor had confided to another magistrate that he thought Chambers's recent concessions to Rebeccaism had 'not been from any want of a wish to do his duty, but rather from an error of judgment'.[4] To Chambers himself, he wrote warmly to commend his 'zeal and activity' at the Pontarddulais clash, where even Rees Goring Thomas admitted he 'had done good service'.[5] While Chambers himself remained uneasy about its consequences, his peers felt they could now rely on him to do his duty against Rebecca. In this spirit, Trevor wrote to Chambers, again, about Shoni Sguborfawr, who was now firmly on his radar – even if Trevor often found the spelling of his sobriquet a struggle and had taken at face value the assumption that his Merthyr origins equalled militant politics:

> We hear to-day 'Scuborfawr' – a great rascal we sent our Police after, is off into the district of Llanelly; he is the ringleader, they say in Llanon district and a Merthyr Chartist. I wish you could pick him up; there is an assault warrant out against him, and he can be held on another, as I hear, for poaching.[6]

At around the same time, on the road just outside Cardigan, Joseph Downes was looking forward to settling down for the night. When he left the disturbed districts behind a few days later, the essay Downes delivered to *Blackwood's* magazine from the relative safety of Builth was not free of sentiment and romance, including a sneaking sympathy for the rebel thrill of what Rebeccaism had wrought, although Downes performatively chided himself for succumbing to it. Recalling his first experience of not having to pay the three-pence toll at a ruined gate, Downes confessed to 'a certain scandalous pleasure.' He remembered idly fingering the unspent coins in his pocket and musing:

> I defy any man—Aristides Redivivus himself, to ride toll free through, or rather over, a turnpike defunct in this manner, and not feel ... a sort of slyly triumphing satisfaction, spite of himself, as of a dog that gets his adversary undermost; in short—without becoming for the moment, under the Circean chink of the saved 'coppers', a rank Rebeccaite! The Lord and the law forgive me, for I surely loved 'Becca at heart at that moment! If the casual saving of a toll could thus operate upon ME, who should, perhaps, never pass there again, can it be wondered at that farmers, to whom this triumph must prove a great annual gain, are Rebeccaites to the backbone, and to a man?[7]

The experience of events surrounding Sarah Williams's death, however, had considerably dampened Downes's outlaw enthusiasm, and he had spent the previous day's ride from Hendy to Cardigan muttering in outrage to his son about the verdict given by the 'assassin jury'. He had then been startled to hear a voice, rising out of the darkness on the road behind them, asking whether Downes had the same sympathy for those arrested after Pontarddulais:

> [A] voice behind asked in English, saucily, if I was going to attend the future trial of the 'Hugheses, and them of the Llanon village, then in Swansea jail?' The tone clearly indicated how alien to the Welshman's feelings were those I was expressing, though but those of common humanity. Giving the voice in the dark such short answer, refusing to

satisfy him, as the question deserved, and with responsive bluffness, we left the man behind ...[8]

Unfortunately for Downes, when he eventually found a bed for the night in an inn at a Cardiganshire crossroads, he discovered the downstairs parlour was crowded with farmers, whose conversation fell suspiciously silent as he entered. Retreating to his room upstairs, he heard the volume of chatter in Welsh rise again, and thought he recognised the voice of his heckler on the road. His suspicions increased when he heard several of the men leaving the inn to fire off guns in the front yard beneath his window. Making sure he had secured his door, Downes fell into an unsettled sleep, broken at intervals until two in the morning by the continuing oratory and argument downstairs.

BLOOD AND BROTHERHOOD

In this strained atmosphere, the Stag and Pheasant gang were stepping up their activities to a degree that left even some of their own members unsettled. Shoni had moved on to instructing any Englishman employed locally to leave the country on pain of death, which Dai expressed his disapproval of but made no move to stop. After their involvement in yet another arson attack on William Chambers Junior's hayricks on a Sunday morning in late September, one of the group also shot one of Chambers's horses. The unfortunate animal was then stuck with a knife and its blood used as a 'sacrament', with the men in the party dipping in their hands as a sign of commitment to the gang's actions.

Shoni wasn't present on this occasion, but had he been, his fondness for animals might have led him to frown on proceedings. It was difficult to make out the rationale behind this arresting act of blood-brothership; customs like the *ceffyl pren* and Mari Lwyd showed that the horse had a particular cultural significance in that part of Wales – some even connected Rebecca's customary appearance on a white horse with the *Mabinogion's* mythical figure of Rhiannon – but horses were more prosaically and, above all, at the time, economically valuable animals. At any rate, Dai related the ritual glibly after the event, describing the dawn raid on Chambers's hayfield as 'a little jaunt' to an acquaintance he met returning from chapel later that morning.[9]

During the attack, however, Dai had himself become uneasy – or so he claimed in a later confession – and had implored the group not to use guns on a Sabbath morning. On seeing that a field of corn was about to be set ablaze, he had, again, protested, urging his men to desist by snapping 'for God's sake do not burn the corn as it is food for man'.[10] While previous, and more official, Rebeccas had been able to keep their 'daughters' in check during attacks, the loose group of anarchic freelancers that Shoni and Dai had set in motion were proving more difficult to control. This kind of spectacular but senseless destruction, a far cry from the justified targets of earlier in the summer, also wasn't quite what some of Dai and Shoni's more sober followers had signed up for. A few of them now began looking for a way to extricate themselves, even if it meant going to the authorities.

William Chambers Junior himself, having tolerated several attacks on his property, along with warning notes to his tenants that they risked their own houses being set on fire due to their association with him, and threats to his own life becoming increasingly open and direct, wasn't sure he could rely on either his fellow gentry or the military for protection. In the silence of an emptied Llanelly House, with the servants' wing now the only source of either activity or companionship, Chambers could think of only one association left to turn to. He began a plaintive note to the board of the Oddfellows fraternity, asking for their help in rallying his own blood-brothers 'who would not desert me in an hour of need'.[11]

The Oddfellows were one of several 'friendly societies' formed in the seventeenth and eighteenth centuries to provide support for their membership of craftsmen and tradesmen in cases of illness, injury or death – another thread in the era's network of mutual aid.

209

Unlike trade unions, they operated legally and with little attempted interference from the authorities – some of whom, like Chambers, were members themselves. And in Wales their attitude towards Rebeccaism, like that of the local chapels, had so far been a mixture of official censure and unofficial indifference. In his letter, Chambers appealed to them to contact their lodges in Carmarthenshire, Cardiganshire, Pembrokeshire and Glamorganshire – all counties now under the sway of Rebecca – and ask them to use their influence to denounce the kind of criminality that he feared was overtaking the movement. He went on to show how serious the situation was: 'Except in the town itself, under the influence of the military, we are in a state almost bordering on civil war.'[12]

CRACKDOWN

While the presence of the military in Llanelli might have been keeping things calm, in Carmarthen it was doing the opposite. On 16 September, a Saturday evening, Guildhall Square was still thronged with marketgoers and buzzing with conversation as people gathered in knots between the market stalls to talk over recent events. Their lively discussion took in proceedings at both Hendy and Pontarddulais, the condition of the prisoners in Swansea, and the recent reductions in the supply of coal, candles and soap to the paupers at the town's workhouse.

It wasn't a good atmosphere for the tense and overworked police, under orders to prevent people congregating in public, to attempt to break up the crowds and send them home. At around half-past nine, an elderly woman was singled out by a local constable and told to stop talking and move on. When she responded angrily to this, he pushed her backwards, with his own uncertain steps suggesting he might be drunk on duty. His action drew the indignation of those around the pair, one of whom retaliated on the old woman's behalf by knocking the policeman to the ground.

So far, this scuffle wasn't anything radically different from the usual street theatre that Carmarthen marketplace saw on Saturday night. But a handful of other police, tearing their eyes away from the scene, had rushed to the Lion Hotel where Colonel Love and George Rice Trevor were meeting. They claimed to the pair that they couldn't keep the peace without military assistance. Alarmed at the size of the crowd they saw gathering in the marketplace, many of whom were being drawn there merely out of curiosity about the initial disturbance, Trevor and Love were anxious that the scene might descend into another riot. Without consulting the town's magistrates or mayor, they ordered out the military to clear the streets 'in any manner that they thought proper'.[13]

What happened next displayed almost a mirror-image of the town authorities' former attitude to military intervention, which had seen them ready to rescind control in exchange for protection against the people. The local magistrate James Morse, who had previously hailed the dragoons' arrival from the window of Carmarthen workhouse, now feared that their presence on the streets would look like an unnecessary provocation. He was present when the troops were called out by Trevor, and later recalled the man being 'much excited' and giving no answer to Morse's protests that this was the wrong course to pursue.[14]

It was, in any case, too late. The infantry, with fixed bayonets, advanced into the marketplace, followed by a group of dragoons on horseback, 'flourishing their swords as if they had gone cracked'.[15] Forcing their way through Guildhall Square and up to King Street, they sent the crowd scrambling and then moved through the town chaotically clearing the streets, evacuating shops, knocking over market stalls and scattering their produce on the ground. The town's mayor – who was only alerted to the military being called out when he saw them galloping past his window with drawn swords – wandered the streets for the whole of the night until dawn on Sunday, imploring anyone he saw to stay calm and keep the peace.

This had been a huge overreaction, strongly criticised afterwards by Carmarthen's civic authorities, but it reflected both Love and Trevor's increasingly hardline position and the volatility on the ground. Their defence was that they were preventing a riot, but there had been no potential riot to prevent. Although the military had inflicted no injuries, the point was more that they had seemed not to care if they did. James Morse, at a subsequent meeting of the magistrates, was still incensed by the scenes he had witnessed: 'Was this a fitting time for Dragoons to ride over people, for swords to be brandished over people's heads, for officers of troops to ride into shops and order people out at an early hour of the night?'[16]

A public meeting was scheduled to censure both the magistrates and the military, despite the former's rush to reassure people that they had had nothing to do with the actions of the latter. This might have absolved them of responsibility in this instance, but it also suggested the weakness of their authority in general. A committee of magistrates demanded to know whether the regional capital 'was to be governed by the Mayor and magistrates or by the military'[17] – was Carmarthen, in fact, under martial law already?

PART FIVE:

'WE ARE ALL OF US REBECCAS'

19
'BECCA THERE IS NOW DEAD'

DÉTENTE

By the end of September, George Rice Trevor's policy of bringing in more and more troops and policemen was at last producing an effect, less through any deliberate strategy than through sheer weight of numbers. Perhaps regretting their failure to take the previous demands of the magistrates seriously, the government now flooded south-west Wales with police and soldiers, and, by mid-autumn, an occupying network of over 2,000 troops and police had almost paralysed the three counties. One absentee landowner expressed dismay at coming back to Wales from abroad to find 'all the little towns filled with troops'. In early October, Trevor appointed twenty new magistrates and sought to cram even more soldiers into Carmarthenshire. He wrote to local magistrates seeking lodgings for them and encouraged the local authorities to use the military for back-up – heedless of the dangerous overreaction this tactic had just produced in Carmarthen's marketplace.

In Thomas Campbell Foster's opinion, the fact that things seemed to be quietening down was due more 'to the close manner in which the people are watched, than to any change of feeling among them'.[1] But Rebeccaism was seeing a certain change in strategy, too. The meetings that Foster attended throughout the late autumn of 1843, still relaying their proceedings meticulously in his reports for *The Times*, saw fewer fiery demands and more interminable discussion on bureaucracy and administration. Meetings took place between magistrates and the public at which the trusts' accounts were pored over and found wanting – some were near bankruptcy and many were unable to account for where the revenue from tolls had gone. There was a sheepish admission from the local authorities of the many petty injustices that had occurred under both the tollgate system and the new system of poor relief, but examining them had become a dull matter of combing through regulations and account-books – and any intention to officially change them was not yet in sight.

Other mass meetings continued, in daylight, with crowds often tramping through the season's torrential rain and ankle-deep mud to attend. Most of them ended by resolving to petition the Queen against the tollgates and the Poor Law, asking her to 'Dissolve the pretend Parliament'.[2] They were appealing now to national authority rather than taking direct action themselves. This somewhat appeased the magistrates, who were content to look at reducing or abolishing tolls and even lowering tithes, and to leave the rest to Parliament – in exchange for a cessation of night-time meetings and the Rebeccaite outrages that tended to follow.

This was a bargain an increasing number of farmers were happy to strike. In between the regular complaints about tolls and tithes, they also began to condemn attacks on private property and the homes of the gentry, agreeing that 'Rebecca' had gone too far. Farmers at Tir-fran even took part in rebuilding a local tollgate. The gentry were also beginning to compromise: at Llechryd, the landowner who had constructed the weir that cut off access to salmon, first ripped up a Rebecca letter he had received warning him to not repair it, but then agreed to give up his lease on the weir. The gathered crowd drew his carriage back to his house, cheering and assuring him that 'Becca there is now dead'.[3]

Such heartwarming conclusions were not repeated everywhere. At one meeting, Rees Goring Thomas held up a copy of the address circulated in Penboyr in which 'Rebecca' urged farmers to collectively petition their landlords for rent reductions. He denounced it as seeking to impose 'a system of terror and threat' and tore it into pieces.[4] Although this meeting resolved to petition the Queen to dissolve parliament, the landed interest now appealed to the farmers to join with them in suppressing any further demands by Rebecca in exchange for taking up their grievances. National authority was looked to at the expense of reinstating the local status quo.

In Radnorshire, the MP John Walsh met with Carmarthen's archdeacon and hatched a plan to ask 'gentlemen freeholders or respectable farmers' to sign a declaration condemning acts of violence, in favour of 'proper modes of representing, and obtaining redress for any real grievances'. A subsequent meeting, however, attracted only two people willing to sign – one a freeholder and the other a bank clerk. Walsh stumped home glumly and concluded in his journal that 'the meeting was not very satisfactory. Without help from without nothing can be done'.[5]

Help from without, however, was gradually filtering in, particularly as financial pressure was brought to bear from various angles. The Home Secretary sanctioned George Rice Trevor's request for fines to be given to those refusing to be sworn in as special constables. At the same time, a Royal Proclamation, signed by Victoria herself, was issued, offering rewards of up to £500 for the arrest of Rebeccaites, along with smaller awards for information which entailed immunity from prosecution if an informant had been personally involved. As always, and especially in a poverty-stricken country, money talked.

REBECCA MOVES HOUSE

But as relative calm began to descend on Carmarthenshire, Pembrokeshire and Cardiganshire, magistrates in neighbouring Radnorshire and Brecknockshire could no longer deny that Rebecca was now at home in their counties. Early October saw the first attack on a tollgate at Brecon, while three gates at Rhayader were taken down in a single night. A public notice from the Radnorshire authorities, issued while more specials were being sworn in, was notably conciliatory, indicating perhaps that John Walsh and other magistrates there had learned from the course of events elsewhere. They acknowledged the impact of the economic crisis even while condemning the 'lawless attacks' on tollgates:

While we are determined to enforce the law, we are at the same time desirous of giving every consideration to all reasonable complaints. We are aware that the depressed state of agriculture renders the burden of maintaining the roads in repair peculiarly heavy at the present moment, and we shall afford our anxious and immediate attention to the best means of alleviating and equalizing these burthens as far as is practicable.[6]

And even in Carmarthenshire, Rebecca was still managing to assert her authority. At Pwll-Trap near St Clears, the scene of one of Rebecca's earliest victories, a tollhouse was still standing, now empty and abandoned. On a Thursday night, despite the presence of a detachment of dragoons in the town, a hundred-strong procession of Rebeccaites called at the dilapidated house of James Thomas, an impoverished amputee. They told him 'he had lived for a long time in a poor cottage, and he should have a better residence'. Packing up the family's furniture and loading it onto a cart, they conveyed the somewhat baffled Thomas and his wife to the unoccupied tollhouse, telling them to make it their new home – on condition of not taking any tolls. The crowd then went to the house of a local magistrate and pinned an uncompromising notice to his doorpost:

> I beg that Rebecca gave possession to James John [Thomas] of the house that was formerly belong to Pwll-trap gate, and if any person will come and throw him out, Rebecca will and her children will remember him in future time, the first that will come there, shall be dragged between four horses.[7]

They then gave a copy of the notice to the town crier along with four shillings, instructing him to proclaim the news locally. The local writer Henry Tobit Evans, recording these events in a book published in 1910, claimed that the same family were still in possession of the tollhouse several decades later.

Other Rebecca actions at this point, however, were veering off-course from their usual tightly organised and disciplined form. During an attack on a tollgate at Prendergast, the night's 'Rebecca' told her followers to wait while she went ahead of them to scout for any military presence, temporarily shedding her bonnet and gun and leaving one of her 'daughters' in charge. On returning to an abandoned clearing, she found that her second in command had usurped the leadership role, picking up the abandoned bonnet and leading the crowd on to attack the gate by another route – and, as it transpired, straight into a clash with police.

At Tir-y-pound farm later in the autumn, a bailiff called on Phillip Phillip and his son to serve him papers for overdue rent. The farmer retorted that when the bailiff returned to execute the warrant, 'the mother and her children would be there to meet them'. Sure enough, when two bailiffs returned, at a signal from Phillip dozens of Rebeccaites emerged from the adjoining farm buildings. They were led by a tall man with a cloak over his work-clothes and his face disguised with a false beard, described by the bailiff as 'similar to a goat's beard'. They demanded the warrant papers from one bailiff and burnt them in front of him.[8]

But as 'Rebecca' stood close to the flames, fear descended into farce as the glue of the false beard became unstuck and the whole thing slipped off his face. The bailiff now recognised this Rebecca as William Harries, a local blacksmith, and was able to identify him in court where both he and the Phillipses were charged with riot and assault. The jury acquitted Harries, but one more Rebecca had been conclusively unmasked.

DOWNFALL

While beards were becoming unglued, so was the commitment of labourers to their work for Rebecca. The greater danger from the vastly increased numbers of police and soldiers was making labourers think twice about doing tollgate demolition work for farmers. William Chambers was told by a tenant in late September that a farmer and collier in his neighbourhood had been overheard arguing, the collier saying: 'Damn you, do you think I will go out to be shot for you for two shillings and sixpence a-night any more?'[9] On the other hand, some farmers were tiring of paying the two shillings and sixpence due to Rebecca on pain of having their own hayricks fired.

Significantly, too, the movement's anonymity and immunity from prosecution was beginning to break down. The judge at Phillip Phillip's trial had said that the defendants had:

> availed yourselves of the disturbances in the country – of the heat and excitement which then reigned predominant in men's minds – men who went prowling about reckless of order and of disgrace, assuming names which have become a bye-word of alarm and violence.[10]

He could equally well have been referring to Shoni and Dai, who were still at large in the outskirts of Llanelli. On 25 September, warrants for the arrest of both men were taken from the magistrates to the London police stationed at Pontyberem, but they couldn't yet be acted on without evidence. The authorities were prepared to use strong-arm methods to obtain it. The bearer of the warrants, William Francis, was instructed to 'use his best endeavours to obtain further evidence'. He subsequently had a long and intense conversation with Thomas Philips of Topsail, who eventually, on condition of his own name not being publicly mentioned, disclosed the names of several others he claimed to be involved in Rebeccaism: among them were Shoni and Dai.

A few days later, Francis accompanied the London police to Gwendraeth and began searching for the pair, dispatching underlings in various directions to scour the local pubs. At around 7 o'clock, Dai was sighted at the Stag and Pheasant, and followed as he headed to another pub nearby, the Plough and Harrow. Too impatient to wait for news of Shoni, three officers were placed at the pub's back door and Francis made his way to the fireside corner where Dai sat. Seized and handcuffed, Dai was taken into custody at Llanelli workhouse.

The next day, as Dai was taken to a cell at Carmarthen jail, Shoni was arrested at another pub at Tumble, just east of Pontyberem where his Rebeccaite journey had begun. Seated on the pub's settee with a gun loaded at his side, he was pinned down and handcuffed before he quite realised what was happening. As more police rushed into the room he fought back, trying to grab his gun in shackled hands, to no avail.

At Carmarthen jail the two were interrogated by George Rice Trevor and a clutch of magistrates, with the radical lawyer Hugh Williams having dashed there to act in their defence. Shoni protested that he had not been 'sent for any particular purpose' to the area, but simply 'came to work' – including for his arresting magistrate, the Swansea industrialist Richard Nevill.[11] Significantly, Shoni's arrest was on charges of general affray and assault, usually involving threatening people with guns, and not for destroying tollgates. Nonetheless, his capture was presented as the decisive taking of 'Rebecca'. The local press, describing Shoni as 'a very lawless and desperate sort of fellow of great physical strength', concluded rather ambiguously that: 'He is known to have led many of the gate-breaking expeditions, though there is no evidence of it.'[12]

Meanwhile, many of the pair's worried associates went to ground and swore each other to silence. Others weighed up the rewards and 'refreshment' on offer from the authorities in exchange for giving evidence. For some, this proved an irresistible lure. Seventeen people were paid and given food and drink for making statements against Shoni and Dai at Carmarthen on Saturday 30 October, and a further nineteen the following Thursday.

One of these was Thomas Philips, the workman who had turned informer on condition of anonymity, and who had also been the man to originally propose William Chambers's assassination at the Stag and Pheasant. The authorities had never seemed competent enough to employ agent provocateurs, and Philips was no doubt simply shifting with the prevailing winds of power, but his behaviour was enough to draw suspicion from at least one of his acquaintances, who cornered him a few days later during Llanelli cattle fair. Philips said of the encounter:

> I was in the shop of Mr. Jno. Bowen, Grocer, Llanelly, and David Thomas, son of the tenant of Cilferryucha beckoned me out. I went out and he asked me how I had suffered Dai Cantwr to be taken at the Plough 7 days before. I said I could not help it, there were so many Policemen there. He said 'I don't know in the world what will come of it now, they will have the burning and all out.' ... I advised him to go round the parties and tell them of it and call a meeting and contrive the best way to get out of it for it was a bad job. He said that he would do so and left me for the purpose immediately.[13]

20
FROM LAWBREAKERS TO LEGENDS

FRIENDS IN HIGH PLACES

As October 1843 drew to a close, Jac Ty Isha and his comrades were still in Swansea jail awaiting trial, but the movement in which they had taken part was already approaching legendary status. The media and political attention given to Rebeccaism meant that the events had by now become a kind of spectator sport. Readers of *The Times* and other national and international newspapers avidly kept up with the latest exploits of 'Rebecca', and, even in supposedly straight-laced Victorian society, individuals had begun using Rebecca's guise for both political and personal self-expression.

Across the country, letters to the press were continuing from people wishing, with varying degrees of seriousness, that Rebecca would pay a visit to the tollgates in their own neighbourhood. In London, porters at University College were sent a 'Rebecca letter' threatening to remove the wooden toll-bar across Gower Street, along with other 'public obstructions'.[1] Assuming the letter was a student prank, they ignored it, but the gate was duly filed off its hinges and later discovered hidden in bushes in the college grounds. Meanwhile in Shropshire, an inhabitant of Ludlow named John Archer caused a stir by wearing women's clothing to evening service at church. While Archer may not have intended to impersonate Rebecca specifically, the local paper's account of the reprimand given in court for this escapade referred to Archer as 'Miss Rebecca'.[2] Evidence given at the trial of the ninth Earl Ferrers, for breaching a promise of marriage, also referred – with no further elaboration – to his habit of dressing up 'after the fashion of the tollgate breakers'. According to the statement of a friend, after dinner the Earl 'used to put a night-cap over his whiskers, and tie his pocket handkerchief over his hat, and then he used to go out at night'.[3]

In early October, a play called *Rebecca and her Daughters, or, Paddy the Policeman* was staged at Liverpool's Royal Amphitheatre. It was set in 'Ponty Puddle', and from the playbill's synopsis of the action, it seemed – for once – to paint the authorities in a more heroic light than the rioters:

> Vigilance of the civil and military authorities; £100 reward for the apprehension of Rebecca, and £10 for each of her daughters; False alarm; Invincible courage of the Yeomanry; Arrival of the London Police in disguise; Paddy Whack undertakes to capture the delinquents; Admonitions to the Constabulary; The inspection; Mysterious appearance of Rebecca and her daughters in the Glen of Llandilo, at midnight; Tried before the Justice of the Peace; Happy denouement.[4]

More earnestly, in November, a letter was published in *The Times* from Thomas Attwood, who as MP for Birmingham had presented the first Chartist petition to the House of Commons in 1839. Although a radical of the moral-force persuasion, Attwood saw Rebeccaism, along with the pro-independence unrest in Ireland, as heralding a threat to the British state itself, the reasons behind which required urgent addressing to avoid turning out as seriously as their historical precedents had:

> Undoubtedly the proceedings in Ireland and in Wales are mere symptoms of a great organic disease. They are the mere mutterings of the thunder of the public wrath, directed against legislative unions and turnpike-gates to-day, but which, under our present system, may probably be exhibited in one deadly and universal war against rents, Customhouses, and Excise-offices, to-morrow. Louis XVI was dancing in a ball at Versailles at the very moment when the towers of the Bastille were trembling over his throne. Charles X was hunting in the woods of Fontainebleau when

Marshal Marmont galloped up to him with the terrible words, 'Sire, it is not a riot, but a revolution' ... These premonitory symptoms are now visible in every quarter of the British empire. Woe unto the statesmen who may disregard them.[5]

A few weeks before the letter's publication, the government had in fact taken its first belated step towards seriously attempting to grasp the reasons behind Rebeccaism. At the end of October Thomas Frankland Lewis, a former MP who owned land on the borders of Radnorshire, arrived in Carmarthen along with two other MPs and a host of administrative staff. They were there to begin a Royal Commission, reporting to the government on what really lay behind the unrest. Lewis and his fellow commissioners – Robert Henry Clive, MP for South Shropshire and second son of the earl of Powis, and William Cripps, a barrister and MP for Cirencester – would spend the next seven weeks touring south Wales and taking statements from those who appeared before them.

REBECCA ON TRIAL

This national public attention meant that the first major trial of Rebeccaite prisoners was also a media event. Opening on the day after the Royal Commissioners had arrived in Carmarthen, the trial of Jac Ty Isha and his fellow rioters was held at Cardiff rather than in Rebecca's country, and squeezed into the judicial schedule by extraordinary special commission rather than waiting for the next Spring Assizes. It also had a jury composed of gentlemen and tradesmen from Cardiff and Merthyr with, in particular, no farmers allowed. These efforts to avoid a sympathetic jury had not prevented a number of jurymen still refusing to serve, raising suspicions that threats from those still loyal to Rebecca had made their way to them.

Cardiff's links with the industrial Valleys were already developing as iron and coal streamed out of the country through its docks, but the place had much less to do with the world of Rebecca. It would be another century before Cardiff would be made the capital of Wales, and in 1843 it was still beginning its dramatic growth from a small market town on the banks of the river Taff to a flourishing city of railways, colleges and intricate shopping arcades. In the middle of Cardiff's high street, presenting a constant hazard to the flow of carts and carriages, sat a town hall built on similar lines to Carmarthen's, with assembly rooms and a courthouse upstairs and a marketplace and jail cells below. Outside it stood a set of stocks – now largely disused – as well as the gallows where Dic Penderyn, the young martyr of the Merthyr Rising, had swung in the summer of 1831.

On Wednesday 25 October, a sea of supporters, reporters and spectators filled the streets and lapped against the town hall's walls. Mid-morning traffic backed up along the high street as the trial's government-appointed judges arrived, guarded by a detachment of London police and escorted by several carriages of the local gentry, all of whom were eager to watch the proceedings. The trial opened at 11 o'clock that morning, when to the irritation of onlookers the court was immediately adjourned until after lunch. At 2 o'clock, it reconvened to try the Pontarddulais Three.

In the cells beneath the courthouse, the Chartist lawyer Hugh Williams was giving the prisoners a final word of counsel. He recommended a plea of guilty, both to riot and to Jac Ty Isha's additional charge of shooting at Captain Napier – who was currently waiting to give evidence in the courtroom – with intent to kill. The group were ushered upstairs where Jac, with his shattered arm still in a sling, dismayed his lawyer and thrilled his audience by pleading not guilty on all charges. The prosecution's evidence then rested on proving Jac's participation in the riot at Pontarddulais, which in turn hinged on his having come dressed in Rebeccaite costume. The prosecution held forth:

Capt. Napier ... will describe to you the prisoners' dress ... 'a white loose dress about him, a straw hat and his face blackened ...Two other persons were taken – one had a straw hat tied down, his coat turned, and his face blackened …The third man had a piece of fern stuck in his hat … [Another] was dressed in a Druid's dress, a white gown, with blue sleeves.'

The evidence … left no doubt of the prisoner's participation in the riot. It was clear that he was there disguised – that he wore a sort of dress which was produced in court – his face blackened. Was that not sufficient to shew that the prisoner formed part of the mob? If his presence there was accidental, he would not have been there disguised.[6]

The jury found Jac guilty on all counts, but recommended mercy on account of his otherwise spotless character. But the sentence handed down by the judge was transportation for twenty years – equating to one year for every minute the jury had spent deliberating. John Hugh and David Jones, having taken Hugh Williams's advice to attract leniency by pleading guilty, nonetheless received a sentence of seven years' transportation each.

The harshness of the judgement shocked the courtroom and was rapidly transmitted to the equally incredulous crowds outside. As the news made its way back to Rebecca's country, mass sympathy for the three convicted men swelled into huge public meetings. In the days that followed, petitions flooded in to the Queen to reduce Jac's sentence in particular – one of them sent by ten members of the same jury which had found him guilty. His mother also personally petitioned Victoria, while his father led a deputation of 300 farmers to meet with William Chambers Junior, whom they begged to intervene in his capacity as a local magistrate. By this point Chambers's sympathy for the movement was running low, and he pointed out in his refusal to get involved that no one had yet been brought to book for the killing of Sarah Williams at Hendy. The scales of justice might not be fair, but in his view they were balanced.

After the Pontarddulais rioters had received their sentences, Daniel Lewis and the Morgan family were expecting the worst when their trials commenced later the same day. The Morgans, having already entered a plea of guilty to assaulting Captain

Napier and his inspector, crowded together in the dock to hear the verdict. They were cautiously relieved to hear that the charges of assault had been dropped and replaced with the less serious one of misdemeanour. The reasoning behind this was that the family had resisted Henry Morgan's arrest in the mistaken but understandable belief that making an arrest on the Sabbath was illegal. This didn't prevent the two sons being sentenced to twelve months in prison and their sister to six, but their parents, on account of their age and previous good character, were allowed to go free.

By the time Daniel Lewis took the stand along with five other rioters for the attack at Bolgoed, Captain Napier was looking frustrated. He explained to the court that his only witness for the prosecution, Daniel's love rival John Jones, had absconded and was unable to be found. In his absence, the trial was adjourned to the spring.

FIVE SHILLINGS A DAY

A few weeks later in Carmarthen's courtroom, Shoni and Dai stood in the dock, together with the Stag and Pheasant's landlord William Walters and their associate Thomas Morris. While Walters was cleared of the charge of riot, and Morris, pleading guilty, was released on condition of good behaviour, Shoni was sentenced to transportation for life and Dai for twenty years. They received the verdict in silence, and then shared a defiant round of laughter as they were taken down to the cells.

This brotherly bravado lasted around a week, at the end of which the pair sent a letter to William Chambers Junior requesting a meeting. He spent several hours with them at the house of the prison governor, where they confessed to even more than they had been charged with, spilling details of arson and assaults as well as of the organisation and meetings they had been involved with. They offered the names of accomplices – many of whom were respectable farmers, publicans and shopkeepers. They also confirmed the accuracy of the rumoured threats by local colliers after the Pontarddulais arrests to 'undermine the road, and to blow up the Dragoons as they passed along it', saying that the action had only not occurred for lack of a suitable opportunity.

While Dai, still a poet at heart, had begun work from his cell on a threnody or lamentation poem which he called his 'farewell song', Shoni had been in touch with some old friends: the Brecknockshire MP Thomas Wood, who had employed him as a special constable and informant, and James Brown, an ironmaster at Blaina who had known him for twenty-five years. Both men wrote to Chambers to plead for mitigation on Shoni's behalf. Brown claimed that Shoni 'had been made the willing scapegoat of others' and that he, 'being fond of prize-fighting and its concomitant evils was never a sticker to his work but at bottom he was possessed of parts and feelings very different from men who usually follow the course of life he had been leading'.[7]

In his own defence, when speaking to Chambers, Shoni referred with cynical realism to the amount of money that had been coming his way under his and Dai's Rebeccaite protection racket. This was far more, he reasoned, than would have been available to him, or any man like him, through honest labour: 'What a fool I should have been to give up so good a trade when I could get my five shillings a day by it, and that much more easily than when at my own work.'[8]

None of it made a difference to his sentence, with George Rice Trevor particularly concerned to not display anything that might be seen as mercy towards either him or Dai. The two were dispatched from Carmarthen to London, there to await their transportation overseas.

Further east in the Welsh coalfield, Jac Ty Isha was finding sympathy from an unexpected quarter. Lady Charlotte Bertie, the eldest child of an impoverished aristocratic family from Lincolnshire, had already shocked her relatives and London society a decade earlier when she married John Josiah Guest, master of the huge ironworks at Dowlais in Merthyr. His being almost thirty years older than her caused less dismay in genteel drawing-rooms than did his position in trade,

his Dissenting religion and of course his Welshness, but the couple
proved surprisingly well matched. Charlotte had immersed herself in
the history and culture of her new home, helping to run her husband's
business, making friends with local radicals like Dr William Price,
and learning Welsh – enough for her to make everyday conversation
with her husband's employees and to publish an English translation
of the *Mabinogion*. By 1843 she had weathered both threats to the
Dowlais works from the Scotch Cattle and the upheaval around the
Newport Rising while maintaining a measure of sympathy for the
local working population – though this was very much based on her
conviction that the workers in her husband's employ were 'good and
true', and even the local Chartists more reassuringly deferential than
the 'rabble of Birmingham'.[9]

When Jac Ty Isha was sentenced by the Grand Jury on which her
husband sat, Lady Charlotte dabbed her eyes and wrote of Jac as
'my poor Welsh rebel with all his faults and all his grievances and
all his romance'.[10] In December, her husband John was a passenger
on the same steam-packet that carried the transported Rebeccaites
on the first leg of their journey to a holding cell in London, and Jac
Ty Isha, discovering this, asked to speak with him. Although Guest
advised Jac to '[be] as quiet and [give] as little trouble as possible',
the two men held what Charlotte later recorded in her journal as
'an interesting conversation', colouring the report with some of her
own romantic projection:

> The poor man entered into a long statement of the agricultural
> grievances of his neighbourhood which appeared to be
> very great. He had not, however, very enlightened views
> on any subject, which is scarcely to be wondered at when
> it is considered that this, his convict journey, was the first
> occasion of his ever going beyond the limits of his own little
> parish of Llanon. His astonishment at first seeing a ship, or
> steamer, is said to have been very great, and his perplexities
> on the Railway at the train moving without horses quite
> unassuageable. 'Steam?' asked he. 'What is steam?' Under

all this excitement his spirits kept up bravely until he arrived in town and was shown the place of his confinement. 'What, in that little narrow hole? Why, it was impossible to live in that!' And his heart seemed at once to be crushed within him and every hope extinguished. Well might the free child of the mountain shudder and sicken at the sight of that cold and narrow cell![11]

Thus, individual Rebeccaites, standing in for the movement as a whole, were becoming immortalised. Their stories were absorbed into the sympathetic, if patronising accounts of benevolent paternalists like Charlotte Guest as much as the political economy of Thomas Attwood, as well as the more sensationalist or comic depictions of Rebeccaism now appearing in print and on stages across the country as the story appeared to be reaching its end. But the story was, at least, one that had been told and shaped by ordinary Welsh people themselves. Rather than passive and picturesque background colour in other people's tourist narratives, they had emerged as main characters, whether heroes or villains, in a narrative of their own.

These various impressions of the movement remained behind as the handful of men who had – rightly or wrongly – become its figureheads were sent out of the country. From Cardiff and Carmarthen they were taken to Bristol, then to London and then to the penal colony of Tasmania. British colonialism had begun here in 1803, making its mark through wars of extermination against the Aboriginal population, and by 1843 only a few survivors remained. During those forty years, Tasmania – known until 1856 as Van Diemen's Land – had also been receiving tens of thousands of convicts who could no longer fit into Britain's overcrowded prison system. Once there, they were set to work building infrastructure, mining and farming for the state and private landowners.

Back in Wales, the fate of those convicted and transported seemed to offer a tragic – or, for the authorities, a satisfying – end to the story of Rebecca's rebellion. But the events they had set in motion hadn't yet quite run their course.

21
THROWING OPEN THE BOOKS

THE VOYAGE OF THE COMMISSION OF INQUIRY

When Thomas Campbell Foster arrived back in Carmarthen, still finishing off his report for *The Times* on the outcome of the Cardiff trials, he raced immediately to Guildhall Square where the government's Commission of Inquiry was in session at the town hall. But, just as had happened five months earlier when he tried to access a magistrates' meeting after the Carmarthen workhouse riot, he found the doors were barred to the press – partly, he learned, on the grounds that witnesses might be tempted to say sensationalist but unsupported stuff to get their names in the papers. He had to be content with loitering in the square outside the building to observe as the day's deputations were seen.

While the county's leading gentry and magistrates, including William Chambers Junior and George Rice Trevor, arrived alone, either in silent composure or bursting with self-important bluster, farmers and labourers trooped under the lintel in large groups, a designated spokesman at their head, the others crowding in behind him to listen carefully and interject at points to ensure no item on their list of collected grievances would be left untouched. Between them came other women and men of all walks of life, including those connected with the trusts – surveyors and contractors as well as the 'toll-farmers', shifting nervously as they recognised copies of their own account-books laid out on the table before the commissioners.

From vox-popping those who filed back out into the pale autumn sunlight from the darkened committee rooms, variously elated, shrewdly sceptical or simply dazed with disbelief after finally having their opinions listened to, Foster got some sense of how the commissioners operated: taking statements, asking questions, cross-referencing the testimony of different individuals, and examining the account-books and other papers of the trusts and the reports of civic authorities and the military officials stationed in the area. As the interviews proceeded, translators switched between English and Welsh, while a small army of clerks scrambled to get down in their dense shorthand everything that was said. Sometimes the interviews began with open-ended questions like 'What do you wish to say to the commissioners?' or 'What complaint have you to make?', which could leave ordinary people open-mouthed as, feeling somewhat spoilt for choice, they were unsure where to begin. At other times, however, the commissioners only wanted information or opinions on a particular issue – usually the turnpike trusts or the New Poor Law – and would cut off any attempt to offer a more holistic analysis of the causes of the unrest.

The commissioners, for their part, often seemed surprised by much of what they heard. They were also surprised at the number of tollgates they had had to travel through to reach Carmarthen – even though this was a fraction of the number that had been there before Rebecca got to work. Why on earth, they asked, hadn't the magistrates intervened in the past few years to stop so many gates popping up on the same road, or to challenge the unfair charging of tolls for a cartload of lime or a single sack of potatoes? Wouldn't actions like these have stopped the past few months' regional rebellion in its tracks? The answers they received – that magistrates were often tollgate trustees themselves, and in any case favoured the trusts, or in some cases just hadn't taken much of an interest in other people's problems – seemed to baffle them further, as though they had found themselves transported back in time to a more blithely feudal era.

Despite having got many things off their chests, Foster's interviewees weren't hopeful about any change in the law beyond tollgates, such as action on tithes or rents or particularly on workhouses, despite having told the commissioners 'openly and warmly' their complaints about them. After all, they pointed out, Frankland Lewis had himself been overall chairman of the Poor Law commissioners until 1839, and his two fellow officials were also known to be supporters of the new system. One disgruntled contributor – a magistrate, no less – remarked to the reporter: 'The sooner you take a house here the better, for we shall give you enough to do in Wales to keep you here; and the Commissioners might as well go back again.'[1]

After spending eleven days taking evidence at Carmarthen, the commissioners moved on for shorter stays at Haverfordwest, Narberth, Newcastle Emlyn, Cardigan and Aberystwyth. Local magistrates and trustees were sent advance notice of the commission's arrival by post, expecting them to attend, and other people in the gentry's circles soon found out via local news and gossip. Ordinary people were meant to be made aware through newspaper advertisements and publicly circulated handbills, in which the commissioners invited 'any parties who may be desirous to come before them and make any statements respecting the administration of the turnpike laws and the causes which have led to the recent disturbances'.[2]

As things turned out, this wasn't an optimal system. Printed notices announcing the commission's arrival went out late, with incorrect timings or locations, and many sessions, because of these bungled logistics, had to be held in haste or without Welsh interpreters. In Newcastle Emlyn, where Foster had previously heard the complaints of a farmers' delegation of around 150, only a dozen or so were attending the official commission there. The reason was that the only public news of its arrival had been carried round the area by a single town crier on a rainy Friday night, while written announcements had been put up at short notice and in English only. The next day was a fair, at which several hundred farmers would be arriving, but by then the commissioners would be out of town and on the road to Cardigan. In the hills around Aberystwyth, people heard the news in good time, but some felt too intimidated at the prospect of making their way from their mud-thatched cottages to the plush coffee-room of the Belle Vue hotel on the seafront where the commissioners were ensconced. Others worried that appearing before the commission was a trap set to catch them as Rebeccaites, and stayed away in case their testimony ended with them being ushered into a police wagon.

This kind of confusion and suspicion, making it even harder for ordinary people to organise themselves to attend and present their problems, annoyed and frustrated the commissioners as much as anyone else. But at least as many people were able to overcome these difficulties, taking the day off work, putting on their Sunday-best waistcoats and jackets, and walking miles into the centre of town to have their say. In Haverfordwest, Narberth and Pembroke, farmers held meetings around a week in advance of the commission's arrival, writing down the views gathered and choosing a smaller group to present them, often reconvening later for their delegates to report back.

The commissioners then passed through Rhayader, Presteigne, Brecon, Llandeilo, Llanelli, Swansea, Bridgend and Cardiff, before finishing up at Merthyr Tydfil on 13 December. Over 10,000 questions had been asked in the course of their inquiries, and the information they obtained covered several hundred densely packed pages. But even before they set off back to London, it seemed as though their minds were already made up as to what needed to be done. Rather than any deeper overhaul of the political, social and economic system of the country, their preliminary findings had concluded that the tollgates were the thing to focus on. The tollgates had achieved the same symbolic importance for the commissioners that they had held for the rioters themselves, but without the same understanding that they were only a final straw and not the entire burden.

Thomas Campbell Foster, doggedly tracking the commissioners around south Wales from one town hall or hotel to the next, and taking the measure of those who went before them, grew increasingly irritated at the prospect of them recommending only superficial changes. He could be forgiven for some exasperation at the fact that the broader problems brought to light already by his own reports, and largely ignored by both local and national authorities, were now being repeated in the pages of the government's commission, but without any action to mitigate them being considered. In one of his final reports, he wrote: 'it is plain no legislative measure can easily be devised to remove the other grievances complained of – in fact, to remove general poverty.'[3]

MOPPING UP

By the end of 1843, there had been almost 300 attacks on tollgates, and the cost of damage done to the property of the trusts was estimated at £10,000. The intervention of a government commission, combined with an increasing police presence and the destabilising effect of the movement's internal tensions, was now dampening down both the number and intensity of disturbances in Rebeccaism's heartland. But elsewhere, the spark was continuing to catch. In November, the *Cambrian* newspaper reported:

> While we have to congratulate our readers on the discontinuance of the lawless proceedings of the Rebecccaites in the counties of Carmarthen, Pembroke and Cardigan, we regret to find, that in Radnorshire, they have commenced their work of destruction with much daring. About two o'clock on Friday last, Rebecca, with upwards of 200 individuals, all disguised, and well-armed with guns and other weapons, entered the streets of Rhyader, and proceeded direct to the respective turnpike gates, and in a very short space of time the north and cast gates, as well as the two recently-erected gates adjoining the bridge, with the posts, etc, were entirely erased to the ground.[4]

This incident also saw Rebeccaites, in the familiar garb of bonnets, cloaks and petticoats, engaging in a shoot-out with police on the bridge over the river Wye. In a subsequent action, another gate was sawn in two and thrown into the river by a fifty-strong group 'shouting "Becca for ever" and discharging firearms'.[5] In December, there were accounts from as far away as Anglesey of Rebeccaites assaulting bailiffs and taking back the property they had seized, and a tollgate on the Holyhead road was demolished with a note left 'informing the tollkeeper that the breach was committed by Sister Rebecca'.[6] Back in Radnorshire, John Walsh MP, after sourly recording 'a meeting of the magistrates, which nobody attended', was further annoyed to receive reports of a threatened attack on the workhouse at Knighton and actual attacks on bailiffs.

Incidents like these would carry on well into 1844, and Radnorshire would in fact be the scene, three decades later, of 'a second Rebecca riots' focused on the privatisation of fishing on the river Wye. But in Rebeccaism's immediate aftermath, these scattered attacks no longer formed part of any larger or coordinated protest movement. As November 1843's hiring fair approached, when farm servants left their year-long contracted service to larger farmers, this 'severing of old interests' was expected to inspire more informing on Rebeccaite farmers by servants and labourers, forced into petticoats, bonnets and sword-belts in the course of Rebeccaism, who now had no retribution to fear from their employers. There was at least one instance of this at Llanon, involving 'a young farmer, very respectably connected'.[7] When financial reward as well as personal satisfaction was on offer, the urge to inform was even greater, and by the following year George Rice Trevor's list of individuals to be paid for giving evidence leading to convictions for Rebeccaite activity stretched to fourteen pages of names.

With the movement's alleged ringleaders already severely dealt with at the showpiece trials in Cardiff, the authorities felt able to treat subsequent cases more leniently. The majority of Rebeccaite prisoners standing trial in early 1844 – including Daniel Lewis – were found not guilty, had their charges withdrawn, were released on condition of good behaviour, or received prison sentences of less than a year. Even John Harries of Talog, who was found guilty of being 'a ringleader, or at least a very active promoter' of the storming of Carmarthen workhouse, was given the relatively light sentence of twelve months' hard labour.[8] At the same trial two co-defendants from Carmarthen, one a tailor and one a coracle-man, were defended by Rebecca's on-again-off-again ally, Edward Crompton Lloyd Hall.

An unfortunate exception to this clemency was David Thomas, who had played Rebecca at Llanfihangel-ar-arth and was given twenty years transportation, with ten years given to seven of his fellow rioters. The subsequent uproar in court did nothing to sway the sentencing. The slight relaxation of tensions also hadn't stopped the need, in late November 1843, for a triple-guard of marines to protect informants from an angry crowd when almost thirty Rebeccaites were committed to bail for rioting at Fishguard – all of them released without charge a few months later as the only witness against them had fled the country.

By the summer of 1844 the military, increasingly kicking their heels in the Welsh countryside, were gradually being filtered out of the area. The London police were sent home, too, although they left behind them a newly established regular police force in Carmarthen. In July 1844 George Rice Trevor, now relieved to be back in London himself, wrote from Hyde Park Gardens to William Chambers Junior. He apologised for having neglected to pay the costs of transporting troops from Swansea to Llanelli, and languidly instructed Chambers: 'Will you be kind enough to pay the money and remind me to pay it you again.'[9] He then sat back, gratefully dropping most of his interest in the whole business along with his pen.

GOVERNMENT THE GREATEST 'BECCA'?

The final report of the Commission of Inquiry was published in March 1844, and entirely vindicated Rebecca's complaints. It began with a general account of the dissatisfaction people had expressed with the behaviour of the tollgate trusts, before a more detailed examination of the way they had been run, which exposed incompetence, mismanagement and abuse of the system. Although it found no deliberate attempt to defraud, the report criticised the frequency and level of the tolls charged and in some cases the conduct of the toll-collectors. After 'long and careful deliberation', the commission recommended that the trusts in each county be consolidated and new boards created to take over management of the roads. On any of the other problems that their interviewees had brought to their attention, however, the report made few recommendations – and it also made the foreboding suggestion that the socially and morally chaotic state of Wales might owe as much to its people's lack of the English language, and their worship in chapel rather than the Church of England, as it might to any of the economic issues outlined.

What had come as more of a surprise, a few weeks earlier, was the Home Secretary Sir James Graham's announcement of some changes to be made to the New Poor Law. This took the form of a new amendment that effectively overturned the bastardy clauses and allowed women to, once again, apply for child maintenance. The Commission's preliminary report, it emerged, had been harsh about the impact of the bastardy clauses in Wales, which backed up longstanding complaints from across the whole country that had up to this point been ignored.

Introducing the new bill in Parliament, the Home Secretary downplayed its importance as just another step in the Poor Law's evolution. Among the many who found this unconvincing was the Radical MP for Finsbury, Thomas Duncombe, who had been part of the Chartist-led opposition to the Poor Law across Britain for the past ten years. While welcoming the changes, he dryly told the House of Commons that he was 'sorry to hear' that this wider public opinion, including several petitions to Parliament, had done less to move the government than 'the turbulent and tumultuary, and he might almost say insurrectionary, proceedings which had occurred in some districts of Wales'.[10] Rattled by the implication that Rebecca's physical-force resistance might have made more of an impact than moral-force petitioning, the Home Secretary snapped back an uneasy denial:

The hon. Gentleman imputed to him, that he had admitted, that it was necessary for the people of this country by the violation of the law, or by turbulent conduct such as had characterized their proceedings in South Wales, to mark their sense of the law, before the attention of the Government would be attracted to their feelings on the subject. He begged to say, that until the riots in South Wales had been entirely subdued, and the majesty of the law completely vindicated by the trial by jury, Her Majesty's Government had not thought of directing their attention to the subject.[11]

Back in Wales, however, the Welsh press were quick to claim credit for Rebeccaism in catalysing opposition to the law. The *Welshman* took the Home Secretary's words and ran with them:

We think it can hardly be denied that the 'warm feelings' of the inhabitants of South Wales on the subject ... must have had at least some effect in producing in the mind of the right hon. Baronet a conviction that it was expedient to repeal a 'portion' of the Poor Law ... The people of the Principality [will], we are sure, perceive with pleasure that a Minister of the Crown ... does not hesitate deliberately to declare before Parliament and in the face of the country, 'that there was WELL-FOUNDED CAUSE OF COMPLAINT IN SOUTH WALES'.[12]

In May, Sir James Graham also announced that the government's legislative response to the commission's report on the tollgates was already at an advanced stage. The Turnpikes (South Wales) Act was introduced a few months later and closely followed the commission's recommendations, consolidating the trusts and simplifying the toll system, including officially halving the toll on lime. But, people asked themselves and each other, did this official action constitute salvation, or was it just a stitch-up?

239

On the one hand, with the national government now unambiguously backing them up, local authorities felt more emboldened to act against the toll-farmers. Thomas Bullin was summoned before the magistrates at Neath to answer several charges of exacting an illegal amount of tolls – including from 'several poor persons who were carrying their potatoes home from a neighbouring field'.[13] In 1889 Alcwyn C. Evans, now entering his sixties but with his teenage part in the Carmarthen riot still a vivid memory, finished his remembrance of the movement by welcoming a recent amendment to the 1844 Act that finally abolished tolls on local roads, adding in a wry aside: GOVERNMENT THE GREATEST 'BECCA'.[14]

The immediate response in Wales to the commissioners' report, however, was indignation and bitterness at the lack of attention paid to problems that went deeper than the tollgates – just as many contributors to the commission had predicted. In April, a correspondent from Carmarthen wrote to *The Times*, astutely identifying both the commissioners' focus on legislative superficiality over systemic problems and their imperialist mindset:

> We Welshmen were asking all the while, where is the redress of grievances? In vain may we seek it in the report. The grievances the commissioners love to dwell upon are the use of the Welsh language and the broken gates. The remedy they suggest for the cure of all the evils and miseries of Wales is the consolidation of the turnpike trusts and the abolition of the language ... Our redressers of wrongs find miseries to be relieved, oppressions to be removed, an irritated, insulted people to be conciliated, and behold what admirably adapted means they suggest for the attainment of the desired end! History presents a thousand instances of such moon-blindness, but they have always been the precursors of some dire catastrophe.[15]

21
WHAT BECCA DID NEXT

'NO MORE MISCHIEF THAN WAS WHOLLY NECESSARY'

In 1848 Thomas Frankland Lewis, the former Chair of the Commission of Inquiry, was, again, travelling through Wales. He took the opportunity one evening on the road to regale his companions with the tale of his involvement with the Rebecca riots, which, at the distance of four years, he now considered 'a very creditable portion of Welsh history'. One of the party recorded Frankland's opinion on the events:

> Their cause, he said, was good. The magistrates, whom the farmers looked upon as their natural protectors, were the creditors of the trusts, and maintained their expensive tolls ... the people saw that their only remedy was to take the law into their own hands – the Rebecca movement was organised well ... It never was diverted from its original purpose, it did no more mischief than was wholly necessary for that purpose.

Recalling the movement's solidarity and reach, Lewis cited the words of one contributor to the commission that 'We are all of us Rebeccas'.[1]

By that same year, the Rebeccaites sentenced to transportation for their role in the movement had settled in the penal colony of Van Diemen's Land. After a gruelling journey by sea lasting over four months, they were one fewer in number than when they had set off. David Jones, having never fully recovered from the injuries he had sustained at the Pontarddulais tollgate, had died shortly after arrival aged just twenty-one. His fellow Rebeccaites, John Hugh and Jac Ty Isha, fared better. Though neither of them returned to Wales,

241

both eventually married and raised families in Tasmania after their release, with Jac Ty Isha living well into his eighties and keeping up a regular correspondence with his family back home.

Shoni Sguborfawr and Dai'r Cantwr stuck together as they were taken from Carmarthen jail to London's Millbank penitentiary, but there their partnership ended. While Dai was transported with the Pontarddulais men and over 200 others on the convict ship the *London* in March 1844, Shoni had left a few days earlier on the *Blundell*, which carried '210 of the worst class' of offenders. The paths the two followed on arrival in Tasmania, though, were similar, studded with periods of solitary confinement and hard labour for drunkenness, insolence, theft and other petty offences, including using indecent language and resisting a constable in Dai's case, and in Shoni's refusing to work unless he received extra rations.

In April 1854 Dai was granted his ticket-of-leave, which allowed him to seek private employment. For the next twenty years he drifted between places, jobs and identities. In the summer of 1874 his body, suffocated by smoke and partly burnt, was recovered from the outbuilding of a hotel, where, it was assumed, he had been drinking himself to sleep when he set the grass beneath him on fire while lighting his pipe. Shoni received a ticket-of-leave two years after Dai, and remained in Tasmania until his death in 1867. A letter from a fellow convict in 1855 referred to Shoni having, with perhaps some newfound generosity, given the writer ten shillings after his wife's funeral.

Dai's poetry was to outlive his tragicomic end, with two ballads under his name sold publicly as broadsheets. Shoni's legend in Rebecca's country, too, lingered long after he left. In April 1845, prior to yet another arson attack on the property of William Chambers Junior, Chambers was told about the worrying words of a local farmer, who had said:

> Skiborfawr had proved himself a good prophet and that his prophecy would soon be accomplished inasmuch as Shoni had said that Mr Chambers would be a dead man. They are

not to suppose that Becca is dead – Oh, No, far from that, she is as alive as ever, and you may depend she will make them know that.[2]

Decades later, his name was still being adopted as a *nom de guerre* – rather like that of Rebecca herself. In 1895, a letter signed as 'Shoni Sguborfawr' was published in the Welsh tinplate workers' union newspaper, *Industrial World*. The writer was applying the flamboyantly violent style associated with his chosen pseudonym to an evolving context of industrial militancy, in words which raised the old spectre of Wales following the example of Ireland's campaign for independence, as well as continuing the eternal debate within radicalism between moral and physical force:

> I ask you, Mr Editor, which is the more likely to settle a dispute first in a tin-plate works? Is it £2,000 or £3,000 in strike pay to the workmen, or 2lbs. or 3Ibs. of Josepii Chamberlain's cordito under the 'boss's' dining-room to blow him to his own place. The two most valued things tin-platers possess are money and reason. These two commodities have nearly failed. What shall we have next? It is not the speeches of her illustrious sons that have won for Ireland what she possesses.[3]

CLOSING CREDITS

William Chambers Junior survived all the threats against his life, though not his property. In 1850 he became the first chairman of Llanelli's Board of Health which managed a large part of the town, but five years later his father's death heralded another protracted court case which ultimately returned his Llanelli estate to the heirs of its original owners in the Stepney family. Chambers moved on with his own family to the Hafod estate in Cardiganshire, but the expense of running it eventually bankrupted him. By 1882 he was back in Kent, the land of his fathers, where he died aged seventy-two.

In 1847, Thomas Cooke left Middleton Hall to take up a position as land agent at a far less chaotic estate in Gloucestershire. He worked there, still writing regularly to his mother, until his death in 1851. His former employer, Edward Adams, went on to squander most of his family's fortune in an unsuccessful attempt to have his younger brother's children declared illegitimate during yet another legal battle over inheritance. Middleton Hall, its mansion entirely gutted by a fire in 1931, is now the site of the National Botanic Garden for Wales.

Edward Crompton Lloyd Hall learned in 1849 that his own illegitimate status meant he wasn't set to inherit the whole of his father's estate, despite being the eldest son. Angrily severing ties with his father, he changed his surname to Fitzwilliams in the belief that the Halls were descended from a noble medieval family of that name, only to find later that there was no evidence of this.

George Rice Trevor succeeded to the title of Baron Dynevor on his father's death in 1852. When he himself died in 1869 with no male heirs, the title passed to his cousin while the family's money passed to his daughters, splitting the dynasty's name from its wealth.

Also in 1852, Colonel Love was appointed Lieutenant-Governor of Jersey. There his career in suppressing democracy faltered when he made an unsuccessful attempt to shut down the radical printing press *L'Imprimerie Universelle*, which had been founded by refugees to the island from revolutionary socialist movements in France, Italy and Poland.

Captain Napier, having collected his £500 reward and a vote of thanks from Parliament, continued to devote himself to lawkeeping as Chief Constable of Glamorgan's police force. He died in 1867 of tuberculosis, apparently having caught a cold while he waited for a train at Cardiff after attending a meeting of the police finance committee.

After the Commission of Inquiry's report had curtailed his activities, Thomas Bullin gave up toll-farming and established a livery stable in Swansea, where he charged the owners of horses a fee to board their animals. His entrepreneurial spirit found another outlet in 1858, when he obtained permission to have a cab standing for hire in Castle Square and became the town's pioneer of private taxis.

Elizabeth Davies, notwithstanding her father's objections, married Daniel Lewis on Christmas Day in 1847. Daniel worked his way up from weaving to become a woollen manufacturer and auctioneer, as well as receiving a Druidic silver medal for his cultural achievements. The two are buried together next to Goppa chapel, a few hundred yards from where the tollgate outside the Fountain Inn once stood.

While Frances Evans remained elusive in the records after her part in the storming of Carmarthen workhouse, in August 1844 a woman of the same name – though better known as Fanny'r Gath, or Fanny the Cat – was charged along with three other women as an accessory to theft in Carmarthen town centre. Her alias suggests that she may have found better prospects among the Carmarthen mob than in returning to domestic service.

Twm Carnabwth, the first Rebecca, is buried at the Baptist chapel in Mynachlog-ddu – possibly the same one where he achieved a more local level of fame for reciting the *pwnc*.

As Rebeccaism began to burn itself out in the final months of 1843, the farmers of Carmarthenshire had begun collecting donations to have a piece of silverware made and engraved. In February 1844 they presented it to Thomas Campbell Foster, offering it with customary modesty as 'a very slight testimonial' of thanks for his help in providing a 'truthful exposition of the actual state of South Wales'. For Foster, this was more personally rewarding than any credit for his reports from the Commission of Inquiry might have been. Back in London, he was to find his Welsh adventure had done him some professional good, too.

Mere weeks after Britain's Home Secretary had announced the subduing of insurrection in south Wales, there were hayricks ablaze, property threatened and Biblical visions of apocalypse reported on the opposite side of the country. The agricultural labourers of East Anglia, like the farmers and workers of south-west Wales, were, again, taking the law into their own hands over rural unemployment and poverty. *The Times* now knew it had the right man for the job, and dispatched Foster to make another series of embedded reports on the uprising. He spent the following few years, before embarking on a far less remarkable career in law and Liberal politics, engaged in intense reporting on social conditions, and popular unrest in response to them, across Britain and Ireland. There was seldom a shortage of stories to be written.

REBECCA FOR EVER?

As many respondents to the Commission of Inquiry had forewarned, the fact that little beyond tollgates had been done about the problems besetting south Wales meant that dissatisfaction remained. Threatening letters, arson attacks and disputes over land – things that stitched together the fabric of precarious rural life – carried on under the radar of national authority, but now, after Rebecca, discontent smouldered rather than blazing. What helped to head off further danger in the years after 1844 was not any action by landowners or magistrates, but a general economic upswing which enabled higher prices for farm produce, higher wages for agricultural labourers and ultimately higher rents for landlords.

Economics, of course, wasn't everything. In 1847 another government commission, triggered by the combined political anxiety caused by the successive spectaculars of the Merthyr Rising of 1831, the 1839 Chartist insurrection at Newport, then Rebeccaism, resulted in the *Report of the Commissioners of Inquiry into the State of Education in Wales*. Known as the 'Blue Books', it was an official three-volume assault on the country's language and religion as the cause of its alleged immorality and backwardness. The outraged public response to this in Wales led to a defiant coalescing of national consciousness around the language and dissenting religion, inspiring a political and cultural effort by Welsh people to shape their own alternative public image and hardening the concept of a particular Welsh identity.

As political unrest continued outside Wales, so it did within. Those disappointed that Rebeccaism hadn't given rise to a general restructuring of society poured their remaining energy and ideas into political education and trade unionism. They took part in Chartism's renewed political reform campaign of 1848, the year of Europe's 'springtime of peoples', as urban workers all over the continent called for democracy and peasants demanded land reform and the abolition of feudal relations. In 1867, Disraeli's Tory government passed the Second Reform Act, which doubled the number of British people eligible to vote and increased the influence of the industrial working class – although women, as well as many working-class men, would have to wait to win the vote for themselves in the suffrage campaigns of the early twentieth century.

Throughout all this, Rebeccaism might have faded from national consciousness, but it remained an indelible part of Welsh culture. Rebecca had bestowed a name that would be carried on into the next two centuries, and an identity that could be stepped into by anyone wanting to take direct action against economic, social or political injustice. In the years after 1844, protestors against everything from enclosures to church rates to taxes on malt were dubbed Rebeccaites and had their actions reported under headlines like 'Rebecca at work again'. Farmers and labourers protesting tithes in the 1880s styled themselves the 'Rebecca of north Wales'.

In the late 1870s, Radnorshire was hit by attacks on privatised salmon weirs on the river Wye, carried out by armed gangs with blackened faces and in Rebeccaite dress. The familiar grim sense of humour, and the flaunting of disrespect for the authorities, was, again, on display as one of the fish taken during a raid on a landowner's weir was later sold at Rhayader market with the label *Bred and fed by John Lloyd, of Huntingdon; butchered by Rebecca.* A second salmon was found nailed to the entrance of the town's market-hall, accompanied by the taunting note: 'Where were the river watchers when I was killed? Where were the police when I was hung here?' The signs of a Rebeccaite revival were unmistakable, as one magistrate admitted:

> The very word 'Rebecca' showed [the protests to be] connected with a feeling that prevailed all over Radnorshire more than 30 years ago ... Then the grievance was the turnpike gates; now it was the river.[4]

Thus Rebecca's name was easily adapted to direct action that needn't have much to do with its original form or location, other than a sense of popular justice. The movement's name and image was carried on into the twentieth and twenty-first centuries, from the 1970s radical magazine *Rebecca*, which targeted establishment corruption, and the political art collective the BECA group, to singalongs protesting at tolls on the Severn Bridge and the 2001 environmental protests in Pembrokeshire by the group Deffro Rebecca ('Wake Up Rebecca'). The latter, whose participants combined Rebecca-style dresses, bonnets and aprons with balaclavas and pipes in reference to Mexican rural radicals the Zapatistas, displayed posters with a text that sums up Rebecca's resonance and its ongoing use: 'We hope to take the spirit of Rebecca and her daughters from its beginnings, Efail-Wen to a new site of social injustice'.[5]

The original Rebecca movement was composed of ordinary men and women who, finding their circumstances intolerable, used what they had to hand – from petticoats to petitions, and from mass meetings to sledgehammers – to challenge and change their world. The extent of their success is perhaps less important than the fact that they made the attempt. Like that of other folk-heroes and legendary outlaws, the persistence of the movement's legacy shows that, when a path we are set on seems likely to lead to disaster and a new destination is needed, Rebecca and her children will always be ready to take the reins.

SELECTED BIBLIOGRAPHY, REFERENCES AND FURTHER READING

PRIMARY SOURCES

Manuscripts and archival material

National Archives, Home Office papers 40, 45, 51

National Library of Wales, General MSS:

11342–12473 12368E (ALCWYN C. EVANS 13), cuttings book and memoirs of Alcwyn C. Evans 13

14536E and 14590E, letters and reports on Rebecca, 1843

18943B 'Anonymous Narrative of a Tour Through Wales, by an English Gentleman'

21209C, letters of Thomas H. Cooke, Middleton Hall

23218, Corbet Hue, 'Journal of a Tour through N W[ales]', 1810

BUTE ESTATE RECORDS L88/163i

LLYSDINAM MS1/B1165, John WALSH, letters of Sir J. Walsh in October and November 1843

Nassau Senior 1: A12, journals of Nassau Senior, 1848–63

Ormathwaite MS FG 1/14, Journal of John Walsh 1843

West Glamorgan Archive Service, Royal Institution of South Wales Collection, 'Notes Connected with the Rebecca Riots in the year 1843'

Parliamentary Proceedings

PP 1844, xvi (ii), *Report of the Commissioners of Inquiry for South Wales*

PP 1846, xxiv, *Commission of Inquiry into the State of the Mining Districts*

PP 1847, xxiv, *Commission of Inquiry into the State of Education in Wales*

Hansard, 3rd series, 1843–9

Newspapers and periodicals
Blackwood's Edinburgh Magazine 1843
Cambrian 1839–45
Carmarthen Journal 1839–45
Hereford Times 1839–45, 1879
Monmouthshire Merlin 1843
New Times 1819
Northern Star 1843
Pembrokeshire Herald 1843–4
Quarterly Review 1844
The Standard 1842
Swansea Journal 1839–45
The Times 1839–46
Welshman 1839–45

SECONDARY WORKS

Articles

Barber, Jill, '"Stolen Goods": The Sexual Harassment of Female Servants in West Wales during the Nineteenth Century', *Rural History* 4:2 (1993), 123–36.

Coward, Adam, 'English Anglers, Welsh Salmon, and Social Justice: The Politics of Conservation in Midnineteenth Century Wales', *Welsh History Review*, 27:4 (2015), 730–54.

Evans, Chris, 'El Cobre: Cuban Ore and the Globalization of Swansea Copper, 1830–70', *Welsh History Review*, 27:1 (2014), 112–31.

Henriques, Ursula R. Q., 'Bastardy and the New Poor Law', *Past and Present,* 37 (1967), 103–29.

Howard, Sharon, 'Riotous Community: Crowds, Politics and Society in Wales, c.1700–1840', *Welsh History Review,* 20:4 (2001), 656–86.

Jones, David, 'Thomas Campbell Foster and the Rural Labourer; Incendiarism in East Anglia in the 1840s', *Social History*, 1:1 (1976), 5–43.

Jones, David J. V., 'The Second Rebecca Riots: salmon poaching in Radnorshire and Breconshire', *Llafur*, II (1976), 32–56.

Jones, E. W., 'Medical Glimpses of Early Nineteenth-Century Cardiganshire', *National Library of Wales Journal*, XIV (1965–6), 260–75.

Jones, Rhian E., 'Symbol, Ritual and Popular Protest in Early Nineteenth-Century Wales: The Scotch Cattle Rebranded', *Welsh History Review*, 21:6 (2012), 34–57.

Jones, Rosemary A. N., 'Popular culture, policing and the disappearance of the ceffyl pren in Cardigan c. 1837–1850', *Ceredigion*, 11 (1988–9), 19–40.

Navickas, Katrina, 'The Search for "General Ludd": The Mythology of Luddism', *Social History,* 30:3 (2005), 281–95.

Rees, Lowri Ann, 'Paternalism and rural protest: the Rebecca riots and the landed interest of south-west Wales', *Agricultural History Review*, 59:1 (2011), 36–60.

Roberts, Peter R., 'The Decline of the Welsh Squires in the Eighteenth Century', *National Library of Wales Journal*, 13:2 (Winter 1963).

Rogers, Shannon L., 'Wasteland to Wonderland: Wales in the Imagination of the English Traveller, 1720–1895', *North American Journal of Welsh Studies* 2:2 (Summer 2002), 15–26.

Sayce, R. U., 'The One-Night House, and Its Distribution', *Folklore*, 53:3 (1942), 161–3.

Scourfield, E., 'References to *Y Ceffyl Pren* (the Wooden Horse) in South-West Wales', *Folklore*, 87:1 (1976), 60–2.

Suggett, Richard, 'Festivals and Social Structure in Early Modern Wales', *Past and Present*, 152 (August 1996), 79–112.

Thompson, E. P., 'Rough Music Reconsidered', *Folklore*, 103:1 (1992), 3–23.

Books

Armand-Louis-Bon Maudet, Comte de Penhouët, *Letters Describing a Tour Through Part of South Wales by a Pedestrian Traveller* (T. Baylis, 1797).

Cordell, Alexander, *Hosts of Rebecca* (London: Victor Gollancz, 1960).

Cragoe, Matthew, *An Anglican Aristocracy: The Moral Economy of the Landed Estate in Carmarthenshire 1832–1895* (Oxford: Oxford University Press, 1996).

Cragoe, Matthew, *Culture, Politics and National Identity in Wales 1832–1886* (Oxford: Oxford University Press, 2004).

Dillwyn, Elizabeth Amy, *The Rebecca Rioter: A Story of Killay Life* (London: Macmillan, 1880; new edn, Dinas Powys: Honno, 2001).

Draisey, Derek, *The Rebecca Riots within ten miles of Swansea* (Swansea: Draisey Publishing, 2010).

Epstein, James, and Dorothy Thompson (eds), *The Chartist Experience: Studies in Working Class Radicalism and Culture, 1830–1860* (London: Macmillan, 1982).

Herbert, Trevor, and Gareth Elwyn Jones (eds), *People and Protest: Wales 1815–1880* (Cardiff: University of Wales Press, 1988).

Hobsbawm, Eric, and George Rudé, *Captain Swing: A Social History of the Great English Agricultural Uprising of 1830* (London: Random House, 1968).

Howell, David W., *Patriarchs and Parasites: The Gentry of South-West Wales in the Eighteenth Century* (Cardiff: University of Wales Press, 1986).

Howell, David W., *The Rural Poor in Eighteenth-Century Wales* (Cardiff: University of Wales Press, 2000).

Jenkins, Geraint H., and J. Beverly Smith (eds), *Politics and Society in Wales 1840–1922: Essays in Honour of Ieuan Gwynedd Jones* (Cardiff: University of Wales Press, 1988).

John, Angela V. (ed.), *Our Mothers' Land: Chapters in Welsh Women's History, 1830–1939* (Cardiff: University of Wales Press, 1991).

Jones, David J. V., *Before Rebecca: Popular Protests in Wales 1793–1835* (London: Allen Lane, 1973).

Jones, David J. V., *Rebecca's Children: a Study of Rural Society, Crime and Protest* (Oxford: Clarendon Press, 1989).

Selected bibliography, references and further reading

Jones, Ieuan Gwynedd, *Mid-Victorian Wales: the Observers and the Observed* (Cardiff: University of Wales Press, 1992).

Jones, Rhian E., *Petticoat Heroes: Gender, Culture and Popular Protest in the Rebecca Riots* (Cardiff: University of Wales Press, 2015).

Jones, T. Gwynn, *Welsh Folklore and Welsh Custom* (London: Methuen & Co, 1930).

Linton, William James, *Threescore and Ten Years, 1820–1890: Recollections* (London: Charles Scribner's Sons, 1894).

Loffler, Marion, *Welsh Responses to the French Revolution: Press and Public Discourse, 1789–1802* (Cardiff: University of Wales Press, 2011).

Lord, Peter, *Words with Pictures: Welsh images and images of Wales in the popular press, 1640–1860* (Aberystwyth: Planet, 1995).

Molloy, Pat, *And They Blessed Rebecca: an account of the Welsh tollgate riots, 1839–1844* (Llandysul: Gomer Press, 1983).

Navickas, Katrina, *Protest and the Politics of Space and Place, 1789–1848* (Manchester: Manchester University Press, 2017).

Owen, D. Huw (ed.), *Settlement and Society in Wales* (Cardiff: University of Wales Press, 1989).

Owen, Trefor M., *Welsh Folk Customs* (Llandysul: Gomer Press, 1987).

Peate, Iorwerth C., *Tradition and Folk Life: A Welsh View* (London: Faber & Faber, 1972).

Poole, Robert, *Peterloo: The English Uprising* (Oxford: Oxford University Press, 2019).

Rees, Lowri Ann, Ciarán Reilly and Annie Tindley (eds), *The Land Agent 1700–1920* (Edinburgh: Edinburgh University Press, 2019).

Skrine, Henry, *Two Successive Tours Throughout the Whole of Wales* (Elmsley and Bremner, 1798).

Smith, David (ed.), *A People and a Proletariat: Essays in the History of Wales 1780–1980* (London: Pluto, 1980).

Thomis, Malcolm, and Jennifer Grimmett, *Women in Protest 1800–1850* (New York: St Martin's Press, 1982).

Thompson, Dorothy, *The Chartists* (London: Temple Smith, 1984).

Thompson, E. P., *The Making of the English Working Class* (London: Pelican, 1968).

Thompson, E. P., *Customs in Common: Studies in Traditional Popular Culture* (London: Penguin, 1993).

Tobit Evans, Henry, *Rebecca and her Daughters, being a history of the agrarian disturbances in Wales known as 'the Rebecca riots'* (Cardiff: Educational Publishing Company, 1910).

Vaughan, Herbert M., *The South Wales Squires* (London: Methuen & Co, 1926, reprinted Carmarthen: Golden Grove Editions, 1988).

Wilks, Ivor, *South Wales and the Rising of 1839: Class Struggle as Armed Struggle* (London: Croom Helm, 1984).

Williams, Daniel G., *Black Skin, Blue Books: African Americans and Wales 1845–1945* (Cardiff: University of Wales Press, 2012).

Williams, David, *The Rebecca Riots: a Study in Agrarian Discontent* (Cardiff: University of Wales Press, 1955).

Williams, Gwyn A., *The Merthyr Rising* (Cardiff: University of Wales Press, 1978).

Williams, Gwyn A., *When Was Wales? A History of the Welsh* (London: Pelican, 1985).

Online

Archives and local history references to Rebecca and Welsh life at the following websites:

www.cragenbeca.co.uk

www.genuki.org.uk

www.llanellich.org.uk

www.sublimewales.wordpress.com

Bassett, Sarah, 'The Stepney and Chambers Families of Llanelly House: Exploring the "Cultivation of Identity" of the Old and New Squirearchy in the Llanelli Landscape, Circa 1706–1855' (Student dissertation, The Open University, 2018), available at *www.oro.open.ac.uk/56401/*

Jones, Rhian E., 'Occupy the Tollgates: The Rebecca riots as myth, meme and movement', Wales Arts Review (November 2015), available at *www.walesartsreview.org/occupy-the-tollgates-the-rebecca-riots-as-myth-meme-and-movement*

Lewis, Samuel, *A Topographical Dictionary of Wales* (4th edn, 1849), available at *www.british-history.ac.uk/topographical-dict/wales*

Rees, Lowri Ann, 'Middleton Hall, Carmarthenshire', East India Company at Home (June 2014), available at *www.bpb-eu-w2. wpmucdn.com/blogs.ucl.ac.uk/dist/1/251/files/2014/06/Middleton-Hall-pdf-final-19.08.14.pdf*

'The Letters of Queen Victoria: A selection from Her Majesty's correspondence between the years 1837 and 1861' (London: John Murray, 1908), available at *www.gutenberg.org/files/20023/20023-h/20023-h.htm*

Wallace, Alfred Russel, 'The South-Wales Farmer' (originally published 1905), available at *www.people.wku.edu/charles.smith/ wallace/S623.htm*

Waterhouse, Martin, 'A New Rebecca? GM Crop Protests', On the Edge: Peripheral Communities and Marginal Anthropology (Ph.D. thesis, University of Glamorgan, 2002), available at *www. pure.southwales.ac.uk/ws/portalfiles/portal/992240/397886.pdf*

ENDNOTES

Foreword

1. See E. P. Thompson, *Customs in Common: Studies in Traditional Popular Culture* (London: Penguin, 1993), pp. 185–351.

2. See, for instance, novels by Elizabeth Amy Dillwyn, *The Rebecca Rioter* (1880); Violet Jacob, *The Sheep Stealers* (1902), and Vivian Annis Bailey's *Children of Rebecca* (1995). Alun Hoddinot's 1962 piece for chamber choir sets to music a poem on the riots by Jon Manchip White. The 1992 film *Rebecca's Daughters*, directed by Karl Francis, is based on a 1948 screenplay by Dylan Thomas. In 2013, a musical by Ian Michael Thomas, based on Alexander Cordell's bestselling 1960 novel *Hosts of Rebecca*, opened at Cardiff Weston Studio at the Wales Millennium Centre.

Prologue

1. *Carmarthen Journal*, 23 June 1843.

2. National Library of Wales, General MSS: 23218, Corbet Hue, 'Journal of a Tour through N W[ales]', 1810.

3. *Hints to Pedestrians, or How to Enjoy a Three-Weeks Ramble through North and South Wales* [1836] (Joseph Onwhyn, 1837) – quoted online at *www.sublimewales.wordpress.com*.

4. Catherine Sinclair, *Hill and Valley, or Hours in England and Wales 1833* (1st edn, New York, 1838; 2nd edn, Edinburgh, 1839) – quoted online at *www.sublimewales.wordpress.com*.

5. Armand-Louis-Bon Maudet, Comte de Penhouët, *Letters Describing a Tour Through Part of South Wales by a Pedestrian Traveller* (T. Baylis, 1797), p. 38.

6. 'Rebecca: Anti-turnpike league' in the *Quarterly Review*, vol. 74 (June 1844), no. 779, 123–54.

7. 'Rebecca: Anti-turnpike league', *Quarterly Review*.

8. *The Times*, 16 December 1843.

9. Statement of Revd P. M. Richards in *Commission of Inquiry into the State of Education in Wales* (1847), Part 3.

10. *The Times*, 16 December 1843.

11. Alfred Russel Wallace, 'The South-Wales Farmer' (1905).

12. Wallace, 'The South-Wales Farmer'.

13. Wallace, 'The South-Wales Farmer'.

14. Samuel Lewis, *A Topographical Dictionary of Wales* (4th edn, 1849).

15. Herbert M. Vaughan, *The South Wales Squires* (London: Methuen & Co, 1926, reprinted Carmarthen: Golden Grove Editions, 1988).

16. Peter R. Roberts, 'The Decline of the Welsh Squires in the Eighteenth Century', *National Library of Wales Journal,* 13:2 (Winter 1963).

17. *New Times*, 21 January 1819.

18. National Archives, Home Office papers 42/35, report of John Phillipps, 24 August 1795.

19. 'Rebecca: Anti-turnpike league', *Quarterly Review.*

20. NLW MSS 14590E, Statement of 'Rebecca's demands and complaints', undated.

21. Letter to the *The Times*, 2 April 1844.

22. Vaughan, *South Wales Squires.*

23. PP 1844, xvi (ii), *Report of the Commissioners of Inquiry for South Wales.*

24. PP 1844, xvi (ii), *Report of the Commissioners of Inquiry for South Wales.*

25. *Welshman*, 23 March 1843.

PART ONE
2 Respectable radicals, rough music

1. Joseph Downes, 'Notes on a Tour of the Disturbed Districts in Wales', *Blackwood's Edinburgh Magazine*, 54 (338), 1843.

2. Henry Skrine, *Two Successive Tours Throughout the Whole of Wales* (Elmsley and Bremner, 1798).

3. *Pigot & Co. South Wales Directory for 1830*, available at *www.genuki. org.uk/big/wal/CMN/Llanelli/Pigot1830.*

4. *Monmouthshire Merlin*, 21 August 1830.

5. NLW MSS 11342-12473 12368E (ALCWYN C. EVANS 13) p. 189.

6. 'Rebecca: Anti-turnpike league' in the *Quarterly Review*, vol. 74 (June 1844), no. 779, 123–54.

7. 'Rebecca: Anti-turnpike league', *Quarterly Review.*

8. *Welshman*, 5 May 1843.

3 Men in the middle

1. National Library of Wales, General MSS: 21209C, letters of Thomas H. Cooke, Middleton Hall, 8 May 1842.

2. Carmarthen Archives, Bryn Myrddin Collection, MS 142, printed address 'A Few Words addressed to the Electors of Carmarthenshire by a Loyal

Reformer, an Advocate for the Ballot, and a Friend to the Dissenter and the Farmer' (Bath, 1835); also see *www.landedfamilies.blogspot.com/2013/02/1-abadam-of-middleton-hall.html*.

3. National Library of Wales, General MSS: 21209C, letters of Thomas H. Cooke, Middleton Hall, 23 July 1842.
4. *Northern Star*, 1 July 1843.
5. *Welshman*, 6 January 1843.

4 'Faithful to death'

1. *New Zealand Gazette And Wellington Spectator*, Volume IV, Issue 274, 23 August 1843.
2. *Welshman*, 17 March 1843.
3. NLW MS 2114C, letter of Edward Davies, 15 January 1901.
4. *Welshman*, 30 March 1843.
5. *Welshman*, 17 March 1843.
6. *Welshman*, 10 March 1843.
7. *Welshman*, 17 March 1843.
8. *Welshman*, 17 March 1843.
9. *Welshman*, 17 March 1843; *Cambrian*, 18 March 1843.
10. *Cambrian*, 18 February 1843.
11. *Cambrian*, 18 February 1843.
12. NLW MSS 27399, prosecuting brief Pembrokeshire Lent Assizes March 1843, *Nathl Rowlands v Howells, Rebecca Riots at Trevaughan*.
13. NLW MSS 11342-12473 12368E (ALCWYN C. EVANS 13), p. 189.

PART TWO
5 A thorough revolution

1. *Pigot & Co. South Wales Directory for 1844: Carmarthenshire*, available at *www.genuki.org.uk/big/wal/CMN/Carmarthen/Pigot1844*.
2. NLW MSS CWRTMAWR 1201F, *Mihangel's Valentine for the 'old mother' in Carmarthen; Carmarthen brought to tune* (Pamphlet, 1854).
3. *Swansea Journal*, 14 June 1843.
4. NLW MSS 14590E, William Chambers Junior, Rough memoranda of complaints before grievance commissioners at Carmarthen. Undated.
5. *Cambrian*, 23 January 1841.
6. NLW MSS 14590E, William Chambers Junior, Rough memoranda of complaints.

7. National Archives, HO 45/454, letter of William Chambers Junior, 25 June 1843.
8. NLW MSS 11342-12473 12368E (ALCWYN C. EVANS 13), p. 194.
9. National Archives, HO 45/454, letter of J. Wood, 21 June 1843.
10. *Pembrokeshire Herald and General Advertiser*, 2 February 1844.
11. National Archives, HO 45/454, letter of E. C. L. Hall, 14 June 1843.

6 Lovers of justice
1. PP 1844, xvi (ii), *Report of the Commissioners of Inquiry for South Wales*.
2. *Cardiff and Merthyr Guardian*, 10 October 1846.
3. PP 1844, xvi (ii), *Report of the Commissioners of Inquiry for South Wales*.
4. *Northern Star*, 1 July 1843.
5. NLW MSS 11342-12473 12368E (ALCWYN C. EVANS 13), p. 197.
6. NLW MSS 11342-12473 12368E (ALCWYN C. EVANS 13), p. 197.
7. *Welshman*, 23 June 1843.
8. *Cambrian*, 23 March 1844.
9. NLW MSS 11342-12473 12368E (ALCWYN C. EVANS 13), p. 199.
10. *Welshman*, 23 June 1843.
11. *The Times*, 24 June 1843.
12. *Swansea Journal*, 5 July 1843.
13. *Swansea Journal*, 5 July 1843.
14. *The Times*, 22 June 1843.

7 Rebecca in the spotlight
1. *The Times*, 24 June 1843.
2. *The Times*, 24 June 1843.
3. *The Times*, 27 June 1843.
4. *The Times*, 27 June 1843.
5. *The Times*, 27 June 1843.
6. *The Times*, 26 June 1843.
7. *The Times*, 24 June 1843.
8. Carmarthenshire Archives, DYN 159/13, 29 June 1843.
9. *Carmarthen Journal*, 23 June 1843.
10. *The Times*, 27 June 1843.
11. *The Times*, 27 June 1843.

PART THREE
8 A losing battle
1. *The Standard*, 29 June 1843.
2. *Welshman*, 14 July 1843.
3. National Library of Wales, General MSS: 21209C, letters of Thomas H. Cooke, Middleton Hall, 3 September 1843.
4. *The Times*, 30 June 1843.
5. *The Times*, 27 July 1843.
6. *The Times*, 5 September 1843.
7. *Swansea Journal*, 28 June 1843.
8. *The Times*, 3 July 1843.
9. *The Times*, 3 July 1843.
10. D. C. Jenkins (ed.), *Selections from the Diary of Thomas Jenkins (1826–1870)* (Bala: Dragon Books, 1986, republished Historia Wales, 2012).

9 All but open rebellion
1. National Archives, HO 45/454, letter of E. C. L. Hall, 30 June 1843.
2. NLW, NLW, BUTE ESTATE RECORDS L88/163i.
3. National Archives, HO 45/454, letter of Col. Love 11, 12, 25 June 1843.
4. *The Times*, 8 August 1843.
5. *The Times*, 8 August 1843.
6. NLW MSS 11342-12473 12368E (ALCWYN C. EVANS 13), p. 211.
7. *Cambrian*, 26 August 1843.
8. National Library of Wales, General MSS: 21209C, letters of Thomas H. Cooke, Middleton Hall, 23 July 1843.
9. *Northern Star*, 28 July 1843.
10. *The Letters of Queen Victoria: A selection from Her Majesty's correspondence between the years 1837 and 1861* (London: John Murray, 1908), letter of Viscount Melbourne, 22 June 1843.
11. *Letters of Queen Victoria*, letter of Queen Victoria, 23 June 1843.

10 Rebecca goes south
1. *Swansea Journal*, 5 August 1843.
2. *The Times*, 14 July 1843.
3. *Swansea Journal*, 2 August 1843.
4. *Welshman*, 25 August 1843.
5. *Swansea Journal*, 7 June 1843.

11 Organised chaos
1. *The Times*, 6 July 1843.
2. *The Times*, 30 September 1843.
3. *The Times*, 30 September 1843.
4. *The Times*, 25 July 1843.
5. *The Times*, 25 July 1843.
6. *Welshman*, 28 July 1843.
7. *The Times*, 8 August 1843.
8. *The Times*, 8 August 1843.
9. *Cambrian*, 23 June 1843.
10. *Cambrian*, 15 July 1843.
11. *Welshman*, 15 September 1843.
12. *Cambrian*, 16 March 1844.
13. National Library of Wales, General MSS: 21209C, letters of Thomas H. Cooke, Middleton Hall, 6 August 1843.
14. *Welshman*, 5 August 1843; *Cambrian*, 30 March 1844.
15. National Library of Wales, General MSS: 21209C, letters of Thomas H. Cooke, Middleton Hall, 24 August 1843.
16. *The Times*, 3 July 1843.
17. *The Times*, 3 July 1843.
18. NLW, LLYSDINAM MS1/B1165, John WALSH, letters of Sir J. Walsh in October and November.

12 Ladies of letters
1. *Welshman*, 1 September 1843.
2. *Welshman*, 1 September 1843.
3. NLW MSS 11342-12473 12368E (ALCWYN C. EVANS 13), p. 226.
4. National Archives, HO/45/642, letter of E. C. Lloyd Hall, 7 October 1843.
5. *Pembrokeshire Herald*, 15 March 1844.
6. *Pembrokeshire Herald*, 15 March 1844.
7. *Cambrian*, 23 December 1843.
8. NLW MSS 11342-12473 12368E (ALCWYN C. EVANS 13), p. 232.
9. Henry Tobit Evans, *Rebecca and her Daughters* (Cardiff: Educational Publishing Company, 1910).
10. *Welshman*, 22 December 1843.
11. *Welshman*, 29 December 1843.

12. National Archives, HO 45/454.

13. NLW MSS 11342-12473 12368E (ALCWYN C. EVANS 13), p. 190.

14. NLW MSS 11342-12473 12368E (ALCWYN C. EVANS 13), p. 190.

15. *Swansea Journal*, 25 October 1843.

13 Out of the shadows

1. NLW, Ormathwaite MS FG 1/14, Journal of John Walsh 1843.

2. NLW, Ormathwaite MS FG 1/14, Journal of John Walsh 1843.

3. National Archives, HO 45/454, letter of E. C. L. Hall, 25 June 1843.

4. National Library of Wales, General MSS: 21209C, letters of Thomas H. Cooke, Middleton Hall, 24 August 1843.

5. *The Times*, 7 August 1843.

6. *The Times*, 7 August 1843.

7. *The Times*, 7 August 1843.

8. Quoted in David Williams, 'A Report on the Turnpike Trusts', *National Library of Wales Journal* 8:2 (Winter 1953).

9. *Swansea Journal*, 23 August 1843.

10. *Northern Star*, 1 July 1843.

11. *Northern Star*, 30 September 1843.

12. *The Times*, 8 August 1843.

13. *Northern Star*, 26 August 1843.

14. *The Times*, 10 August 1843.

15. George Eyre Evans, 'Rebecca Riots: Unpublished letters, 1843–44', The Transactions of the Carmarthenshire Antiquarian Society and Field Club, vol. XXIII.

14 'More than one hundred thousand strong'

1. *The Times*, 29 August 1843.

2. *Northern Star*, 9 September 1843.

3. National Library of Wales, General MSS: 21209C, letters of Thomas H. Cooke, Middleton Hall, 24 August 1843.

4. William James Linton, *Threescore and Ten Years, 1820–1890: Recollections* (London: Charles Scribner's Sons, 1894), p. 90.

5. Linton, *Threescore and Ten Years, 1820–1890*, p. 90.

6. NLW MSS 14590E, letter of George Rice Trevor, 6 September 1843.

7. NLW MSS 14590E, letter of William Chambers Junior, 2 September 1843.

8. NLW MSS 14590E, undated letter.

9. *Welshman*, 27 September 1843.

10. *The Times*, 30 September 1843.

11. *The Times*, 6 October 1843.

12. *The Times*, 30 September 1843.

13. *The Times*, 30 September 1843.

14. *The Times*, 28 September 1843.

15. *The Times*, 28 September 1843.

16. *Welshman*, 1 September 1843.

PART FOUR

15 Rebecca rules

1. *The Times*, 9 September 1843, letter from 'Another Constant Reader'.

2. *The Times*, 13 September 1843, letter from 'CIVIS'.

3. *The Times*, 28 July 1843.

4. *Cambrian*, 5 September 1843.

5. NLW, BUTE ESTATE RECORDS L88/163i, letter of 7 August 1843.

6. NLW, BUTE ESTATE RECORDS L88/163i, letter of 7 August 1843.

7. CUL, Graham papers, letter 15 September 1843.

8. *Welshman*, 29 December 1843.

9. PP 1844, xvi (ii), *Report of the Commissioners of Inquiry for South Wales*.

10. NLW, Ormathwaite MS FG 1/14, Journal of John Walsh 1843.

11. *Welshman*, 29 September 1843.

12. *Welshman*, 1 September 1843.

16 Raising the stakes

1. *Poor Man's Guardian and Repealer's Friend*, 2, 9, 16 September 1843.

2. *Northern Star*, 9 September 1843.

3. *Northern Star*, 2 September 1843.

4. *The Times*, 5 September 1843.

5. *Welshman*, 15 August 1843.

6. *Carmarthen Journal*, 8 September 1843.

7. West Glamorgan Archive Service, Royal Institution of South Wales Collection, 'Notes Connected with the Rebecca Riots in the year 1843'.

8. West Glamorgan Archive Service, 'Notes Connected with the Rebecca Riots'.

9. *The Times*, 28 October 1843.

10. *Cambrian*, 3 September 1843.

11. *The Times*, 14 September 1843.

12. *The Times*, 14 September 1843.

13. NLW, Bute Estate records, L88/258, letter of Capt. Napier 11 September 1843.

14. *Swansea Journal*, 13 September 1843.

15. *The Times*, 20 September 1843.

16. *The Times*, 16 September 1843.

17. National Archives, HO 45/454, letter of E. C. L. Hall, 22 September 1843.

17 Death at Hendy

1. Joseph Downes, 'Notes on a Tour of the Disturbed Districts in Wales', *Blackwood's Edinburgh Magazine*, 54 (338), 1843.

2. *Swansea Journal*, 8 September 1843.

3. Downes, 'Notes on a Tour of the Disturbed Districts in Wales'.

4. *The Times*, 9 September 1843.

5. NLW MSS 14590E, letter of 13 September 1843.

6. NLW MSS 14590E, statement of John Jones (Shoni Sguborfawr), undated.

7. NLW MSS 14590E, letter of 13 September 1843.

8. National Library of Wales, General MSS: 21209C, letters of Thomas H. Cooke, Middleton Hall, 16 September 1843.

9. National Library of Wales, General MSS: 21209C, letters of Thomas H. Cooke, Middleton Hall, 28 September 1843.

18 Are the government mad enough?

1. See Hansard 24 August 1843, HL Deb, 24 August 1843, vol. 71, cc1005-10.

2. *The Times*, 22 September 1843.

3. Letter of 17 September 1843 in George Eyre Evans, 'Rebecca Riots: Unpublished letters, 1843–44', *The Transactions of the Carmarthenshire Antiquarian Society and Field Club*, vol. XXIII.

4. Letter of 26 August 1843 in Evans, 'Rebecca Riots: Unpublished letters, 1843–44'.

5. NLW MSS 14590E, letter of Goring Thomas, 9 September 1843, letter of George Rice Trevor, undated.

6. Letter of 25 September 1843 in Evans, 'Rebecca Riots: Unpublished letters, 1843–44'.

7. Joseph Downes, 'Notes on a Tour of the Disturbed Districts in Wales', *Blackwood's Edinburgh Magazine*, 54 (338), 1843.

8. Downes, 'Notes on a Tour of the Disturbed Districts in Wales'.

9. NLW MSS 14590E, statement of David Howell, 13 December 1843.

10. NLW MSS 14590E, statement of David Davies, 9 September 1843.

11. NLW MSS 14590E, draft letter of William Chambers Junior, undated September 1843.

12. NLW MSS 14590E, draft letter of William Chambers Junior, undated September 1843.

13. *The Times*, 22 September 1843.

14. *The Times*, 22 September 1843.

15. *The Times*, 22 September 1843.

16. *The Times*, 22 September 1843.

17. *The Times*, 22 September 1843.

PART FIVE

19 'Becca there is now dead'

1. *The Times*, 14 October 1843.

2. *Cambrian*, 21 October 1843.

3. *The Times*, 14 October 1843.

4. *The Times*, 28 September 1843.

5. NLW, Ormathwaite MS FG 1/14, Journal of John Walsh 1843.

6. NLW, HARPTON COURT 1 2419. Notice dated 11 October 1843.

7. *The Times*, 19 October 1843.

8. *Cambrian*, 6 January 1844.

9. PP 1844, xvi (ii), *Report of the Commissioners of Inquiry for South Wales*.

10. *Cambrian*, 6 January 1844.

11. NLW MSS 14590E, statement of John Jones (Shoni Sguborfawr), undated.

12. *The Times*, 5 October 1844.

13. NLW MSS 14590E, statement of Thomas Phillips, 12 December 1843.

20 From lawbreakers to legends

1. *Swansea Journal*, 4 October 1843.

2. *Hereford Times*, 18 November 1843.

3. *The Times*, 16, 19 February 1946.

4. See Henry Tobit Evans, *Rebecca and her Daughters* (Cardiff: Educational Publishing Company, 1910).

5. *The Times*, 11 November 1843.

6. *Swansea Journal*, 25 October 1843.

7. NLW MSS 14590E, letter of James Brown, undated January 1844.

8. *Welshman*, 19 January 1844.

9. 19 May 1839, 'Lady Charlotte Guest – Extracts from her journal 1833–1852' at *www.genuki.org.uk/big/wal/GLA/Guest*.

10. 6 December 1843, 'Lady Charlotte Guest – Extracts from her journal 1833–1852'.

11. 6 December 1843, 'Lady Charlotte Guest – Extracts from her journal 1833–1852'.

21 Throwing open the books

1. *The Times*, 7 November 1843.

2. Letter of George Rice Trevor, 26 October 1843 in George Eyre Evans, 'Rebecca Riots: Unpublished letters, 1843–44', *The Transactions of the Carmarthenshire Antiquarian Society and Field Club*, vol. XXIII; PP 1844, xvi (ii), *Report of the Commissioners of Inquiry for South Wales*.

3. *The Times*, 13 November 1843.

4. *Cambrian*, 11 November 1843.

5. *Cambrian*, 30 December 1843.

6. *Swansea Journal*, 29 November 1843.

7. *The Times*, 29 November 1843.

8. *Cambrian*, 23 March 1844.

9. Letter of 19 July 1844, in Evans, 'Rebecca Riots: Unpublished letters, 1843–44'.

10. Hansard, 10 February 1844.

11. Hansard, 10 February 1844.

12. *Welshman*, 16 February 1844.

13. *The Times*, 16 November 1843.

14. NLW MSS 11342-12473 12368E (ALCWYN C. EVANS 13), p. 239.

15. Letter from 'E. T.', *The Times*, 2 April 1844.

22 What Becca did next

1. NLW, Nassau Senior 1: A12, journals of Nassau Senior, 1848–63.

2. NLW MSS 14590E, anonymous statement made to William Chambers Junior, undated.

3. *Industrial World – Organ of the South Wales, Monmouthshire & Gloucestershire Tinplate Workers' Union*, May 1895.

4. NLW, Llysdinam MS1/B1558.

5. See 'A New Rebecca? G M Crop Protests', Martin Waterhouse, 'On the Edge: Peripheral Communities and Marginal Anthropology', (Ph.D. thesis, University of Glamorgan, 2002).